AFRICAN FOLK MEDICINE

african folk medicine

PRACTICES AND BELIEFS OF THE BAMBARA AND OTHER PEOPLES

PASCAL JAMES IMPERATO

YORK PRESS INC. / BALTIMORE

Library of Congress Cataloging in Publication Data

Imperato, Pascal James.
  African folk medicine.

  Includes bibliographies and index.
  1. Bambara tribe--Medicine.   I. Title.
DT551.42.I46   615'.882'096   77-5465
ISBN 0-912752-08-4

Manufactured in the United States of America.

York Press, Inc., 101 East 32nd Street, Baltimore, MD 21218.

Library of Congress Catalog Card Number 77–5465
ISBN 0–912752–08–4

To

Lowell E. Bellin, M.D., M.P.H.
Commissioner of Health, City of New York
(1974-1977)

and

Dominique Amadou Traoré
(1890-1972)
Officier de la Légion d'Honneur Française

Who have both dedicated themselves
to the cause of better health care
for all the peoples of the world.

Contents

Africans, being a prescientific people, do not recognize any conceptual cleavage between the natural and the supernatural. They experience a situation rather than face a problem. They allow both rational and nonrational elements to make an impact on them. I think, too, that the African can hold contradictory ideas in fruitful tension within his mind without any sense of incongruity, and he will act on the basis of the one which seems most appropriate to the particular situation.

Preface

This book is an introduction to the traditional medical beliefs and practices of various African peoples. It uses the Bambara people of Mali as a base, since most of my work in Africa was with the Bambara. They are one of the largest and most important ethnic groups of the West African savannah and sahel. As members of the greater Manding family of peoples, they share certain linguistic and cultural affinities with adjacent ethnic groups, especially the Malinke, who live to the west of them. The Malinke live not only in Mali like the Bambara, but also in adjacent Guinea, Senegal, and Gambia. The traditional medical beliefs and practices of those Malinke who live in Mali are similar, often identical, to those of the Bambara.

The Bambara have been studied carefully since the early part of this century, first by missionaries and colonial administrators, then by trained anthropologists and other types of scientists. Rev. Joseph Henry, a missionary priest stationed in Segou in the central Bambara country, published the first book on the Bambara, *L'Ame d'un Peuple Africain*: *Les Bambara*, in 1910. This work, and the articles which he wrote, represent the earliest anthropological studies of the Bambara. Father Henry was a keen observer, a methodical gatherer of facts, and an excellent writer. His monograph, richly illustrated from photographs taken by his colleagues, still stands as a major overall work on the Bambara. Although primarily an observational and impressionistic work, it touches upon most of the diverse aspects of Bambara religious beliefs and social organization. Traditional medical beliefs and practices are discussed briefly, and no details are presented.

Maurice Delafosse, a contemporary of Father Henry, was a colonial administrator and trained linguist and ethnographer who spent almost a quarter of a century in French West Africa beginning in 1894. Delafosse gained renown for his excellent studies of the languages, history and cultures of many West African peoples, reflected in his forty-three publications. His three volume work, *Le Haut Sénégal-Niger*, considered a masterpiece of its kind, is a rich and detailed description of the peoples and history of much of present day Mali. Concentrating as he did on linguistics and history, Delafosse did not delve deeply into traditional medical beliefs and practices, except to provide some generalizations.

Following Henry and Delafosse was Louis Le Barbier, whose small 42-page monograph on the Bambara, *Les Bambaras, Moeurs, Coutumes, Religions*, was published in 1918. Although providing useful details on religious beliefs, cults and social organization and customs, Le Barbier did not describe traditional medical beliefs and practices. But his work as well as the works of Henry and Delafosse constitute the initial corpus of re-corded anthropological information on the Bambara.

Five major researchers studied the Bambara and wrote about them in the decade following Le Barbier's work. Louis Tauxier (1878-1942) was a French colonial administrator who wrote two major books, *La Religion Bambara* (1927) and *Histoire des Bambara* (1942). The former was the first major work on the Bambara since Father Henry's 1910 publication. It contains a detailed description of Bambara religious beliefs and extensive information on traditional medical beliefs, witchcraft and sorcery. The major criticism of this work that has been made by subsequent generations of scholars who have conducted field research among the Bambara, is that the information in it was not obtained firsthand. This is a valid criticism, but that his information was gathered second-hand does not really lessen the value of Tauxier's work. A good deal of the information that Tauxier provides was obtained from his Bambara interpreter, Baba Bolo, a blacksmith, while Tauxier was serving in the Cercle[1] of Issa-Ber (now the Cercle of Niafunke). The population of this cercle is predominantly Peul, but Tauxier states that there were 17,000 Bambara there at the time he conducted his study (December, 1912–August, 1913). Although Issa-Ber is not in the Bambara country, Tauxier had access to a fairly large expatriate Bambara population and a good informer-interpreter.

Moussa Travélé, a Bambara interpreter in the service of the French colonial administration in the then French Sudan (now Mali) wrote a number of publications dealing with Bambara religious beliefs and social organization in the 1920's and 1930's. These are of high quality and written in French. Henri Labouret, a linguist and anthropologist, made a major contribution to our knowledge of the Bambara in his monograph *Les Manding et Leur Langue* (1934). Charles Monteil, a colonial administrator, known for his superb monograph on the ancient city of Djenné (1903), published a history of the Bambara in 1924, *Les Bambara du Segou et du Kaarta*. Labouret's work contains some general information on traditional medical beliefs and practices, but the major focus of his work is linguistic and sociologic. Monteil's work does not touch upon traditional medical beliefs and practices in a significant way.

---

[1]Cercle — a political subdivision.

Georges Cheron, a colonial administrator, conducted studies among the Malinke and described a then-new spirit medium cult, the *dyidé*, that was widespread among the Malinke and Bambara in the 1930's. A number of French administrators, missionaries, scholars, and African interpreters .and school teachers contributed to our knowledge of the Bambara in the period prior to World War II. Among these are Abiven, Bazin, Lem, Monod, Mauny, and others, who described various aspects of Bambara history, social organization, language, and religion.

Between 1931 and 1933, Marcel Griaule led the famous Dakar-Djibouti Expedition of anthropologists across Africa. While in the French Sudan (Mali) he came into contact with the Bambara, Bozo, Malinke, Dogon, and other ethnic groups. It was the Dogon, the cliff dwellers of West Africa, who fascinated him the most. And for the next 20 years, until his death in 1956, he studied and described their complex religious and cosmologic beliefs, social organization, and other aspects of their culture. Under his guidance, a number of his students undertook to study not only the Dogon, but also other ethnic groups in Mali, especially the Bambara. It is they who since the 1940's have produced the largest corpus of works on the Bambara. Their methodical studies were carried out in the field over a period of many years and have resulted in an authoritative and comprehensive group of publications.

Germaine Dieterlen's *Essai Sur La Religion Bambara* (1950) is a detailed study of Bambara religious and cosmologic beliefs. In addition, Madame· Dieterlen has written numerous articles on other aspects of Bambara culture. Recently she and her Malian student, Youssef Cissé, published *Les Fondements de la Société d'Initiation du Komo* (1972), a book dealing with the *komo* society. Solange de Ganay has published numerous articles dealing with Bambara social organization, customs, cosmology, and graphic signs. Viviana Paques, whose field work was conducted in the southern and western Bambara country, has written a number of important publications dealing with Bambara social organization, religion, and certain initiation societies. Her major work is *Les Bambara* (1954), a comprehensive monograph dealing with social organization, religion, demography, the physical and climatologic characteristics of the Bambara country, economics, and a wide variety of cultural matters. Much of this information is presented through the optic of the western and southern Bambara country where there are numerous nuances of difference from the central and eastern Bambara country. Nonetheless, this book is the best general work on the Bambara and their homeland.

Dominique Zahan spent ten years, from 1948 to 1958, in the Segou area of the Bambara country. There he served as Chief of the Immigration Section of the *Office du Niger*, one of Africa's largest irrigation schemes. A student of Griaule's, he undertook a number of carefully planned and executed studies which are reflected in his numerous publications. Of all those who have studied the Bambara, none have contributed more to our knowledge of them than Dominique Zahan. His studies have spanned an enormous horizon covering religion, art, cosmology, linguistics, social organization, and traditional medical beliefs. Professor Zahan's major books to date on the Bambara are *Sociétés d'Initiation Bambara, Le N'Domo, Le Kore* (1960) and *La Dialectique du Verb Chez Les Bambara* (1963). The former deals with two of the six Bambara initiation societies and the latter with spoken language and its significance. Professor Zahan's book on the *Tyi Wara* initiation society is to appear shortly. In 1974, Zahan published a small English language book, *The Bambara*, which essentially summarizes some of his previous publications in French.

Zahan's article, "*Principes de Médecine Bambara*," in the Belgian journal, *Zaire* (1957) presents a general overview of the basic beliefs about disease causation among the Bambara. It is one of the few recent articles which deals with general beliefs about disease causation among the Bambara.

Claude Meillassoux has published a number of studies dealing with Bambara society, both ancient and contemporary. Among the latter is his excellent English language book, *Urbanization of an African Community, Voluntary Associations in Bamako* (1968). In this work he describes the social developments among uprooted rural migrants to Mali's capital.

In preparing this present work, I have drawn upon the publications of all of these authors to provide a general overview of Bambara social organization, religion, cosmology, and general beliefs about disease causation. My treatment of these aspects of Bambara life has had to be succinct; I have made no attempt to make it comprehensive. Readers interested in obtaining more information about these aspects of the Bambara will find a list of references at the end of each chapter. While trying to be succinct in providing the general social and cultural background of the Bambara, I have also tried to draw upon information gathered by others over a period of more than 60 years. In general, the works of more recent scholars tend to build upon and enlarge the works of earlier scholars. The regional nature of some field studies more than accounts for the nuances of difference with similar studies carried out by others. And the lapse of a few decades between studies reveals sharp differences easily explained by the profound changes in Bambara society. In presenting Bambara cosmology and religion, I have drawn upon all of these sources in addition to my own field studies and have presented what I consider to be the best consensus. The scope and detail of the material in this book has been geared to provide the reader with a sufficient background against which to understand Bambara medical beliefs and practices.

While a number of authors from Joseph Henry to Dominique Zahan and Claude Meillassoux have touched upon traditional medical beliefs and practices, nowhere is this information extensive nor pulled together in one place. Rather it is scanty and widely scattered. I have made special efforts to pull all of this previously published information together in this book, providing the reader with the source from which it comes, and to add my own observations. Prior to 1960, there were fewer than half a dozen articles written on traditional medicine among the Bambara. The earliest of these by Dr. J. Peyrot, entitled "Us, Coutumes, Médecine des Bambaras," was published in 1905 in the *Annales d'Hygiene et de Médecine Coloniales*. Almost 40 years elapsed until another article appeared, Ben Sai's article on indigenous medicine and medicinal plants in the Sudan, published in Dakar in the journal *Notes Africaines* (Volume 21, 1944). Bacou's two papers published in *Notes Africaines* (Volume 22, 1944) appeared next. One deals with the treatment of leprosy in the western Bambara country and the other with the treatment of dysentary. In 1947, Dominique Traore published a paper in *Notes Africaines* on indigenous methods for rodent destruction in houses. Then followed Dominique Zahan's paper in 1957, mentioned above, on principles of Bambara medicine.

Dominique Amadou Traoré, a leading expert on West African herbal medicines, published his monumental pharmacopeia in 1965. Entitled, *Médecine et Magie Africaines*, it is a compilation of thousands of remedies employed for various disease processes in northern Nigeria, Upper Volta, Ivory Coast, and Mali. Traoré was born in northern Nigeria around 1890 and placed into indigenous slavery as a child. He graduated from the Normal School at St. Louis in Senegal and spent many years as a teacher in Upper Volta, Mali, Niger, and Ivory Coast. At the same time he recorded the indigenous herbal remedies used for various diseases and thus produced a major written African pharmacopeia. While recording these herbal remedies, he was associated with the *Institut Français d'Afrique Noire* and had the support of Georges Cheron when the latter was the Commandant of the Cercle of Bobo-Dioulasso in Upper Volta.

By the early 1950's, Traoré had finished the manuscript for his pharmacopeia. Unfortunately, he could not find a publisher for it. But finally he succeeded in finding one willing to publish it if it were subsidized. It took several years for him to collect the necessary donations from Africans and Europeans to get the required three thousand dollars. The money and the manuscript were entrusted to a French national returning from the Sudan to Paris. Traoré never heard from him again. Both the money and the manuscript disappeared. Traoré then rewrote the manuscript from his notes, a task which required more than two years. This manuscript was eventually published in 1965 under the title *Médecine et Magie Africaines*. It is a regional West African pharmacopeia in that it includes remedies from many ethnic groups from several countries. Unfortunately, it sometimes does not identify remedies as to where and among whom they were recorded. Statements are made about the efficacy of some of the remedies, based both on direct observation and on self-experimentation. Traoré administered a number of his recorded remedies to himself as well as to others. Occasionally, he became seriously ill from toxic side effects.

I have described Dominique Traoré and his work in some detail because it was at his urging and under his guidance that I undertook my studies of traditional Bambara medicine. This book is the result of those studies. I arrived in Mali in late 1966 and lived and worked there in a continuous fashion until early 1972. I was sent to Mali by the United States Public Health Service to organize and direct a smallpox eradication and measles control program and to develop mobile medical services. Ultimately, I became responsible for directing a mobile health program which delivered a variety of diagnostic, curative, and preventive health services to the entire population of Mali, including immunizations against smallpox, measles, yellow fever, cholera, and meningitis.

The program's activities were carried out by mobile teams of infirmiers (nurses) and vaccinators working in a carefully structured organization which eventually reached most of the country's population. All of these activities were organized within the framework of the national mobile medical service, the *Service des Grandes Endemies*. The professional cadre of this service was composed of experienced infirmiers who over the years had visited virtually every village in the country. When all of the infirmiers of the *Service des Grandes Endemies* were gathered beneath one roof, there was hardly a village in Mali that one could mention that was not familiar to someone present. My working closely with this group of Malians, who themselves had a profound knowledge of their country, greatly enlarged the richness of my experience. My acceptance in villages and nomad camps was not only enhanced by my service-rendering role as a physician, but also because of my association with infirmiers who were known and respected. This combined with the nature of my work, gave me access to parts of the country little visited then by foreigners. I worked in each of the country's 42 cercles and 228 arrondissements (administrative districts), and traveled by truck, plane, canoe, boat, on horses, camels, donkeys, and on foot. It is difficult to estimate the total distance I covered in Mali; my travel by truck alone totaled about 150,000 miles.

During my five years in Mali, I conducted a large number of medical and anthropological field studies among the Bambara, Tuareg, Peul, Songhoi, and Dogon. I began my studies of traditional medical beliefs and practices among the Bambara in 1967 in collaboration with Dominique Traoré, who I always addressed as "Monsieur Dominique." At the time he was a retired schoolteacher, but worked out of a small office given to him at the *Pharmacie Populaire* in Sikasso, in southern Mali. In August, 1967 Mali's socialist regime launched a cultural revolution which intensified in early

1968. At that time, Monsieur Dominique was told by officers of the local branch of the *Union-Soudanaise-RDA* (Mali's then ruling party) in Sikasso to sever his working relationship with me because I was an American. He hesitated at first, but, given the extreme anti-West thrust of the cultural revolution and threats to deprive him of his small room at the *Pharmacie Populaire* and of his meager pension, he had no choice but to comply. Our relationship was only suspended for a few months, until November, 1968, when a military coup overthrew Mali's socialist regime.[2]

I continued my studies of traditional Bambara medicine until the end of 1971. I undertook further studies in 1973 when I returned to Mali and during two field visits which I made to Mali in 1974. Because I was able to travel throughout the entire Bambara country, I obtained information from the broadest possible base. Interviews were conducted with elders, village chiefs, herbalists, diviner-healers, Koranic teachers, spirit medi-

---

[2]Monsieur Dominque completed a second volume of his pharmacopeia in 1968 and had difficulty getting it published. He asked for my assistance and together we went to see C. Robert Moore, then the United States Ambassador to Mali. Ambassador Moore was extremely interested in the project and suggested we contact the National Academy of Sciences in Washington, D.C. There, the late Dr. Zgymunt Deutschman, who had been involved in U.S. health programs in Africa for several years, was enthusiastic. Since he was due to visit nearby Dakar in a few weeks time, he agreed to come to Bamako specifically to discuss the project. A week before his scheduled arrival, Monsieur Dominique contacted me and told me of the threats made against him by the local party officials in Sikasso. He reluctantly asked me to turn over the copy of his pharmacopeia then at the U.S. Embassy in Bamako to the Director General of Public Health. This I did and shortly thereafter, Modibo Keita, then President of Mali, issued an executive order to have the government subsidize the publication of the pharmacopeia; but complications followed. The overthrow of the Keita regime followed, putting into question the government's promise to pay for the publication of the book. Monsieur Dominique then obtained an audience with the new president of Mali, in early 1969 and came to my office immediately thereafter with the news that the president agreed to have the government publish his pharmacopeia. Monsieur Dominique was instructed to contact the *Institut des Science Humaines* in Bamako to work out the details. Then, after months of delay, the director told him that his book could not be published until he obtained photographs of all the plants mentioned. This was an inordinate demand, viewed by Monsieur Dominique as an attempt to stop the publication of his book. The time, effort and cost required to photograph thousands of plants would have been prohibitive.

After several months he gave up and requested that the institute return his original manuscript. He was told it had been misplaced and after several months he was informed that it was lost. He had a copy, however, and asked that I revive interest in the book's publication with the National Academy of Sciences. In 1970 I met with Robert O. Blake, then U.S. Ambassador to Mali. Because of the complicated history of this book and the fact that only one copy now remained, we decided it was simply too risky to become involved in its publication. Monsieur Dominique passed away in 1972 and never published his second pharmacopeia. It was left in the possession of his family in Sikasso.

ums, blacksmiths and a wide variety of other people. Herbal remedies, their preparation and administration were recorded as well as stated observations about their efficacy. Extensive interview surveys revealed that certain remedies were more common than others and that many were almost universally known throughout the Bambara country. In this book, I have presented these commonly-used remedies for the most part.

In villages, herbs were always described to me by their Bambara names which I recorded. Monsieur Dominique provided scientific identification of some and for this I am profoundly grateful. The majority were identified in Berhaut's *Flore du Senegal* (1967) (Dakar, Librairie Clair-afrique). In addition to obtaining information about herbal remedies, I also carefully observed and studied the traditional health care delivery system in its current sociologic context and obtained detailed information about current concepts of disease causation. As part of other anthropological studies I conducted, I surveyed current cosmological and religious concepts among informed village elders.

Dramatic changes in Bambara society over the past several decades due to Islamization and the impact of western technology have relegated many of the beliefs and practices included here to a position of historical interest only, for many of the Bambara. These changes have not been uniform in extent and degree across the Bambara country. I have attempted, however, to indicate some idea of the nature of these changes.

Most of my own findings are presented here for the first time, although some, such as those relating to smallpox, measles, and cholera have been previously published in part in the medical literature. I acknowledge with thanks the kind permission of the editors of *African Arts*, the *Bulletin of the New York Academy of Medicine*, the *Transactions of the Royal Society of Tropical Medicine and Hygiene*, and *Tropical and Geographical Medicine* to use in this volume various materials that have been published previously in those journals.

In addition to including references to records dealing with the Bambara, I have also referred to studies conducted among other ethnic groups in Africa. There is an enormous body of publications dealing with traditional medical beliefs and practices in Africa. I have made no attempt to achieve geographic balance in discussing these studies. Rather, I have chosen those studies which best serve as a comparison to beliefs and practices among the Bambara, or which describe unique practices and beliefs. No doubt some readers will miss a work or works of particular interest to them. The references cited, however, should more than satisfy the needs of both the general reader and those who are specifically interested in African folk medicine, for whom this book has been written. This is a very heterogeneous audience of general readers, anthropologists, physicians, public health administrators, health care planners, and

Africanists. The simultaneous satisfaction of the needs of such diverse groups requires a broad general treatment complemented by extensive references from which specialists can obtain further information. I have given the book this focus.

This book is in effect a compilation of the knowledge of Bambara healers, herbalists, Koranic teachers, diviners, patients and old sages. It would be an impossible task to individually thank the hundreds of people who assisted me in this study. I am deeply grateful to all of them for their patience, help, cooperation and hospitality. I also want to thank the many Malian administrators and medical officers in the Cercles of San, Segou, Dioila, Koutiala, Bamako, Bougouni, Kangaba, Koulikoro, Kolokani, Banamba, Nioro, Kita, Bafoulabe, Kayes, Yelimane, and Kenieba for their invaluable help.

Dr. Alan Beck of the New York City Department of Health first suggested I write this book and gave me his constant encouragement. I want to express my sincere appreciation to Professor David Brokensha and to Professor Jan Vansina who reviewed the first draft of the manuscript and provided many useful suggestions. My sincere thanks go to Mrs. Earlene Price and Mrs. Susan Riscica for their careful preparation of the typescript.

1

Introduction to Mali and the Bambara

The Republic of Mali is a landlocked country situated in the heart of West Africa. It covers some 479,000 square miles (1,240,000 square kilometers), sharing common borders with Mauritania and Senegal on the west, Algeria on the north, Guinea and Ivory Coast on the south, and Upper Volta and Niger on the east. Mali's present borders are the legacy of 68 years of French colonial rule during which a number of sizeable changes were made in the country's frontiers (Brasseur 1974, Foltz 1965).

The Bambara, comprising some two million people, are the largest ethnic group in Mali. They are sedentary agriculturists who live chiefly in an inverted triangular area in west central Mali covering 400,000 square miles of flat savanna and sahel.[1]

The Bambara hold a dominant political, social, and economic position in modern Mali, and their language, *Bamanan-kan*, is the *lingua franca* in much of the country. Also known as the Bamana, the Bambara belong to the great Manding family of peoples. The term Manding is used to cover a number of West African groups who share a similar culture and who speak related forms of the same language. The three most important Manding groups are the Bambara; the Malinke (Maninka) who live west of the Bambara in Mali and in Guinea, Gambia, and Senegal; and the Dyula who are a merchant group living north of the Bambara in Mali and the Ivory Coast. The Malinke number about 800,000 and the Dyula about 600,000. These and neighboring groups are discussed below.

Mali's total population is about 5,200,000, but there are another estimated 2,000,000 Malian nationals living in adjacent African states and in Europe. The national capital is Bamako, situated on the banks of the Niger River. The country is primarily agricultural, most of its population

---

[1]The sahel is the strip of semi-desert that lies immediately south of the Sahara desert. Its name comes from the Arabic word *sahil*, meaning shore or borderland. To the south of the sahel is the savanna.

Map of modern Mali showing major towns, cities, and rivers, as well as the surrounding countries.

being subsistence farmers and to a lesser extent herdsmen. The population is concentrated in the southern parts of the country which are traversed by the Senegal and Niger River Basins. The northern half of Mali lies within the Sahara Desert and is sparsely inhabited by Maure and Tuareg nomads. Although there has been some minimal industrial development, the country is still among the poorest in the world. The average annual budget of the Government of Mali in recent years has been about $50,000,000, about half that of the New York City Department of Health.

Early History

Because of its physical location, the country has been a commercial and cultural crossroads between West and North Africa for centuries. Mali is the heir to a number of early African empires and kingdoms which flourished between the 9th and 19th centuries. The earliest of these was the Ghana Empire which was a federation of kingdoms which primarily covered what is now northwestern Mali. The empire, which had its capital at Koumbi Saleh (in southern Mauritania near the Mali border), lasted from the 9th to the 12th centuries, but reached its height about 1,000 A.D. The Mali Empire (12th to 17th centuries) was born out of a small kingdom situated at the headwaters of the upper Niger. Its founder, Sundiata Keita, who ruled from about 1230 to 1255, extended its frontiers to encompass most of the western part of present-day Mali. The empire reached its peak in the middle of the 14th century under Kankan Moussa (Mansa Moussa), the famous emperor who made an overland pilgrimage to Mecca via the Sahara and Egypt in 1324 and 1325. Under him the borders of the Mali Empire were extended to cover much of present-day Mali, Senegal, Gambia and parts of Mauritania. The empire went into decline in the 15th Century (Guilhem 1961).

The Songhay Empire of Gao (1335-1600) developed in the extreme eastern part of present-day Mali among the Songhay people and eventually extended over much of present-day Mali and part of Niger and Upper Volta. It reached its peak under two famous emperors, Sonni Ali Ber who ruled from 1464 to 1492, and Askia Mohammed who ruled from 1493 to 1528. The empire was effectively destroyed by the Moroccans who invaded it in 1591 (Guilhem 1961).

During these centuries, small but culturally and commercially important city states formed, notably Djenné in the 9th century and Timbuctoo in the 12th. Timbuctoo, founded along the left bank of the Niger as a seasonal Tuareg nomad camp, became a thriving commercial and cultural center by the 14th century. It passed successively under the domination of the Manding Empire of Mali, the Songhay Empire, the Moroccans, Tuareg, Bambara, and Peul (Miner 1965).

Moroccan domination and control of political events in the western Sudan, the area occupied mostly by Mali, did not last for more than a century. In the early 17th century a number of strong kingdoms developed in the central part of Mali, notably the Peul Kingdom of Macina (1600–1862), the Bambara Kingdom of Segou (1600–1862) and the Bambara Kingdom of Kaarta (1633–1854). In 1810, a Moslem teacher, Cheikou Amadou, overthrew the ruling Peul dynasty of Macina and established a theocratic state in central Mali known as the Peul Empire of Macina (Ba and Daget 1962). The Senufo Kingdom of Kenedougou developed in southern Mali in the 17th century and lasted until 1898 when its capital, Sikasso, was taken by the French. In the latter part of the 19th century, Samory Touré, an Imam warrior, established political control over much of southern Mali as well as over large areas of adjacent states. He was captured by the French in 1898 and exiled to Gabon.

Political events in the second half of the 19th century in Mali were dominated by the development and extension of the Tukulor Empire and the gradual French penetration of the region. Eventual French annexation of what is now Mali was the result of several decades of diplomatic maneuvering and military confrontation with indigenous political states, especially the Tukulor Empire founded by El Hadj Omar Tall.

In 1854 El Hadj Omar conquered the Bambara Kingdom of Kaarta, then Segou (1862), and finally Macina (1862). He died in 1864 and his son, Amadou, succeeded him as head of the Tukulor Empire, but with less effective control over it. Amadou ruled from Segou from 1864 until 1892 when he was driven out by the French. Another son of El Hadj Omar, Mountaga, succeeded him in Kaarta and a nephew, Tidjani, ruled over the former Peul Empire of Macina. Neither ever fully recognized the supremacy of Amadou (Oloruntimehin 1972).

Topography

The topography of Mali is generally flat, consisting of plains and plateaus, but the southern part of the country is hilly, covered by extensions of the Futa Djallon highlands of Guinea. The Manding Mountains, which rise between 1,000 and 1,500 feet above sea level, extend from the Guinea-Mali frontier to 50 miles east of Bamako. They are composed of sandstone and eroded cliff formations through which many affluents of the Senegal and Niger Rivers cut a course. The highest peak in the western part of Mali is Mt. Mina (1,739 feet). The eastern part of the country is quite flat except for the Bandiagara Plateau and Cliffs. The latter, which run from southwest to northeast for some 150 miles, reach an altitude of 3,300 feet and are among the most spectacular land formations in West Africa. To the east of them are found the spectacular Hombori Mountains which consist of isolated sandstone mesas some of which rise to over 3,000 feet and include the highest point of Mali (3,772 feet).

In the eastern part of the country the only marked relief is found along the banks of the Niger River after it makes its great bend to the southeast at Bourem. This relief consists of tall sand dunes, hills, and several spectacular rocky pillars near Ansongo. The Adrar des Iforas is an eroded sandstone plateau in northeastern Mali in the cercle of Kidal. A part of the Hoggar mountain system of the Sahara, it rises to 1,600 feet in altitude.

The central part of Mali is covered by the flood plains of the Inland Delta of the Niger. Northern Mali lies within the Sahara. In the extreme north are vast plains known as the Tanezrouft and Taoudeni which are covered in many areas by sand dunes and shifting sand. The salt mines at Taoudeni, which have been worked since the 17th century, still provide

Mali with much of its salt. It is carried down by camel caravans and truck convoys across some 440 miles of the Sahara to Timbuctoo (Imperato 1975).

River Systems

Mali is traversed by the Senegal and Niger rivers and their tributaries. The Senegal River is formed at the small town of Bafoulabé by the convergence of the Bafing and Bakoye rivers. It flows for 560 miles in a northwesterly direction into neighboring Senegal and Mauritania and then into the Atlantic Ocean. The river rises between the month of July and October and is low in April and May, the end of the dry season (Keita 1972).

The Niger River traverses Mali for 1,010 miles, a third of its total length. It rises in the highlands of Guinea and Sierra Leone and flows into Mali in a northeasterly direction. Just beyond Bamako, its flow is broken by cataracts at Sotuba but a few miles beyond at Koulikoro, it spreads out in a broad flat valley. Beyond the town of Segou the Niger forms a vast inland delta and then receives its main tributary, the Bani River, at Mopti. Beyond Mopti it breaks up into two major channels, the Bara Issa and the Issa Ber, and a number of smaller branches. These spread out over the flat

The great mosque built entirely of mud brick at Mopti in central Mali. The wooden poles protruding out to the exterior serve as scaffolding for masons who resurface the outside with a stucco of mud after the end of the rainy season each year. The minerets are topped by ostrich eggs. With the spread of Islam, mosques of this type are increasingly common in the Bambara country.

flood plains to form a number of shallow seasonal lakes. Just above Diré, the two main branches join again and the river then flows past Kabara, the port of Timbuctoo. Beyond Kabara, the river changes from a northeasterly to an easterly direction until it reaches Bourem where it makes its great bend towards the southeast. It then flows past Gao and Ansongo and into the Niger Republic just beyond Labezanga. The Niger River rises in response to the rainy season. The Upper Niger crests in August and the crest reaches the inland delta in September and the Niger Bend by December. The river is navigable in Mali for large craft from Koulikoro and Gao during the high water periods, August to January (Gallais 1967).

Climate

In terms of both climate and vegetation, Mali can be divided into three zones. The southern Sudanic climate zone extends up to 15° north

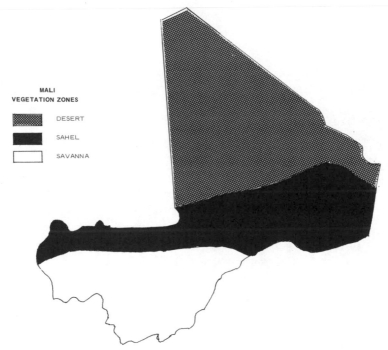

The three vegetation zones of Mali. The climate is generally hot and dry in all three zones. During the rainy season, beginning in June and ending in October, most of the rain falls in the south. In the Sahara region to the north, rainfall is scant. Most of Mali's population lives in the southern half of the country.

latitude. It receives from 20 to 60 inches of rainfall per year, the heavier rains being in the more southern areas of the zone. In this zone average temperatures vary from 75°F to 95°F. North of the Sudanic climate zone is the *sahel* (a transition zone between the Sahara and the savanna) whose southern portions receive about 20 inches of rain per year and whose northern areas receive about 7 inches. Temperatures here vary from 80°F to 100°F. To the north of the sahel is the Sahara climate zone where maximum temperatures range from 120°F to 140°F. Rain in the Sahara is sporadic and scanty (Brasseur 1974).

In all of these three zones, the climate is hot and dry. There are, however, two major seasons. The dry season, which extends from November to June is characterized by progressively rising temperatures, especially from April through June. From November through January the *alize* blows cool air from the northeast causing a brief cool spell with temperatures falling to 70°F. In February, the *harmattan* blows hot dry air out of the Sahara, continuing into June. During this period, temperatures in the Sudanic zone and sahel rise to a daily average of 105°F.

In mid-June the rainy season begins when a monsoon wind blows from the southwest bringing with it considerable moisture. The beginning and end of the rainy season are characterized by severe thunderstorms accompanied by much wind. Most of the rain falls during July and August, usually every few days. It is rare for a daily rain to last for more than a few hours. The rainy season is fairly cool but humid. Once the rains end in October, the climate becomes warm again and is uncomfortably humid until the cool *alize* winds begin to blow (Brasseur 1974).

Population

Mali has about 5,200,000 people, 90 percent of whom live in rural areas. The population density varies from 70 persons per square mile in the central part of the country to less than five in the north. Bamako, the largest town, has a population of about 320,000. Between January and April this is swelled by an influx of about 30,000 seasonal workers, known as *barani*, from Nara, Nioro, and other areas. Only a few other towns have sizeable populations — Mopti (50,000), Segou (40,000), Kayes (30,000), Sikasso (25,000), and San (18,000). A number of towns are undergoing rapid growth because of the presence of new local industries. These include Koutiala, Bla, and Fana.

In 1971 there were some 20,000 more women than men in the country, mostly accountable by the exodus of young males to neighboring African states. The birth rate in 1971 was 55 per 1,000 persons, the mortality rate 30 per 1,000 persons, and an annual growth rate of 2.5

percent. If this rate continues, the population will double in 20 years. The age distribution of the population is overwhelmingly young, 60 percent being below 20 years of age. Life expectancy is 35 years. Most deaths occur in young children below two years of age (*Annuaire Statistique*, 1975).

There are several major ethnic groups in Mali and a number of smaller ones, some of whom share common cultural and linguistic characteristics with one of the major groups. The largest are the Bambara (Bamana) who number close to 2,000,000, 38.4 percent of the total population. They live in much of central and southern Mali along the middle Niger valley. In the southwest and west live the Malinke (Maninka) who number 300,000. They are the heirs to the ancient Mali Empire and are culturally closely similar to the Bambara, speaking a related language. The Peul (Fula) number about 550,000, ten percent of the population. They are concentrated in the inland delta of the Niger in the administrative Region of Mopti, but smaller numbers are found elsewhere in the country. The Sarakole (Soninke), who number about 420,000 live in the sahel in northwestern Mali, and are descendants of the Ghana Empire. The Songhay live along the Niger Bend in eastern Mali and number 300,000. The Dogon, whose culture and art forms have gained renown in recent years, live on the Bandiagara Plateau. They number 240,000. The Senufo and Minanka who live in southeastern Mali number 430,000 and their neighbors to the northeast, the Bobo, number 100,000 in Mali. The Bozo and Somono fishermen of the Niger number 20,000. There are several smaller groups in the country among whom are the Tuareg nomads of the northeast who number about 30,000, the Maure nomads of the sahel who number about 60,000, the Diawara (80,000), Khassonke (80,000), Tukulor (10,000), and Dioula (60,000) (N'Diaye 1970).

Most of these groups are agriculturists except for the Peul, Tuareg, and Maure who are primarily pastoralists, and the Bozo and Somono who are fishermen. The Sarakole and Dioula are merchants, in addition to being farmers. In western central and southern Mali, Bambara is the *lingua franca*. It tends to be the *lingua franca* along with French, the official language, in most administrative centers since such a high proportion of educated administrators are Bambara. In the inland delta, Fulfulde, the Peul language, is the *lingua franca* and in eastern and northeastern Mali, Songhay is widely spoken, even by many Tuareg and Maure.

Administration

Mali is divided into six regions, each headed by a governor. These regions are Kayes, Bamako, Segou, Sikasso, Mopti, and Gao. They are in turn divided into smaller units called *cercles* of which there are 42. Each

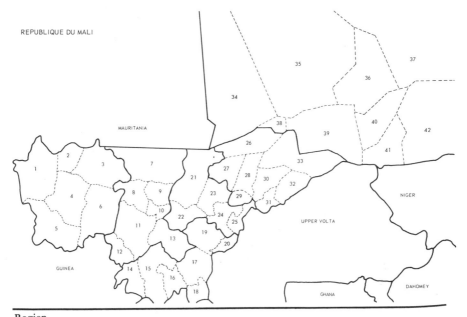

REPUBLIQUE DU MALI

MAURITANIA

GUINEA

NIGER

UPPER VOLTA

GHANA

DAHOMEY

Region					
Kayes	Bamako	Sikasso	Segou	Mopti	Gao
Cercle					
1. Kayes	7. Nara	14. Yanfolilla	21. Niono	26. Niafounke	34. Goundam
2. Yelimane	8. Kolokani	15. Bougouni	22. Segou	27. Tenenkou	35. Timbuctoo
3. Nioro	9. Banamba	16. Kolon-	23. Macina	28. Mopti	36. Bourem
4. Bafoulable	10. Koulikoro	Dieba	24. San	29. Djenne	37. Kidal
5. Kenieba	11. Bamako	17. Sikasso	25. Tominian	30. Bandiagara	38. Dire
6. Kita	12. Kangaba	18. Kadiolo		31. Bankass	39. Gourma-
	13. Dioila	19. Koutiala		32. Koro	Rharous
		20. Yorosso		33. Douentza	40. Gao
					41. Ansongo
					42. Menaka

Mali is divided into six regions, each headed by a governor. The regions are divided into cercles, each with a commandant as its administrative officer.

governor coordinates the services and economic activities of the cercles in his region. The cercles are headed by commandants who supervise administrative and economic activities. The headquarters of the cercles are usually large villages or towns termed *chef lieu* and possess basic services such as police, health, and justice. The cercles are divided into *arrondissements* of which there are presently 228. Each is headed by a *chef d'arrondissement*. The *chef lieu* of the arrondissement is usually a small village with a school and dispensary. Each arrondissement consists of several villages headed by chiefs. Important functions of the heads of the arrondissements are the collection of taxes, the recording of deaths and births, and the settling of local family disputes.

The Bambara and Neighboring Groups

The Bambara belong to the large group of Manding peoples. The Manding are the largest cluster of peoples who live in the savanna of West Africa. They speak different forms of what was once the language of the Mali Empire. Today there are regional forms of this language spoken by these people and referred to by the names of the ethnic groups involved. There are approximately 10 million people living in nine West African states who speak Manding languages (Atkins 1972). The most important of these are the Bambara, the Malinke (Manika) and the Manding diaspora groups of Dyula who number half a million or so.

The generic term *Manding* is derived from the place name Mande (Manden), the nucleus of the old Mali Empire which lies on the upper Niger along what is now the frontier between the republics of Mali and Guinea. It is from this area that most of the Manding peoples trace their historical expansion. In the past, the term *Mande* has been used by scholars to cover this group of people. However, this term is more inclusive than *Manding* and also covers many other groups living in the peripheral coastal areas where similar and related languages are spoken. The present distribution of Manding personal names among non-Manding peoples, and the presence of Manding loan words in other West African languages, indicate that the influence of the Manding language was greater in the past than it is today (Atkins 1972).

Although the Manding language is spoken by large numbers of people and is the main language of trade and commerce in the western savanna and contiguous coastal areas, it has not been a written language. There is evidence, however, that it has been written locally in Arabic script in Moslem communities (Atkins 1972). Also, traditional graphic symbols and ideographs have been used extensively by the Manding and their neighbors for religious purposes (Dieterlen 1950; Ganay 1950; Zahan 1950; Dieterlen and Cissé 1972). It is presumed that these indigenous systems of writing developed in the last two centuries. There are considerable regional variations in these systems of graphic signs.

Secrecy and the guarded word are of great importance among Manding peoples, and therefore there have always been strong forces opposing the development of openly written forms of language (Zahan 1960). Such has not been the case relative to cryptic and esoteric ideographs. Among these peoples, traditions and history have been preserved through the prudent use of the spoken word, passed from one generation to the next by the Manding caste of bards, *dyeli*, who are regarded as the guardians of language (N'Diaye 1970).

The principal ethnic groups comprising the Manding are the following.

Bambara (Bamana)

The Bambara, including their caste of Somono fishermen on the Niger, live in central and west-central Mali. They look to Segou and Kaarta as their cultural centers rather than to the Manding heartland since these were the important centers of the Bambara kingdoms of the 17th and 18th centuries. Over the last century and more especially in the past few decades, Islam has been gradually spreading among these people. But many of them are still animist, remaining faithful to their ancient religion. The Bambara are primarily agriculturists, but those living in the central and northern regions keep sizeable herds of cattle, sheep, and goats. They live in villages that vary in size from 100 or so inhabitants to over 1,000, the average village having about 500 inhabitants. Through their conquests, the Bambara carried the Manding language as far north as Timbuctoo and Mauritania and eastward into the heart of the inland delta of the Niger. The Bambara form of the Manding languages was used by the French colonial administration as a *lingua franca* and they carried it throughout West Africa.

The Bambara live in a roughly inverted triangular area in west-central Mali covering 400,000 square miles of savanna and sahel. They are industrious farmers who grow millet, corn, and manioc and who keep small herds of goats, sheep, and cattle. The Bambara are polygamous, patriarchal, patrilineal and patrilocal. Marriage involves a bride price paid to the parents of the bride. This consists of clothing, textiles, cattle, and in recent years cash payments.

According to tradition, the Bambara arrived on the banks of the middle Niger near the present town of Segou in the early 17th century (Guilhem and Toe 1963). The Soninke, descendants of the Ghana Empire were living there at the time. In 1712, Mamari Coulibaly, known as Biton Coulibaly, founded a kingdom around the town of Segou. He became the *fama* (king) of what was to develop into a powerful political state. To the northwest, another powerful Bambara chief, Sey Bamana, established a kingdom, known as the Kaarta Kingdom (Imperato 1977).

Biton Coulibaly gradually conquered a huge area around Segou, and administratively and militarily organized his state in an admirable manner. He formed the *ton-djon*, a special standing army which started as a royal guard composed of captured enemy soldiers and slaves. He extended the borders of Segou northeastward to Djenné and drove the enemy Massassi Bambara into Kaarta where they formed a separate

A village in the eastern Bambara county. The houses and walls are built of mud brick, with mud dug from large holes in the ground which fill with water in the rainy season, as seen in the foreground.

kingdom of their own. When he died from tetanus in 1755, he was succeeded by his sons, both of whom were killed by the *ton-djon*. They then made one of their own members king. In 1760, N'Golo Diarra, a *ton-djon* was made king. He ruled until 1787 and became Segou's greatest king and founder of the Diarra dynasty which lasted until 1862 (Guilhem 1961). He conquered the Peul, and the cities of Djenne and Timbuctoo. When he died in 1787, his son Monson became king (1787–1808). After his reign the kingdom began to decline. In 1862, Segou fell to the Moslem Tukulor warrior, El Hadj Omar Tall, and in 1864 his son, Amadou Tall, became the King of Segou until 1892 when the French drove him out, as mentioned earlier.

The Bambara kings were in effect priest-kings, because they headed the state religion and presided over all of the cults. When the Tukulor conquered the Bambara, they attempted to impose Islam by force, with little success. Although the Bambara kings were not Moslem (except for one, Ali, one of Biton Coulibaly's sons, who was murdered by the *ton-djon*), they tolerated the Moslem Soninke people in their midst. The latter were vital to the trade of the kingdom and were Segou's main means of commercial exchange with Timbuctoo, North Africa, and the coast. The Tukulor were officially intolerant of the Bambara religion in both Segou

*A close-up view of a Bambara village in eastern Bambara country, showing
a maze of buildings, courtyards, veranda, and walls.*

and Kaarta, but were unsuccessful in destroying it. As had been the case in
the Mali Empire, Islam was the religion of the court but not of the masses.

The Kaarta Kingdom of the Bambara never achieved the administrative and political cohesion of its sister Kingdom of Segou. Its last king
was put to death by El Hadj Omar Tall in 1854 when he captured the capital
of Nioro.

Between Kaarta and Segou lies a large area known as the
Beledougou. Neither Segou nor Kaarta were ever able to bring this area
under their control, nor were the Tukulor successful in conquering it.
Composed of small powerful chiefdoms which united as required against a
common cause, the Beledougou preserved its ancient traditions and the
traditional Bambara religion better than any of the other Bambara areas.

Malinke (Maninka)

The Malinke trace their origins to the Manding heartland and are
distributed from the mouth of the Gambia River, across southern Senegal,
through western Mali and northern Guinea, and on into the Ivory Coast.
Even though the rulers of the Mali Empire adopted Islam, the Malinke
remained largely animist, as they still are today. Like the Bambara, they
are farmers, but keep few cattle or other livestock since they live in tsetse-
infested areas (see section on trypanosomiasis, Chapter 12). Unlike

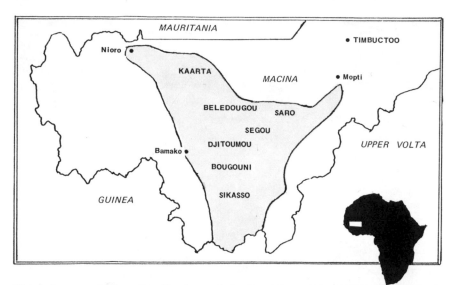

Shaded area shows distribution of the Bambara in Mali. Names in the shaded area indicate traditional Bambara regions. Today the Bambara are Mali's largest ethnic group. They number about two million people—over a third of the country's population. They belong to a large linguistic family (some ten million people) who speak one of the Manding languages.

Bambara villages, Malinke villages tend to be small, most numbering fewer than a few hundred inhabitants. The Malinke live in some of the unhealthiest areas of the savanna, around the headwaters of both the Niger and Senegal rivers where trypanosomiasis and onchocerciasis have a very high incidence. In contrast to most of the Bambara country, the Malinke country today remains rather isolated, with few good roads or even tracks.

Dyula

The term Dyula is used to designate the Manding language which is spoken in the Ivory Coast, Upper Volta, and Ghana. The term is also applied in these areas to all native speakers of Manding, regardless of their origins, and to all those who are native to these areas but who trace their ancestral origins to the Manding homeland. The actual Dyula language is a compromise between Malinke and Bambara and is regarded by these peoples as a form of pidgin, an expected attitude towards a trade language spoken by second-language speakers. Dyula also means, "itinerant trader," a generic term used to describe the commercial diaspora of Manding peoples towards Ghana and the Ivory Coast. The Dyula are primarily Moslem, but many of them retain animist practices. It is thought by some scholars that the Dyula are originally of Soninke (Saracole) origin.

They number close to 200,000 and are primarily traders living in large towns and commercial centers.

Khassonke

The Khassonke number about 70,000 and live on the Upper Senegal near Kayes in Mali. They are considered to be of mixed Malinke and Peul origins. They are primarily subsistence farmers and possess few cattle except in the northern savanna because of the presence of the tsetse fly. The Khassonke are animists, living in small villages scattered through rather mountainous terrain. Only in recent years have they begun to embrace Islam to any appreciable degree. They are close neighbors to both the Bambara and the Malinke and speak a form of Manding similar to that spoken by the Malinke. The principal disease problems among them are onchocerciasis and trypanosomiasis, both of which have greatly interfered with agricultural development in the region.

Wasulunka

The Wasulunka live to the southeast of the Manding heartland around the Guinea-Mali frontier, and number about 50,000. They are subsistence farmers and hunters, but because of the tsetse fly they can keep only small numbers of cattle, sheep, and goats. They are animists who are undergoing a gradual conversion to Islam. The Wasulunka are thought to be of mixed Peul and Malinke origins, but are quite distinct from the Khassonke who live well to the north of them.

Soninke (Saracole, Marka)

The Soninke number about 360,000 and consider their homeland the northern savanna and sahel of western Mali, southern Mauritania, and eastern Senegal. Diasporic groups are found in central Mali near Segou and San and in northern Upper Volta and have been present in these regions for several centuries. The Soninke are staunch Moslems and are thought to be of mixed Peul, Bambara, Berber, and Malinke origins. They are intrepid travelers and itinerant merchants who can be found in large colonies not only in West Africa, but also in Central and East Africa and Europe. Their homeland is a region of exodus from which a considerable proportion of the young male population has migrated. This has created serious social problems in that women and children are often left behind by husbands who rarely return, except for short periods of time to exhibit their wealth and recount their good fortunes. In northwestern Mali, the Soninke live in extremely large villages containing several thousand inhabitants. They practice shifting cultivation and raise small herds of sheep, goats and cattle. The principal disease problems among the Soninke of the northern savanna are endemic syphilis and trachoma (see Appendix A).

Bozo

     The Bozo, who number close to 50,000, are itinerant fishermen who live by fishing and the boat trade on both the Bani and Niger rivers. Some of them also engage in agriculture in the flood plains of the inland delta of the Niger. Although the Bozo are Moslem, they still retain many animist practices, especially those related to the river and fishing. They live in large villages along the river banks in central Mali and begin their seasonal migration downstream when the rivers begin to fall in January. From then until August they live in large temporary camps consisting of many families, often numbering close to 200 people. The principal medical problems among the Bozo are schistosomiasis (a blood fluke infection) and malaria (see Chapter 12 and Appendix A).

Bambara Status and Language

     The Bambara have clearly had close political and commercial ties not only with their immediate neighbors who have just been described in some detail, but also with groups farther away on the west African coast and in the Sahara. The islands of Soninke traders who lived among them brought them into not only commercial contact with the outside world, but also into contact with new ideas. Islam eventually took root among the Bambara not through sudden force, such as that imposed by El Hadj Omar Tall, but via Moslem traders, especially the Soninke.

     Under the French colonial administration, and since Mali became independent in 1960, the Bambara have moved into ever-growing towns in large numbers. Although most of the Bambara are still rural farmers, they constitute sizeable populations in Mali's major towns, Bamako, Segou, San, Kayes, Bougouni and Mopti. A large proportion of the civil service of Mali consists of Bambara personnel and most top political and administrative posts are filled by them.

     Their language, *Bamanan-kan*, is the *lingua franca* in most of Mali. Some of the reasons for this were mentioned above. It developed into a major commercial language, was dispersed even more widely by the French who used primarily Bambara interpreters and administrative assistants, and is the language of Mali's educated elite of administrators and teachers, most of whom are themselves Bambara. Whereas the Peul, Tuareg, Bobo, and Minianka went to extraordinary means to avoid placing their children in colonial schools, the Bambara and Malinke more readily complied. This resulted in the formation of educated cadres who were overwhelmingly Bambara-speaking. This plus the numerical superiority of the Bambara over other groups served to make *Bamanan-kan* even more of a *lingua franca* than it already was in what is now Mali.

The Bambara language is easy to pronounce. Words are composed of a radical, often monosyllabic, to which are added suffixes and prefixes to form the plural, the masculine and feminine, diminutives, and the tenses of verbs. A large number of words in use in the language have been borrowed from Arabic and some from French and there are many onomatopoeas. There is no definite article in Bambara nor in other Manding dialects. The plural of nouns is expressed by the suffix *ou*, which is only slightly pronounced. Those nouns already ending in *ou* in the singular, keep this suffix in the plural (Molin 1956). Some words ending in *i* in the singular, keep the *i* before adding *ou* for the plural. Others do not. As a general rule, nouns are not pluralized if followed by an adjective. The adjective takes the plural form, the noun remains singular. There are some exceptions to this rule (Molin 1956).

Wherever possible, I have used the singular spelling of nouns, even though the plural sense is meant.

At the present time, Mali is attempting to standardize the orthography for *Bamanan-kan*. This is not an easy task, especially since several dictionaries have already been published (Bazin 1906; Molin 1955; Delafosse 1955). Also, over the past century, explorers, administrators, missionaries, and scholars have used a variety of spellings for many words. Spellings used by Francophones often differ from those used by Anglophones. The former, for example, write *Segou*, the latter *Segu*. The French spell the word for village *dougou*, the Anglophones, *dugu*. In presenting the writings of others, I have used whatever spelling they have used. In general, I myself have used the French orthography because it is still the standard at present.

References

Annuaire Statistique, 1972. 1975. Bamako: Direction Nationale du Plan et de la Statistique.

Atkins, G. 1972. *Manding, Focus on an African Civilization.* London: University of London.

Ba, A.H. and Daget, J. 1962. *L'Empire Peul du Macina*, Volume I (1818-1853). Paris: Mouton and Co.

Bazin, H. 1906. *Dictionnairie Bambara—Francais.* Paris: Imprimerie Nationale. Reprinted in 1965 by Gregg Press, Westmead, England.

Brasseur, G. 1974. *Le Mali.* Paris: La Documentation Francaise.

Delafosse, M. 1955. *La Langue Mandingue et Ses Dialectes*, Tome II, *Dictionnaire-Mandingue—Francais.* Paris: Bibliothèque de l'Ecole Nationale des Langues.

Dieterlen, G. 1950. *Essai sur La Religion Bambara.* Paris: Presses Universitaires de France.

Dieterlen, G. and Cissé, Y. 1972. *Les Fondements de la Société d'Initiation du Komo.* Paris: Mouton.

Foltz, W.J. 1965. *From French West Africa to the Mali Federation.* New Haven: Yale University Press.

Gallais, J. 1967. *Le Delta Intérieur du Niger. Etude de Géographie Régionale*, Tome I et II. Dakar: IFAN.

Ganay, S. de 1950. Graphies Bambara des Nombres, *Journal de la Société des Africanistes* 20:295–305.

Guilhem, M. 1961. *Précis d'Histoire de l'Ouest Africain*. Paris: Ligel.

Guilhem, M. and Toe, S. 1963. *Précis d'Histoire du Mali*. Paris: Ligel.

Imperato, P.J. 1975. *A Wind in Africa*. St. Louis: Warren H. Green.

Imperato, P.J. 1977. *Historical Dictionary of Mali*. Metuchen, New Jersey: Scarecrow Press.

Keita, R. 1972. *Kayes et le Haut Sénégal*, Tome I et II. Bamako: Editions Populaires.

Miner, H. 1965. *The Primitive City of Timbuctoo*. Garden City, New York: Doubleday and Company.

Molin, Msgr. 1955. *Dictionnaire Bambara—Français et Français–Bambara*. Issy-Les-Moulineaux, Les Presses Missionaires.

Molin, Msgr. 1956. *Grammaire Bambara, Ancienne Grammaire de Msgr Sauvant*. Issy-Les-Moulineaux, Les Presses Missionaires.

N'Diaye, B. 1970. *Groupes Ethniques au Mali*. Bamako: Editions Populaire.

Oloruntimehin, B.O. 1972. *The Segu Tukulor Empire*. London: Longman.

Zahan, D. 1950. Pictographic Writing in the Western Sudan, *Man* 50:136–138.

Zahan, D. 1960. Ataraxie et Silence Chez les Bambara, *Zaire* 14:491–504.

2

The Therapeutic Process

In Western society, levels of perception of illness vary greatly from one individual to another. Once perceived, illness is managed by a therapeutic process which is in most instances initiated by either the patient or by someone close to him. Symptoms of fever, malaise, pain and change in normally perceived physiologic functions, which are commonly associated with many disease states, do not prompt all patients to initiate the therapeutic process. Some ignore symptoms for a considerable period, hoping that they will disappear. Another group will ignore symptoms for a short time and begin to treat themselves when these symptoms do not abate. Others will initiate self-treatment as soon as symptoms appear and still others will seek out the advice of a physician at the onset of awareness that something is wrong.

Home Remedies in Western Society

It is easy to lose sight of the fact in this era of scientific diagnosis and treatment of disease, that home remedies abound in Western society. Such remedies vary from family to family and between specific ethnic groups. Common components of these therapeutic regimens include bed rest, the implementation of certain dietary practices, and the use of over-the-counter medications. While some of these have been shown to have a scientific basis for efficacy, others have not. The latter are often not discarded because there is generation transfer of the empirical observations of their effectiveness. Chicken soup is given to those sick with influenza and severe upper respiratory tract infections. Scarves are wrapped around the necks of children suffering from severe laryngitis. Tea is forced upon those who have been diagnosed as having intestinal disorders. The variety of such folk remedies is enormous.

Success is often attributed to such treatments in Western society because they are employed for the management of self-limited illnesses; and the same observation applies to folk remedies used in African societies (see also pages 24-25 below). The patient will recover whether or not they are used, a point difficult to prove to the proponents of these treatments. A strong case can certainly be made for their usefulness as non-specific supportive measures, both in the physical and the psychological sense. And indeed, some but not all are given greater credibility through approbation by practicing physicians.

The Physician in Western Society

At some point, most ill individuals seek help by consulting a physician. In doing so, they anticipate positive results from the treatment he prescribes. An increasing number of patients also expect a detailed explanation of how they became ill. When they visit a physician they are consciously aware, often in a vague way, of the general standards inherent in quality medical practice. It is expected that the physician's office have the physical characteristics well-known to most in Western society. So one anticipates finding a waiting room, a nurse or receptionist, examining rooms with standard furnishings, and instrument cabinets and diplomas on the wall. Patients expect the office to be clean and neat, in a sense somewhat antiseptic.

In addition to these physical standards, patients anticipate certain procedural standards. The physician will first elicit the chief complaint with such phrases as, "What seems to be the trouble? What is bothering you?" And this will be followed by an interrogatory encounter in which details of the illness are elicited. "When did it start? How did it start? Have you ever had this before?" These are some of the many questions patients expect to be asked.

The physician will also take down a medical history in an orderly fashion, eliciting all of the patient's past illnesses. He is expected to inquire about possible familially transmitted diseases such as diabetes mellitus. The intelligent patient also expects inquiry into his social and occupational activities, as these may have a bearing on his problem.

A physical examination is conducted beginning with an examination of that area of the body to which the illness is confined. Where such localization does not exist, the physician will conduct the examination according to the long-established procedure by first examining the head, eyes, ears, nose and throat, taking the blood pressure, pulse, respiratory rate and temperature. Patients expect this and would be suspicious of the physician's competency or perhaps alarmed if their chief complaint were a sore throat and he began his examination by checking the feet.

Once the examination is completed, two possibilities result. A diagnosis may be made simply on the basis of the history and physical examination. Secondly, the physician may be unsure of the diagnosis and may have to order a number of diagnostic procedures to rule out other possibilities. In the majority of instances, a diagnosis is made on the basis of a history and physical examination and the patient given a therapeutic regimen. A small proportion of these patients may require hospitalization for treatment. Among the remainder, the diagnostic work up is performed either on an outpatient basis or else the patient is hospitalized. Often a treatment regimen is begun among this group of patients, it being directed at that disease which ranks first in the differential diagnosis. It is not unusual that physicians practice what is known as *shot-gun therapy*. This is the institution of a therapeutic regimen aimed at all possibilities in the differential diagnosis and results in the patient taking a large number of different medications. Needless to say, this is poor quality medical practice in a setting where diagnostic resources are available.

Patients generally expect that the treatment regimen will terminate their illness. If it doesn't, then they will usually consult another physician and in some instances they will be referred to a specialist by their primary care physician.

Patients will not usually consult a physician whose practice digresses widely from the commonly perceived standards considered as indicators of quality care. If per chance they do, on perceiving this situation they will abandon the practitioner and not return. Although standards of high quality may be perceived by patients in the practice of a given physician, he may in fact be practicing poor quality medicine. Only the *cognoscenti* of his own profession would know that he has not kept up with modern medical advances, that his diagnostic acumen has diminished, and that therapeutic advances have passed him by. But often none of these deficiencies catch up with him because he deals primarily with self-limited disease processes. Thus it is common to hear patients speaking in glowing terms of a physician who among his knowledgeable colleagues is not highly regarded. Statistics are on his side in a sense, because in most instances he can muddle his way through. His failures and his disastrous mistakes rarely come to the attention of his clientele, especially in large urban centers.

In the United States, medical consumers have become increasingly aware of those standards and qualifications which spell out good medical care. A physician who has a faculty appointment at a medical school and who is on the staff of a teaching hospital is judged better than one who is not. This is because he must continuously meet the quality standards incorporated into the operation of such institutions. There are, of course, physicians who are not associated with such institutions who deliver higher quality medical care than those who are. But in general, physicians who must constantly meet high standards do practice better medicine, and their hospital and medical school appointments are a certification of this fact. An individual's competency is also attested to by his certification by specialty boards and his membership in certain professional societies.

Sickness and Its Treatment in African Cultures

The process of illness perception is much the same in Africa as in Western society. In general, individuals react to alterations in normal physiology and to symptoms by concluding that they are ill. A variety of home remedies are tried first consisting of measures which closely parallel those employed in Western society. The sick person is the focus of attention and receives recovery wishes from relatives, friends, and neighbors. Often the patient will lie on a bamboo litter or straw mat outdoors in a courtyard or in front of his home, and therefore is extremely accessible to well wishers. They offer their own therapeutic advice. In Western society, a sick person may at most have family members, some friends, and occasionally some neighbors as a circle of therapeutic advisers. But he rarely has as many persons involved in his care as does the African patient.

Home Remedies

Part of the home regimen is the use of herbal preparations which are often obtained in market places or else cut fresh out in the bush. In most African societies there is a well-known pharmacopeia of such home remedies. Their preparation and use are well known, as are the sites where they may be found. In a sense these preparations correspond to the over-the-counter pharmaceuticals used in Western society. People know how to administer them and how often. Just as it is known that aspirin is administered in a dose of ten grains every four hours for fever, herbal infusions are drunk at given intervals to achieve the same purpose. In Western society, it is common knowledge that aspirin tablets are swallowed and not administered as a suppository or in a solution that is rubbed over the surface of the body. The mode of administration of items in the African household pharmacopeia is similarly well-known. There is then considerable similarity in the two systems of medical care, at least at the outset.

Natural and Supernatural Causes of Illness

When the illness does not respond to home remedies, it is not considered to be ordinary in nature. Rather, it is viewed as being serious in nature and probably due to some supernatural cause. Thus there exists a belief in a dualist system of disease causation, a departure from the western world's scientific canons of pathogenesis (Conco 1972). Warren (1975) has recently described the complex system of words used by the Bono of Ghana for naturally- and spiritually-caused diseases. As he clearly shows, in Africa disease states are not all believed to be due to an ultimate spiritual cause. Many are understood to have natural causes. Others have argued that all diseases are believed to have ultimate supernatural causes, even minor illnesses. This point of view, however, has not stood up well in the light of more recent and careful field investigations which show the existence of a dualist system in many African societies. The patient is rarely left to himself to decide whether or not a supernatural cause is involved. His family, friends and neighbors who are familiar with the routine of his daily life and his social connections play no small role in deciding this.

Role of Marabouts in Treating Illness

The next step is for the patient to go to a traditional practitioner who deals with the supernatural causes of disease. In many African societies there are several categories of these practitioners. Among Islamized Bambara, the *marabouts* (Koranic teachers) are clerics who, in addition to interpreting the Koran, diagnose the supernatural cause of illness, neutralize it and prevent its further action. When a patient visits a marabout he is told *why* he became ill. In Western society, the physician tells his patient *how* he became ill. "You have influenza," a physician will say. "You contracted it by breathing in the virus." The marabout usually will say something like, "You have this illness because your ancestor spirits are angry that you have ignored sacrificing to them." Such a reply coming from a physician to a patient in New York City would be viewed as absurd as a marabout in Bamako, Mali, telling a patient his illness was due to a virus invading the respiratory tract. In each situation, the patient expects the practitioner to provide what society views as a standard.

A marabout, like a physician, is judged in terms of competence and quality of service by his clientele. The yardsticks used are obviously somewhat different, but there are striking similarities. The physical setting in which he practices is usually his home. It contains physical elements which the patient expects to find and whose absence would raise doubts about the marabout's competency. There are sand piles for telling the future, cowrie shells (the white shells of a marine snail) for divination, cryptic Arabic phrases written on wooden tablets, and talismans composed of leather pacs containing bits of paper on which passages from the Koran are written.

The marabout begins his encounter with a patient in much the same way as does a physician. He asks, "What is wrong? What do you feel?" Once he is told this, he asks the patient about his social relationships and in so doing sifts through information which may contain indications of conflicts with friends, relatives, or enemies. The patient's religious and social conduct is simultaneously evaluated, the marabout looking for some disharmony of sufficient proportions to which the illness can be ascribed. Invariably, a marabout elicits more than enough information to ascribe the illness to several possible supernatural causes. However, after interrogating the patient, he will determine the specific reason that the illness has occurred, either by reading passages from the Koran or Arabic medical texts, or by interpreting the position of cowrie shells thrown on the floor (Imperato 1969).[1] After the performance of this expected ritual the reason is given to the patient.

The treatment process may require several return visits or it may be implemented at the time of the initial consultation and be repeated by the individual at home. Inherent in these treatment regimens is the participation of the patient by his performance of prescribed ritual acts. Treatment failures are almost never attributed to a marabout, but to improper performance of prescribed rituals. And if these have been performed correctly and the illness remains, the marabout will decide that the supernatural cause is more powerful than he originally thought. In this case he will prescribe a new regimen or refer the patient to another marabout, renowned for his learning.

As with the Western physician, most disease states brought to marabouts are self-limited and resolve on their own. Treatment failures in Western society are often ascribed to some deficiency on the part of the treating physician, rarely to something the patient did or did not do. Among Bambara Moslems, the patient's key role in the implementation of the treatment regimen inherently ascribes to him considerable responsibility for failure. Success is always attributed to the marabout. And if after the intervention of even the most renowned of marabouts, the patient does not improve, it will be attributed to God's will. Marabouts, therefore, unlike the Western physician, possess several fail-safes—the patient's

---

[1] Most Islamic clerics who treat illness in sub-Sahara Africa do not have access to Islamic medical texts. In addition, many have a poor understanding of Arabic, so that these texts would be of very limited use to them.

failure to perform the ritual as prescribed, the nature of the supernatural cause, and Islamic fatalism.

Marabouts are judged not only according to their successes but also according to their training. Those who have studied in urban centers of Islamic training in West Africa enjoy greater prestige than those who have been trained in small villages. At the apex of this hierarchy are those who have spent time in either North Africa or in Mecca. The latter, because of their having been to the geographic origins of Islam, are viewed as possessing the highest degree of supernatural power.

Marabouts do not physically examine their patients. As a consequence, Africans accustomed to maraboutic medicine find it strange when, upon consulting a Western-trained physician, they are examined. They would see nothing wrong in the physician treating them without ever examining them.

The Western medical practitioner is concerned about how — not why — his patient became ill. He is not at all concerned with why his patient became ill. He would push aside as irrelevant any patient inquiry along these lines. Perhaps the only exception to this is the practice of psychiatry where an attempt may be made to probe deeply into the whys of subjective feelings.

African folk medicine rests upon a foundation of beliefs shared and inculcated at a very young age. Traditional practitioners to be successful in meeting the expectations of society must provide both an answer and an antidote to why a patient is ill. They are eminently successful at the former because their training and experience equip them to provide a ready answer. And they rarely fail at the latter because most illnesses are self-limited, with credit for cure being given to the healer (Maclean 1971).

References

Conco, W.Z. 1972. The African Bantu Traditional Practice of Medicine: Some Preliminary Observations. *Social Science And Medicine* 6:283-322.

Imperato, P.J. 1970. Indigenous Medical Beliefs and Practices in Bamako, a Moslem African City. *Tropical And Geographical Medicine* 22:211-220.

Maclean, U. 1971. *Magical Medicine*. London: Penguin Press.

Warren, D.M. 1975. The Role of Emic Analysis in Medical Anthropology: The Case of the Bono of Ghana. *Anthropological Linguistics* 17:117-126.

3

Disease Causation and the Spirit World

In Africa man constantly lives in a close and intimate relationship not only with the individuals of the society to which he belongs, but also with a pantheon of diverse spirits. It is not surprising then that disease and misfortune are believed at times to result from these two types of relationships. Mild disease of a self-limited nature does not generally suggest a supernatural etiology. Serious illness does, whether it is an individual case or an epidemic. It does not respond to simple treatments and therefore is ascribed a serious cause. There is then a dualist theory of disease causation encompassing diseases due to natural causes and those due to supernatural causes (Conco 1972; Warren 1975).

African Beliefs in Supernatural Forces Related to Disease

There are four principal broad categories of supernatural forces in sub-Sahara Africa believed responsible for illness and misfortune: spirits, ghosts, witchcraft, and sorcery. While this statement may not hold true for all societies, it does for many. Most African peoples believe in a Supreme Being who is called by a variety of names and who is believed to have created the universe and all the beings and forces within it. Many of the cataclysms and disastrous changes that occur in the universe are ascribed to this Supreme Being—as the ultimate cause; but he is believed to act through lesser spirits to achieve these ends. He is not held responsible for personal and individual misfortunes and illness, and as a consequence no one in animist societies attempts to intercede directly with him to reverse such events. Among Moslems in Africa, God is viewed as often permitting illness and misfortune to occur through the agency of other proximal causes, often supernatural. Beliefs differ in various African societies with respect to the relationship between God and the pantheon of spirits and ghosts in the world. In some societies all spirits and ghosts are believed to be subordinate and under the Supreme Being's direct control; in other groups, the degree of control is believed to be much less; and among still other peoples, spirits are considered to be diverse manifestations of the Supreme Being (Evans-Pritchard 1937).

Ghosts and Spirits

Spirits, as viewed by most of the peoples of Africa, are extra-human powers of which there are several categories. For an individual the most important of these are the ghosts of deceased ancestors and relatives. As viewed by many Africans, a ghost is a portion of the spiritual element which remains behind on earth after a person's (or an animal's) death (Beattie and Middleton 1969). Many African societies possess elaborate formalized mechanisms for appeasing and pleasing the ghosts of ancestors and kin. Ancestor worship, among other things, prevents or minimizes the displeasure of forces capable of causing illness and misfortune. Among certain groups, such as the Banyoro of Uganda, the ghosts of ancient folk heroes and kings, known as *cwezi*, exert a powerful influence in the affairs of the living and they are appeased and prevented from doing harm through the Cwezi Spirit Cult (Beattie 1963). Another group of ghosts are those of the recently deceased who are not related to an individual, but who may have been harmed or insulted when alive.

Hunters in many societies must take precautions against the ghosts of animals they have slain since these ghosts are capable not only of impeding the hunter's future ability but also of inflicting illness on him and his family. There is also widespread belief in the spiritual powers of many inanimate things such as trees, mountains, rivers, thunder, lightning, and clouds. These are nature spirits.

In Islamized areas, there is a strong belief in *jinn* or genies as they are often called. *Jinn* are spiritual beings and not the ghosts of deceased humans. While some *jinn* are believed to be benevolent, most are malevolent and act either on their own or for someone who controls them. They are believed to assume a number of terrifying corporeal forms and also human or animal forms if they so wish. *Jinn* are said to be circumcised Moslems and are grouped into a number of different tribes. In contrast to them are the *shetani*, another group of spirits who do not assume a corporeal form. *Shetani* are believed to cause illness by possession of an individual, either on their own initiative or under the influence of a living human who possesses the power to control them. *Jinn* do not usually cause illness through possession (Gray 1969). In addition to these two groups of spirits, many Islamized African groups retain a strong belief in the ghosts of ancestors, kin, the recently deceased, and of elements and inanimate objects.

The pantheon of spirits and ghosts which play so important a role in causing illness and misfortune are dealt with through spirit cults and spirit mediums. Through spirit mediums, misfortune and illness are explained, their cause identified and a prescription given for appeasing the offending spirit or ghost.

Witchcraft and Sorcery

Beliefs in witchcraft and sorcery were once common in the Western world and are now looked upon by most Westerners as the hallmarks of superstitious societies. This attitude has made it difficult, if not impossible, for many foreigners in Africa to understand the considerable differences between witchcraft and sorcery, between witches and sorcerers, and to appreciate the significant role these beliefs play in the lives of those who espouse them. These beliefs are social and not psychological phenomena (Middleton and Winter 1963). That they are complex is well appreciated by those who have attempted to study them.

During the latter part of the nineteenth century and the early part of this century, many descriptions of traditional African medicine were written by missionaries, administrators, explorers, hunters, and traders. Through no fault of their own, many of these observers failed to recognize the existence of two distinct systems, witchcraft and sorcery, operating within the societies they were studying. More often than not, the two were either confused or grouped together. Many of these descriptions have now become hallowed by the passage of time and often have gone unchallenged. It was not until 1937 that the differences between these two beliefs in Africa were differentiated by Evans-Pritchard in his book, *Witchcraft, Oracles and Magic among the Azande*. He provided the first clear distinction between witchcraft and sorcery and elucidated their relationship to spirit mediums, spirit possession, divination, and the indigenous healing of illness.

Middleton and Winter (1963) have pointed out that the distinction between witchcraft and sorcery does not exist among certain African groups. Although such groups are in a minority, they do comprise an exception to the rule, and they render an understanding of these beliefs easier. The Nandi of Kenya are an example of an important group of people for whom there is no distinction between witchcraft and sorcery (Huntingford 1953). In addition, it must be pointed out that those suspected of being witches may also practice sorcery, as among the Luo of Tanzania (Imperato 1966). These exceptions, however, are not widespread, so it can be stated in general that believers make a clear distinction between witchcraft and sorcery.

Witchcraft

Witches are individuals who possess an innate malicious power which works to cause harm to either health or property (Imperato 1966). The mystical power possessed by witches is known as witchcraft substance and is believed to be found in the gastrointestinal tracts of witches where it grows in strength and size with advancing age. Witchcraft substance is thought inherited within certain families. It may be dormant in an individual for many years, unknown to him; he may be unaware that he is a witch until accused. An individual's witchcraft often functions without his being aware of it (Evans-Pritchard 1937). Witches are thought to operate primarily at night, and their power is believed to attack the spiritual portions of their victims' organs.

For the most part, witchcraft is thought to be restricted to women, although there are exceptions to this. Old women are often accused of being witches, and it follows that they are thought to be very powerful ones because of the strength accrued by their witchcraft substance through age.

Sorcery

A sorcerer is an individual who consciously engages in bad magic for the purpose of harming someone; anyone, therefore, can engage in sorcery, as opposed to witchcraft, if he so wishes. Although the materials possessed by sorcerers are considered magical and the rites associated with their use believed to inflict harm, there is no evidence in a scientific sense that this is the case. Sorcery usually involves the use of materials such as herbs, hair, nail parrings and other objects over which a secret formula is pronounced imparting a magical maleficent power to the substances. These materials are used in a variety of ways to achieve their imagined end. They may be deposited near the doorway of the intended victim's house, hidden in the ceiling of his house or under his bed, or buried in the ground near a wall of his house. Theoretically, one can see sorcery being practiced, but there are no specific observers who will attest that the materials and rituals used achieved their intended ends. Because the practice of sorcery is secretly carried out, few outsiders have observed it. Middleton and Winter (1963) state that while beliefs in sorcery may be widespread, the actual practice of it is probably rare.

From the perspective of modern science it is impossible to observe witchcraft in operation. Africans believe it is at work, but they do not themselves claim to see it. A notable exception is the claim of some Luo who say they have seen witchcraft substance at night as a round, red, glowing ball of fire moving across the countryside (Imperato 1966).

It is quite logical to ask why African societies possess beliefs in two maleficent systems, witchcraft and sorcery, when it would seem that one alone might suffice. The fact that beliefs in both witchcraft and sorcery are found almost consistently in most societies in Africa has been the object of considerable study in recent years. Middleton and Winter set forth the convincing argument that because witchcraft is usually confined to the members of one sex, another factor, namely sorcery, must be found to complete the belief system of misfortune and disease causation. The roots of accusations of witchcraft and sorcery generally lie in disputes among individuals who share important social relationships.

If, for example, the child of a woman who possesses many children falls seriously ill, the woman will suspect the person she thinks is most envious of her. If she has a co-wife in a polygamous marriage who is barren, this woman will be immediately suspected of being the cause of the child's illness. The accusation in this instance can be expressed in the idiom of either witchcraft or sorcery if women are believed to be witches. If, on the other hand, the husband of these two women becomes ill a week after having a serious altercation with an older male cousin, he will suspect his cousin of having caused his illness. In this instance the accusation cannot be made that the cousin is a witch, since in this society only women can be witches; therefore the accusation of sorcery will be made.

Witchcraft and sorcery have been carefully studied in Africa by a number of scholars. Both phenomena are extremely complex in Africa and in some societies the lines of difference between them seem rather blurred. Witchcraft has been discussed in detail by Douglas (1967, 1970); Horton (1967); and Parrinder (1958), among others.

Bambara Beliefs in Supernatural Cause of Illness

The Bambara possess an elaborate system of belief in the supernatural causation of illness. This encompasses a belief in ghosts, spirits, witchcraft and sorcery onto which are grafted Islamic beliefs in geographic areas where many have been converted to Islam. There are some slight regional variations in some of their beliefs. Good health is of the utmost importance to the Bambara, as shown by the place that inquiries about health enjoy in their routine greetings. After saying "Ini sogoma" (Good morning), one asks "Era sira?" (Did you sleep well?), and then "I kakene?" (How are you?), the reply to which is "Torote" (I suffer no illness).

Spirits and Ghosts

The Bambara believe that the human soul has two portions—the *ni*, the most important and essential element, and its double, the *dya*. In addition, man and some other creatures possess a spiritual force known as the *tere*, which can be conceived of as being one's character. At death, all of these elements are dissociated. The *ni* rests temporarily in the ancestral altars after the appropriate rites are performed and the *dya* enters the water where it is guarded by Faro, the most powerful of the Bambara spirits. The *tere* becomes a free force, the *nyama*, which roams about freely (Dieterlen 1951).

The Bambara believe in reincarnation. (See p. 44.) The child born in a family receives the spiritual elements of the person who died most recently before his birth. The *ni* of the deceased leaves the ancestral altar at the same time that the *dya* leaves the water. The *dya* enters the body of the newborn and becomes his *ni*, and the *ni* of the deceased becomes his *dya*. Whatever the sex of the child and the deceased relative, the *ni* is always the sex of the infant and the *dya* the opposite sex. Thus, a female child born after the death of an uncle receives his spiritual elements, the *ni* of the child being female and the *dya* male. In a sense this reincarnation would require no manipulation by Faro since the uncle's *dya* is female and it becomes the *ni* of an infant girl and is thus of the correct sex. His *ni*, which is male, becomes her *dya* which is supposed to be male. If the child is a boy, Faro intervenes directly to alter the sex of the spiritual elements (Dieterlen 1951).

Domestic and wild animals also possess the *ni* and the *dya* elements. In some regions it is believed that plants also possess these two elements. However, in other areas it is believed that plants possess only a *ni*, with the exception of wild tomatoes with possess both. This species of tomato, called *ngoyo* in Bambara, is used in sacrifices to Faro. Domestic animals which are closely associated with man also possess a *tere* which upon death becomes a *nyama*. Wild animals, however, do not possess a *tere*. However, they do possess a *nyama* which is released when they die. This *nyama* is not associated with a *tere* (Labouret 1934). Such spiritual forces are also found in inanimate objects such as hills and mountains, rivers and ponds, minerals, caves, and elements such as the wind, rain, thunder, lightning and the sky. In contradistinction to the *nyama* of men, the *nyama* of inanimate objects and elements does not emanate from a *tere*. It is, in effect, always there and operative.

The *nyama* of living beings — men, animals, insects and plants and trees — become operative when they die. In some areas, the *nyama* of trees are believed to be operative even while the trees are alive. Men are surrounded by these spiritual forces, *nyama*, which can do him considerable harm. During the course of his daily existence a man will destroy plants and kill insects and animals, the *nyama* of which will work to harm him. In addition, he may inadvertently incur the malevolent power of the *nyama* of inanimate objects and of elements. Certain physical locations such as caves and mountain peaks are avoided by ordinary people since they may fall ill by coming into contact with the *nyama* which reside there. Many eruptive diseases such as smallpox and urticaria are attributed to such *nyama* (Labouret 1934).

Nyama are immortal and cannot be destroyed. If man offends them or if he has killed their previous living material support, he suffers dire consequences which usually take the form of illness and misfortune. To rectify this situation he performs regular sacrificial rituals which appease these spirits and which atone for his transgressions. Similarly, he regularly performs ritual sacrifices of animals over the ancestral altars to appease the *nyama* of the ancestors (Henry 1910).

One might well ask what happens to the *nyama* of the animals killed in such routine sacrifices. The *nyama* of these animals are captured during the ritual and fastened to the material support, either an altar or a fetish, over which the sacrifice is made. Consequently, they cause no harm. A similar mechanism applies to animals which are killed for consumption and plants which are harvested for food. It is believed that Faro, having directed man to do these acts, keeps the *nyama* of these animals and plants under control (Tauxier 1927). (See also pp. 33-34 and 47.)

Villages generally possess protector spirits, known as *dassiri* which reside in such material supports as trees, animals, or unusual rock formations. These spirits act to counteract the *nyama* of animals, men, and inanimate objects which seek to harm the village as a whole. In many villages the *dassiri* is an acacia tree (*Acacia albida*), but it may be any type of tree. Animals such as donkeys, lizards, pythons, and goats also serve as village *dassiri*. An annual ritual sacrifice lasting three days is held in most

A large baobab tree surrounded by an enclosure of thick brush that serves as a dassiri—the abode of village protector spirits.

villages with everyone participating. A bull is generally slaughtered and each head of a family makes a sacrifice of millet porridge and kills a chicken (Henry 1910). During the year, the chief of the village makes two sacrifices to the *dassiri*, one at the start of the rainy season and one after the harvest. In some villages, it is believed that the *dassiri* is the abode of all ancestral *nyama*.

Requests for fertility are often made of *dassiri* by women who are barren. As part of their ritual they pour white millet porridge over the tree or on the rock and promise to name any offspring after the *dassiri*. This ritual is still common in the town of Kita where the *dassiri* is a tall rock standing on the edge of town.

The Spirits of Animals

In some areas of the Bambara country, it is believed that certain wild animals possess several *nyama* that reside in various parts of the anatomy. Some of these are considered so dangerous that a hunter will not bring this part of the animal into his village even after he has performed the required ritual to appease the *nyama* (Labouret 1934). Bambara hunters are organized into societies which have social, religious and magical functions. On the surface, it would appear that such individuals would be especially vulnerable to the nefarious effects of *nyama* since they kill so many wild animals. However, a hunter wears a talisman, called *dozoboli*, on his shoulder which captures the *nyama* as soon as the wild animal is killed.

Most patronymic groups among the Bambara possess animal totems known as *tne* or *tana*. These animals possess protective powers for their appropriate patronymic group and as a consequence are not allowed to be harmed, killed, or eaten (Imperato 1972). Periodic ritual sacrifices are made to them. The consequences of killing a family totem are serious for the individual. It is believed that the *nyama* of the dead animal will inflict serious illness and misfortune on his family. But in addition, his *tere*, or character, if it is good, will leave him and become a free roaming *nyama* inflicting on him no end of injury. Illness takes the form of a severe anemia and diseases of the mouth, nose, eyes, ears, and anus. Deafness is attributed to this type of transgression which can only be rectified by the appropriate ritual sacrifices. In most instances an animal that is a totem is believed to have rendered an important service to the ancestors of a patronymic group (Tauxier 1927).

The killing of animals by Europeans near villages has historically created serious problems. Tauxier, for example, recorded that in 1907 an epidemic of influenza occurred in the village of Songhobougou, and this was attributed to the *nyama* of a vulture which had been shot near the village by a French administrator. In 1957 a European shot and killed a bustard (a large bird) near a village in the Segou region, and an epidemic of measles which occurred shortly thereafter was attributed to the angry *nyama* of this bird. Measles carries a very high mortality in this part of the world, sometimes close to 50 percent (Imperato, unpublished observations 1969) (see chapter 11); thus the villagers were extremely angry at the European. When presented with the facts as seen by the villagers, he laughed at the representatives who came from the village to complain. They requested that he pay for an animal to be sacrificed to appease the *nyama* of the bustard. He refused. A few days later the European died from acute strychnine poisoning. One of his servants who was from the village had placed it in his food on orders from the village elders.

Spirits and ghosts may inflict illness by acting exteriorly on a victim or they may possess the person. Possession is believed to be the usual mechanism. The ghosts of ancestors are permitted to express what it is they want through a spirit medium. Often, a spirit medium will advise the patient to enter into an ongoing relationship with a spirit since the latter may bestow favors, as well as cause illness. In order to enter into such a relationship, the patient must himself become a spirit medium. (See also chapter 4.)

Witchcraft

The writings of the earliest scholars who studied the Bambara (Henry 1910; Monteil 1924; Tauxier 1927 and Labouret 1934) present a confusing picture of witchcraft and sorcery because none of them distinguished between the two groups of beliefs. The Bambara themselves believe in both witches and sorcerers, although the difference is not always clear to all of them. However, I have found that knowledgeable informants know the difference; they ascribe illness to one or the other depending on the circumstances. There are among the Bambara a number of different types of practitioners, diviners, herbalists, charm makers, fortune tellers, spirit mediums, and anti-sorcerers. Often there are areas of functional overlap between these categories, adding somewhat to the confusion.

Witches are known as *souba* in the Bambara language. Other appellations include *soubaka*, *souya-maou*, and *soubara*. The nature of witches is summed up in a well-known Bambara aphorism: *Bemba bi souba-ou da ni wolola e, n'ka dougouma ou t'ou don*, "God makes witches from the time of their birth, but people of their village do not know them."

Witches are believed to cause illness by attacking the victims' *dya*. The witches may assume various animal forms, such as birds, bats, or snakes or other reptiles. They generally attack their victims at night over an extended period of time, devouring, it is believed, vital organs such as the heart and liver.

Although witchcraft is inherited, it does not necessarily become manifest in a given individual. Both men and women can be witches, but women are more frequent. Accusations of witchcraft were once frequently made against old women and individuals who behaved in some slightly deviant manner. Such unusual behavior aroused suspicions about their being witches.

As seen by the Bambara, witches never cease to cause misfortune and illness because they must continuously eat the souls (*dya*) and vital organs of humans whenever witchcraft becomes manifest. This permanent attribute means that they are a menace as long as they live. Tauxier (1927) states that certain spirit mediums were believed to be able to cure witches of their witchcraft.

According to Tauxier, witches usually attacked individuals in the villages where they lived, which from the sociological point of view created enormous disruption and heightened feelings of anxiety, fear, and hatred. Emotions ran very high in such circumstances and the absence of sure defenses against witches led to drastic measures against those suspected of practicing witchcraft. The Bambara believe that witches often work together in a sort of cult and so when one person was accused of being a witch an attempt was made to force her to name her accomplices.

With the continual spread of Islam and the deepening of Koranic beliefs among those Islamized, beliefs in witches have waned. The Moslem Tukulor who conquered much of the Bambara country in the mid-19th century abolished poison ordeals for detecting witches and the killing of accused witches by burning (Tauxier 1927). At the present time, although the Bambara still profess to believe in the existence of witches, few concretize such a belief through accusation of specific individuals. Islam has provided substitute supernatural causes to which illnesses may be attributed. Islamization and a decline in witchcraft beliefs have led to an abandonment of the *Nama* cult, one of the six Bambara secret societies. One of the principal functions of the Nama was to protect villages from witchcraft and sorcery.

Sorcery

The Bambara maintain that anyone can practice sorcery if he so desires. Sorcery is aimed at a specific individual and so, unlike witchcraft, is not a menace to an entire community. Individuals can avoid being the victims of sorcery if they take care not to arouse anger and jealousy among their social contacts. The Bambara maintain that certain categories of diviners, spirit mediums, and healers practice sorcery on the side at the request of someone who wishes to harm the intended victim. This has led to the erroneous classification of many of these categories of practitioners as sorcerers by some field investigators.

Sorcery is a technique and can be learned by anyone. The act of sorcery is referred to by the Bambara as *nyenyini* and those suspected of engaging in it are also called by the same name, or *flelikela*. There are a number of techniques used, and they can be grouped into two broad categories. First there are those techniques which use material substances of some kind, and second there are those which use spirit agents.

Both of these types of techniques have been described in great detail by Henry (1910) and Tauxier (1927). Among the material substances used are actual poisons of plant origin, generally called *donkono*. These are slipped into the victim's food or drink. In this same category is the *korte*, a small grain of cereal, bone, stone, or wood which is dispatched through the air by one practicing sorcery. The *korte* then enters the body of its victim, usually through the skin. Prior to release of the *korte*, rituals are pronounced over the *korte* to confer on it the power to harm the intended victim. Other *korte* are said to fall into the intended victim's food or drink. Often, actual poisons are given to the victim, a common one being strophanthin (from the dried seeds of strophanthus plants).

Sorcery is also practiced with nail parings, hair, or some other material obtained from the intended victim. Rituals conducted over these items are believed to cause illness in the victim. Magical substances may also be buried beneath the floor of a victim's house or be placed on the path to his doorway by the sorcerer.

SOME REMOTE CAUSES OF ILLNESS AMONG THE BAMBARA*

Cause	Controlling Agent	Description
Korte	Sorcerers	A small physical form the size of a granule which is believed to penetrate the skin and enter the body.
Donkono	Sorcerers	Donkono are actual poisons which are surreptitiously placed in food or drink.
Kenke	Sorcerers	Granules that remain after the *korte* is made. They arrive with the rain.
Sirikoun	Sorcerers	A magical fetish composed of animal horns, hair and hide and cotton threads. The intentional pronouncement of magical formulae over it is believed to cause illness in the intended victim. They are often worn from a belt.
Basi	Diviner-Healers	Charms used for both protection and for inflicting illness.
Danga	Moslem Clerics	Danga are curses inflicted by Moslem clerics (*moriba*) who are referred to as *morijugou* in this role.
Dyina	Jinn (genies)	In Moslem areas live genies who are believed capable of causing illness.

*Illness may also result from disruptions in relationships between man and a variety of village, regional and ancestral spirits.

Sorcery is believed to be practiced frequently through the use of spirit agents. A common technique among the Bambara is the use of the *sirikoun* which is an oracular fetish. It consists of the tail of an animal, usually a bull, around which is tied a cotton thread and seven small pieces of straw. The tail is kept in a small sac of red cloth. *Sirikoun* are usually used for divination, but they can also be used to cause harm to a victim by directing the *nyama* which resides in the animal tail to afflict the intended victim.

Spirit mediums, who in Bambara are called *soma*, *nyabouin*, and *gne-fla*, may practice sorcery against someone at the request of a client. The victim is possessed by a *nyama* over which the medium has control.

Other Bambara Spirits and Islamic Spirits

In addition to the spirits and ghosts already described as causative agents of disease is a special group of spirits known as *woklo* or *woklani*. Most *woklo* are invisible, but some appear in the form of elves with long red beards, long fingernails, and feet which are turned backwards. They are believed to live on the edge of villages, often near large baobab trees. While some *woklo* are benevolent, many are not. When angered, *woklo* attack their victims, who develop severe tropical ulcers which do not heal readily. It is believed that *woklo* enjoy hitting small children who roam outside after dark. Such injuries are inflicted not by intent, but because *woklo* inflict them accidentally while playing with the children. Children who must walk outside after dark are often given a large hat to wear to protect them from the *woklo*.

A belief in *jinn* (p. 27) is widespread now in Islamized areas of the Bambara country. Faro, the chief spirit, subordinate only to God, is now referred to by Moslem Bambara as a water geni. Similarly, other supernatural personalities in the animist pantheon are considered as genies. The *nyama*, which in the animist religion play so important a role in man's life, are incorporated into the Moslem concept of sheltani spirits who are capable of possessing individuals.

References

Beattie, J. 1957. Initiation into the Cwezu Spirit Possession Cult in Bunyoro, *African Studies* 28:1.

Beattie, J. and Middleton, J. 1969. *Spirit Mediumship And Society In Africa*, London: Routledge and Keegan Paul.

Conco, W.Z. 1972. The African Bantu Traditional Practice of Medicine: Some Preliminary Observations, *Social Science and Medicine* 6:283-322.

Dieterlen, G. 1951. *Essai Sur La Religion Bambara*, Paris: Presses Universitaires de France.

Douglas, M. 1967. Witch Beliefs in Central Africa, *Africa* 37:72-80.

Douglas, M. 1970. *Witchcraft Confessions and Accusations*. London: Tavestok.

Evans-Pritchard, E.E. 1937. *Witchcraft, Oracles and Magic among the Azande*. Oxford: Oxford University Press.

Fortes, N. 1949. *The Web of Kinship Among The Tallensi*. London: Oxford University Press.

Gray, R.F. 1969. The Shetani Cult among the Segeju, in *Spirit Mediumship and Society In Africa*. London: Routledge and Keegan Paul.

Henry, J. 1910. *L'Ame d'Un Peuple Africain: Les Bambara*. Paris: Picard.

Horton, R. 1967. African Traditional Thought and Western Science, *Africa* 37 (Part I):50-72, (Part II):155-187.

Huntingford, G.W.B. 1953. *The Nandi of Kenya*. London: Oxford University Press.

Imperato, P.J. 1966. Witchcraft and Traditional Medicine among the Luo of Tanzania, *Tanzania Notes and Records* 66:193-201.

Imperato, P.J. 1969. Traditional Attitudes towards Measles in the Republic of Mali, *Transactions of The Royal Society of Tropical Medicine And Hygiene* 63(6):768-780.

Imperato, P.J. 1972. Door Locks of the Bamana of Mali, *African Arts* V(3):52-56.

Labouret, H. 1934. Les Mandingues et Leur Langue, *Bulletin du Comité d'Etudes Historiques, et Scientifiques de l'A.O.F.*, Paris: Larose, Vol. XVII.

Middleton, J. and Winter, E.H. 1963. *Witchcraft and Sorcery in East Africa*. London: Routledge and Keegan Paul.

Parrinder, G. 1958. *Witchcraft, European and African*. London: Faber and Faber.

Tauxier, L. 1927. *La Religion Bambara*. Paris: Librairie Orientaliste Paul Geuthner.

Warren, D.M. 1975. The Role of Emic Analysis in Medical Anthropology: The Case of The Bono of Ghana, *Anthropological Linguistics* 17:117-126.

4

Bambara Social Organization and Religious Beliefs

Social Organization

The Bambara live in villages which vary in size from two hundred to several thousand inhabitants. Villages, called *dugu*, are grouped into territorial units known as *kafo*, which in turn comprised the kingdoms of Segou and Kaarta which developed in the 17th century and lasted into the 19th. The French colonial government maintained the *kafo*, which they called *cantons*. These were replaced by administrative units known as *arrondissements* when Mali became independent in 1960.

The Bambara are patriarchal (the father is the authority figure), patrilocal (the family lives near the father's relatives), and patrilineal (descent is traced through the male line). Each extended family (a mother, father, and their children, and various relatives) is headed by an elder called the *fa*. He is elected by all of the elders of the extended family from among the eldest living generation, the generation which is closest to the ancestors. Succession to the post of family leadership thus passes between the brothers of the oldest generation before passing on to any of their sons. The heads of nuclear families (consisting of mother, father, and children) are responsible to the *fa*. There are usually several *fa* in a given village who in turn are responsible to a village chief, the *dugu tigui*.

A village chief is chosen from among the oldest living generation of the family which founded the village. The village chief is not only the chief administrator of the village, but also its religious chief. He is master of the earth and, as the descendant of the village founder, is the only person who can relate to the earth spirits which are of enourmous importance to an agricultural people.

Village chiefs in turn were once responsible to area chiefs, the *kafo tigui*, who ruled over several villages. They in turn were responsible to the *fama*, or king, who in the eastern Bambara country ruled from the town of

Ségou. Much of the western Bambara country was organized into the Kaarta kingdom and the *kafo-tigui* reported to the *fama* who resided mostly at Nioro. In principle, kingship passed through the males of the oldest living generation of the ruling family before passing on to the next generation; but often sons succeeded their fathers directly.

The heads of extended families, the *fa*, are in ultimate control of most of the material possessions of the family including land, animals, and harvests. They must, however, assure the material well-being of the family and pay dowries for the males when they marry. The administrative roles of area chiefs, *kafo tigui*, have been abolished. But they still continue certain religious roles as before.

The Bambara possess age sets which group young males and females into a hierarchical structure. These age sets have undergone considerable structural modification in the past two decades and have disappeared in some areas. Circumcision of males and excision of the clitoris in females (see chapter 13) were once performed around the age of 15. More recently, these operations have been carried out at much lower ages, often at the age of six or seven. Boys below the age of six years were grouped into an age set called *bilakoro-dogomani*, from 6 to 10 into a set called *bilakoro-dogoma*, and from 10 to 15 into a set called *bilakoro-koroba* (Paques 1951). Girls were grouped in a similar fashion. Within each village, each age set had a chief, called the *ton-tigui* for the boys and the *musso-tigui* for the girls.

Every three years, the young boys and girls who had reached around 15 years of age were circumcised at the same time, but separately. Now this is done much earlier. They form a group known as the *fla-n-bolo* (two hand), one for the girls and one for the boys. Three successive *fla-n-bolo* are grouped into a *fla-n-ton*. All of the *fla-n-ton* form a larger grouping called the *ton*. It takes nine years to complete a *fla-n-ton*. As a new *fla-n-bolo* enters the *fla-n-ton*, the oldest one leaves, since it usually consists of people who are married or about to be married.

The Ton

The *ton* is one of the cornerstones of Bambara society. Its principal functions are collective work and entertainment. For the men, collective work takes the form of farming fields and making baked mud bricks. This is often done for people who do not have enough men in the family to do it. Whenever they do collective work in someone's field, they are compensated with either cash (which is a recent form of remuneration), or with payment in the form of food, livestock, or a share of the crop. All these become the communal property of the *ton* and are kept for communal celebrations, for buying materials, for making dance costumes, or for purchasing gifts for members of the *ton* who are soon to be married. The girls collect funds by doing such tasks as spinning and hairdressing.

The boys and girls in any given *fla-n-bolo* are coupled and have a special relationship in which sexual relations are prohibited. The girl performs domestic functions for the boy and carries food and water out to him whenever he tills the fields. The boy in turn serves as the guardian of the girl's virginity until she marries, and suffers both physical punishment and public shame if he fails to do so. The relationship finally ends when one of the two marries. This relationship between boys and girls in the *ton* is gradually disappearing. Women and men remain in the *ton* until they marry which is usually in their late twenties or early thirties.

Status Groups

Bambara society is structured into three major status groups, the freemen, called *horon*, the slaves, called *dyon*, and the artisan guilds, called *nymakala*. The latter consist of the blacksmiths (*numu*), the leatherworkers (*garanke*), the weavers (*guesse dala*), the bards (*dyeli*), and the calabash (*gourd*) and woodworkers (*koule*). Although the artisan groups are often referred to as castes, this term, which may imply a low social status, is misleading since the artisans do not have a low social status in Bambara society. They possess a separate social status and quite often are in leadership positions. The blacksmiths, for example, often head initiation societies or else occupy important positions in them. The bards, besides being praise singers, are also the keepers of oral tradition and history, and intermediaries in settling disputes.

The *dyon*, or slaves, do have a lower social status than the freemen. Within this group are the *woloso*, individuals who are second- and third-generation slaves. Although slavery no longer exists legally in Mali, it is still a sociologic fact of life in the country among all ethnic groups, including the Bambara.

Freemen, artisans and slaves are all endogamous, even today; that is, marriage across group lines is rare, and usually occurs only among the educated elite. Polygamy is the rule among all Bambara social groups.

Initiation Societies

The Bambara have six principal initiation societies known collectively as *dyow* into which all circumcised males are progressively initiated. (Zahan [1974] has a good discussion of these socieites, and much of the material below is based on his discussion.) The word *dyow* means "secret." There are also a number of societies which are restricted to limited geographic areas. These initiation societies unite men across village and patronymic group lines and serve as a political stabilizing force in the Bambara country (Henry 1910; Zahan 1960). These societies are not merely social in their functions and purposes, but also religious. They constitute a vehicle through which men acquire increasing levels of knowledge through a gradual initiatory process.

The first of these societies is the *n'tomo* made up of five classes. Young boys enter the *n'tomo* five years before their circumcision and spend one year in each class of the society (Zahan 1960). Children leave the first society once they are circumcised. The classes of the *n'tomo* are respectively known as Lions, Toads, Birds, Guinea Fowl and Dogs. While in each of these classes, boys progressively acquire increasing levels of knowledge about the nature of man and his life's purpose. In the Lion class they learn about the birth of man's spirit, in the Toad class about life and death, in the Bird class about human thought, in the Guinea Fowl class about man's relations with the cosmos, and in the Dog class about man as a social being.

Upon leaving the *n'tomo*, boys are circumcised and, by the removal of their foreskins which represent the female element, they are changed from androgynous (male/female) creatures into men. They are then directed toward women as social partners.

Once out of the *n'tomo*, boys are initiated into the most secret of the six societies, the *komo*. The purpose of this society is to impart higher levels of knowledge to initiates through a variety of rituals from which women are excluded. The *komo* focuses on the issues of generation differences, marriage and society, and on a moral level on the differences between good and evil. As with the *n'tomo*, rituals are often accompanied by material representations, especially masks. The *komo* masks are large helmet-shaped sculptures with long open jaws and serrated teeth. Those of the *n'tomo* are face masks with horns, often covered by cowrie shells and red beads. Initiation into the *komo* lasts for about a year, but unlike the *n'tomo*, boys do not leave it for good. Rather they remain part of it for the rest of their lives.

The *nama* is a society whose chief purpose is to control sorcery and to solidify heterosexual relations[1] and promote the reproduction of human beings. Initiates are prepared for marriage and are taught the social codes necessary for communal life.

The *kono* is a society whose rituals teach initiates judgment and which reinforce knowledge of good and evil. It stresses the role of the conscience, man's interior voice. The *kono* mask is sculptured in the form of an elephant and a bird, the former representing intelligence, the latter spirit. The ears are large, symbolizing the strength of man's inner voice, his conscience, influencing his judgment, influencing his choice between good and evil. The *kono* mask hears all that is said of men; no secrets are hidden from this diety.

---

[1]Overt homosexuality is rare among the Bambara. Homosexuals are not tolerated in Bambara villages. They seek refuge today in large towns in Mali or in cities and towns in adjacent countries.

The dance of the Tyi Wara. *The antelope headdress to the left represents* Tyi Wara, *the spirit who taught the Bambara how to farm. The headdress at the right is a female figure with a baby on its back. These headdresses are used annually in dances during ceremonies of the* Tyi Wara *society.*

The *tyi wara*, is the only society of the six which is also open to women. The *tyi wara* commemorates a deity of the same name who taught the first men how to farm (Imperato 1970). It teaches people to be good farmers, both physicially and morally, and imparts to them profound knowledge of crops and the instruments and techniques of farming. It also teaches them the relationship between the sun and the earth, the two cosmic realities necessary for agriculture.

Once initiated into these five societies, men are ready to enter the *kore*, that final society that teaches them knowledge of God and puts them into a relationship with the supreme being. The *kore* functions around a central belief of the Bambara in re-incarnation. Man, if he fulfills certain conditions, may undergo endless re-incarnations. The Bambara believe that unless the *kore* intervenes man loses a portion of his spiritual nature each time he returns to earth. This is because God keeps a portion of this spiritual nature each time a man dies. After several re-incarnations, the entire spiritual nature is kept by God, and the person ceases to be re-incarnated. The *kore* prevents God from assimilating a part of a man's spiritual nature each time he dies, thus insuring endless re-incarnations (Zahan 1960). The *kore* teaches men not to fear death and that death is ultimately union with God.

Initiation into the *kore* is long and complex. There are eight classes. The Monkey class teaches initiates about their own animality; the Whipmaster class teaches command of speech; self-flagellation is performed during some of the rituals associated with this class. The Hyena class teaches self-control and condemns greed, idle inquisitiveness, and gluttony. The Firebearers class purifies, initiates, and frees them from their predjudices. These four classes of the *kore* are considered preparatory for the four which follow. They constitute spiritual training whereas the remaining four symbolize man's union and communication with God.

The Horse class represents the joys of those who possess perfect knowledge and who have achieved union with God. Members of this class are called *kore dugaw* and act as buffoons and behave as if they were free of all social conventions. They even eat human excrement. The Battered class teaches man self-sacrifice. Initiates inflict wounds on their skin with thorns during the rituals associated with this class. The Lion class teaches God's nobility, serenity, and justice. The Plank-bearer class, called *karaw*, is the most important. Initiates carry long planks which bear abstract sculptured designs. They symbolize man's union with God.

The six initiation societies of the Bambara are not only important social institutions, but also essential vehicles through which the Bambara acquire knowledge and religious instruction. Thus, the Bambara religion is best understood if one has some knowledge of Bambara social organization. Zahan (1974) points out that the six initiation societies form an inseparable whole. The *n'tomo* is the introduction, while the *kore* is the climax of man's knowledge and religious instruction.

Bambara Religious Beliefs

The Bambaras' concepts of disease are intimately related to their religious beliefs. Just as an understanding of the Bambaras' social organization is important for comprehending their religion, an understanding of their religion is important if one is to comprehend their views of disease.

The Bambara conceive of the creation of man as a series of events which originated with a supreme being called *Bemba* or *Ngala* (Zahan 1963). According to their myths, which are highly developed and complex, Bemba created the world out of a great void known as *gla*. A voice came out of this void and created its double. Then from out of this coupled voice came a humid substance which formed itself into hard and shining bodies. After many movements and transformations, the two *gla* produced an explosion which gave rise to a hard and powerful material which came down vibrating. This vibration gave rise to the designs of things as yet uncreated. Then the mind of man detached itself from the *gla* and went down onto the uncreated things in order to name them and to give them awareness. In the process of this creation, Bemba emerged and created sound and light, all beings, all actions, and all sentiments and emotions. As a result of this, a series of disorders took place which upset creation in which man thus far played an important role (Paques 1954).

Bemba then created two powerful spirits, *Faro* and *Pemba*. Faro, the master of the spoken word, then created seven heavens and *Teliko*, the spirit of air. Then, in the form of water, Faro spread life across the earth and created two twins from whom the Bozo fishermen of the Niger River were born. The other spirit, Pemba, moved across the earth in a swirling fashion and gave form to the land. After passing across the face of the earth for seven years, Pemba transformed himself into the seed of a *balanzan* tree, *Acacia albida*, rested on the ground, germinated and became a tree. Then with the dust he had created in his travels across the land and with his saliva, he created a woman, *Moussa Koroni*, who is the earth, to whom he gave a soul, *ni* and its double, *dya*. He united with her in creating the plants and the animals (Paques 1954).

Men paid homage to Pemba and Moussa Koroni, who in turn gave them directives for their lives. All women on earth came to copulate with Pemba which aroused the jealousy of Moussa Koroni and drove her to create disorder in the world. She instituted circumcision and excision (see chapter 13) and told men everything she had learned from Pemba. Because of this, everything she touched then became impure, and sickness and pain were introduced into the world as well as death. Pemba tried to drive her away. Faro finally reached her, but even he was unable to subject her to his control. Finally she died, but before she did, she revealed agriculture to men. Pemba then demanded men's blood in return for which he made them young when they had grown old. He also taught men how to make fire. But because Pemba abused his power, man turned away from him and worshipped Faro. In turn, Faro gave women twins who had moveable limbs. Pemba, angered by this, unleashed death on men. To compensate, Faro taught men to speak (Zahan 1963). When this series of events was over, Teliko tried to take power away from Faro, and men followed him, abandoning Faro. Faro finally defeated Teliko and punished men for helping him by giving them articulated limbs suitable for manual labor which they were all then obliged to perform. Births then became single, instead of twin, but in compensation, each being was given a double, the *dya* which rests in the water. (See section on Twin Births, chapter 9, below.)

       After all of these events, Faro traveled all over the world restoring order. He established the seasons and the rains and then classified living beings into different categories. Men were separated into different races and castes. He finally established his control over all events and all beings, but this order created by Faro is considered to be but a phase in time and space. Twelve waters are believed hidden and upon Faro's orders they will rise and spread out over the world. They will make men speak the language of the future and will create a new world conceived of by Bemba (Paques 1951).

       There are variations in the mythology of creation in the Bambara country, but the essential elements are present in all of them. In some accounts, Pemba, Faro, and Moussa Koroni are presented as personifications of Bemba and not as distinct spiritual beings. They all have the nature of Bemba. In addition, some accounts include another divine person, *Ndomadyiri*, the heavenly blacksmith. Ndomadyiri was formed by the action of the wind and by the evaporation of water. He is the element earth. He is what remains after the elements air and water are withdrawn. He is thus linked with idea of fixity. He is also linked to the notion of a tree, the source of the first human life (Zahan 1974).

       Ndomadyiri is often thought of as being a tree. He is the chief healer and herbalist and the ancestor of all blacksmiths who are the healers among the Bambara. The materialization of this mythology is found in the forms of altars, sacrifices and rituals. Pemba is represented by a piece of timber with a central cavity on which are carved twenty-two lines three times over, symbolizing the transfer of his power to Faro. The acacia tree is no longer a cult object, but the animists reserve a special place for it because of its former significance. Faro is thought to live in water, especially in the Niger, but he can be anywhere. His face is white because he took it from Teliko, the air spirit who was an albino; and Faro's chest is made of copper. Albinos and copper are the two sacrifices of choice to Faro, and during the time of the Bambara kingdom of Segou, albino human beings were sacrificed on an annual basis. Certain plants such as the tomato (*ngoyo*), which are like blood, are cultivated in villages for sacrifices to Faro (Paques 1954), as mentioned in chapter 3.

The Bambara conceive of man as a microcosm of the universe. The principle of duality contained in the original plan of creation is present in him as twin souls which compensate for the separation of the sexes. In man Faro is represented by the *ni*, the soul, and the *dya*, the double. Pemba is represented by the *tere*, the character, and the *nyama*, the character when it leaves its material support after death. Mousso Koroni is represented by the *wanzo*, the nefarious force which resides in the prepuce and clitoris. This is removed by circumcision and by excision. At death all of these elements become dissociated. The dya rests in the water where it becomes the *ni* (soul) of a newborn of the same family. The *tere* becomes a free force (the *nyama*) which can be dangerous and vengeful. It rests on the *pembele* (the altar to Pemba) where it joins the forces of the ancestors (Paques 1954).

It is also believed that all living and dead animals, plants and inanimate objects, such as minerals, possess a *ni* and a *dya*. Whenever an animal dies, its *dya* becomes re-incarnated as the soul of a newborn of its species but its *nyama* can roam the world and cause mischief and illness. (See pp. 32-34.) So if a man kills an animal or even an insect, its *nyama* can avenge itself against him. This problem is handled by resorting to the help of benevolent protective nature spirits (Tauxier 1927; Dieterlen 1951).

Protective and Malevolent Spirits

Protective spirits are individual, familial, or communal, and are either nature spirits or ancestral spirits. They have as their main function the promotion and preservation of the spiritual and material well-being of the individual or the community. The *dasiri* is a communal protective spirit responsible to Faro. Its abode is often a rock or a tree and occasionally an animal. The *dangu* is another communal protective spirit which absorbs all of the impurities, evil and undesirable things of individuals and the community. Its abode is frequently-used areas such as crossroads where all passersby are sure to pay it homage. With this spirit people may leave the *nyama* of animals they have killed and in doing so be freed of their vengeance (Henry 1910).

The *nyama* of ancestral spirits reside in material supports known as *boli*. These are objects made of mud, bone, feathers, cotton, and other materials over which blood sacrifices are periodically made by the head of the family. Sacrifices are often made over *boli* in times of sickness. Sacrifices are also made over individual altars to Faro on behalf of a single person or for all of his family (Henry 1910).

The Bambara believe in malevolent spirits whose *nyama* are vengeful because they have been abandoned and are without cult; but, unlike the Dogon, the Bambara do not have a special prelate who deals with these spirits. Rather, people resort to the *dangu* to protect them, or they use amulets made by magicians and diviners (Dieterlen 1951). There are a number of cults for a variety of local areas such as the forest, wells, streams, fields, the sky and trees where it is believed that special nature spirits live (Henry 1910). The women in many regions have a cult to a spirit which specifically protects them and which resides in a tree known as the *mousso-ka-dyiri*.

Bambara Animism and Islam

For the most part the Bambara are either animist or Moslem. The difference between Islam as a religion and a civilization and the Bambara religion, which is a religious and social system, appears profound. Yet this theoretical difference is often observed in reality not to be so great. This is because Islam in Mali is characterized by a series of conversion gradations in which Islamic culture is slowly assimilated and the Bambara religion gradually abandoned.

The process of religious change of this kind in Africa is slow, passing through three successive stages over several generations (Trimingham 1959). In the first or preparatory stage, Islamic cultural elements infiltrate the society. There is never a violent confrontation between Islam and animism. The former offers new values without uprooting the latter. The second stage is characterized by a gradual break with animism and an adoption of Islam; but in this process no more of the old animist cult is abandoned than is absolutely necessary. Thus people who claim to be Moslem and who are in fact in this transition stage are practicing both religions. The third stage witnesses the complete adoption of Islam, not only as a religion but also as a way of life. Yet even in the third stage Bambara elements can always be found because in this process of religious change there is reciprocity in culture contact. Certain elements of the Bambara religion are rejected because they are incompatable with the new religion. Material expressions of the Bambara religion such as masks and statues are destroyed and prohibited because Islam is opposed to the materialization of the spiritual (Imperato 1970, 1975). Islam, however, cannot change certain psychological attitudes and attitudes towards spirits and magical powers. An accommodation is reached by association with the spiritualism and magical practices of Islam which are counterparts to those already present among the Bambara, derived from similar elements in the religion of pre-Mohammed Arab pagans. The presence of animist elements in a universal religion such as Islam naturally assists in its assimilation by animists (Trimingham 1959).

Islam gives new values to old Bambara customs. Circumcision of males and excision among females, for example, are given Islamic legends of origin based on the myth of Abraham. Thus they are practiced because God ordered them to be and not because they were the customs of the ancestors founded on native African myths of creation. Similarly, other pre-existing practices are given new Islamic value. This is a process of assimilation and not mere adoption, because Islam transforms these practices sufficiently so that they conform to its laws and dogmas.

There are many elements of the Bambara foundation which cannot be assimilated without Islam's becoming denatured and losing its true identity. Such irreconcilable elements and practices present a problem and persist for a while, but eventually Islam changes conceptions of life and gains total acceptance, and at this point the established Islamic clergy are able to mobilize public opinion and purge the new religion of these elements (Marty 1920). It takes several generations before Islam comes through as a way of life, compatable with the Islam of the law books and the Koran, but yet distinctly African and Bambara because of the basic foundation (Delafosse 1922). What emerges then is a Moslem community based not on blood relationship, but on religious affiliation which possesses recognized leaders, rules and regulations and norms of conduct and communal rites (Levtzion 1968).

Even though the process of conversion is gradual and smooth, confrontations between Bambara beliefs and Islam do occur on several planes, retarding the adoption of Islamic elements for many generations (Imperato 1975). Islamic law requires society to be patrilineal, bringing it into direct conflict with matrilineal animists.[2] It also prescribes private ownership which is a concept requiring several generations before it is assimilated by ethnic groups such as the Bwa among whom communal ownership is the norm. Because conversion to Islam from animism is a long and gradual process, spiritual dualism exists among those undergoing conversion (Trimingham 1959).

Trimingham has likened the process to that structure of an embroidered textile in which the basic fabric is animist. An Islamic pattern is woven on top of this to the extent where the background can no longer be seen. However, it is still there as a firm foundation, providing for the

---

[2]This particular conflict with Islam does not occur among the Bambara, since they are patrilineal.

variations one encounters in the Islam of different ethnic groups. Religious
life then is composed of two structures, the animist foundation and the
Moslem superstructure (Boyer 1953). In practice, people are not conscious
of this spiritual dualism to the point where they are torn between the two.
In practice, the two co-exist, woven together, as Trimingham explains, like
the warp and the weft of different textures into a cloth of complicated
design. Clerics combine animist and Moslem functions, those of the
animist healer and spiritualist and those of the Moslem cleric. The
religious and magical are not differentiated; rather they are combined into
the one person who represents both the Islamic and animist traditions.
Magical practice also persists because everyone still believes in it and also
because Moslem clerics find it economically profitable.

It becomes clear from this explanation of Islamization among the
Bambara why so much contradiction is found in the figures presented by
various authors and the Malian government for the ratio of Moslems to
animists in a given locale. Quite obviously, a simple ratio of two religious
categories cannot and should not be used to characterize a situation in
which several categories actually exist. Even in predominantly animist
communities, the fear and shame of being despised for being an animist
intimidates many people into declaring themselves Moslem to government
officials. Consequently, census takers tend to come up with artificially
inflated figures for the number of Moslems present.

Whether a person or a community is thoroughly Moslem will depend
on the criteria used to evaluate their religious practices. While the act of
profession does indicate a change toward Islam, it alone is not a
dependable indication of the religious status of either an individual or a
community. The status of communal and family cults must be examined, as
well as the functional role of the Moslem clergy in family and community
life. Once the Moslem clergy assumes an important role in family and
community life, the community is considered Moslem.

Bambara Religious Concepts and Disease Concepts

Concepts of disease causation and disease management are
intimately bound to both the Bambara religion or to Islam. (For a detailed
discussion of medicine in an Islamic community, see chapter 7, dealing
with Timbuctoo.) The Bambara have a dualist theory about disease
causation, recognizing both natural and supernatural causes. Logically,
they then employ natural techniques and empirical knowledge for treating
those diseases thought to have a natural cause, and they resort to the
supernatural when a supernaturally-caused disease is suspected. Eventually Islam has a profound effect on the spiritual management of disease
because it displaces the means used by the Bambara and dislodges the

Bambara healer from his central social position. Islamic clergy fulfill a role analagous to magicians and healers in societies which are in transitional stages of conversion. Even though these practices adopted from folk beliefs are not recognized by Islam, partially Islamized societies permit them, and indeed demand them.

Islam is a monotheistic religion which does not possess a sacredotal body. It does, however, possess a clergy, leaders who serve as the interpreters and teachers of religious law. This clergy falls into three main groups, those appointed for public worship, teachers and masters of cannon law. In most areas of the Bambara country, one cleric fulfills all of the functions. In Islamic societies the cleric stands apart because he is a lettered man who can read and write in Arabic. He performs specific religious functions, leads in prayer, teaches children the rudiments of the religion, conducts marriage ceremonies, officiates at naming ceremonies, washes the dead and leads the funeral prayers at the cemetary.

A number of terms are used for Moslem clerics, a common one being *marabout* which is a French term which was first widely used in North Africa and carried over into black Africa. Although the Bambara have adopted this French term into their language, they more frequently use the term *moriba*, meaning "great Moslem." The Dyula of Mali, Upper Volta, and the Ivory Coast use *karamogo* which means "literate man." The Moslem clergy are loosely organized on a local level with a chief cleric, the *imam*, at their head (Lewis 1966).

The Islam of the Bambara is remarkable for the absence of saint cults which are a focal point of the religion among the white Africans of the Sahara and the sahel. There are exceptions, as among the Wolof of Senegal and the Peul of Mali. The latter consider Cheikou Ahmadou, the first Peul emperor of Macina to be a saint, and his burial place at Hamdallaye has always been well cared-for. (The term *baraka* in North Africa connotes a holiness given by God to saints, which can be absorbed by people and objects with whom they are in contact. In West Africa *baraka* is the *nyama* —free force—inherent in all beings, men, animals, plants, and inanimate objects. Thus, an animist concept is given a Moslem name.)

The unofficial religion that predominates among the Bambara represents an accommodation on the part of Islam to existing religious beliefs. Magic and religion are not clearly separated. Both Bambara cult leaders and Islamic clergy add the role of magician to their vocation. Moslem clergy make and sell innumerable charms which are magical in nature because they draw upon the power of God and His angels for the benefit of the wearers. Islamic clergy substitute new amulets for the old Bambara ones.

These amulets are of two general kinds and are often used for protecting against or curing disease. One contains a verse of the Koran written on a bit of paper along with names of genies and angels and mysterious formulas. Instructions are given for the use of charms and the taboos which must be observed if they are to remain powerful and effective. Amulets are sewn up into leather sacs and worn around an appropriate part of the body. The second variety consists of verses of the Koran written on slate or wood and washed off with water which is then either rubbed on the body or drunk. Such charms fall into four categories — those which are protective in action, those which gain health and wealth for the wearer, those which can harm an enemy or cause disease, and those which render bad magic innocuous.

Moriba also engage in bad magic or in what is often termed "black magic," whose aim is to cause illness and death or to harm someone in some other way. Those clerics who perform black magic are known among the Manding as *morijuga*. Witchcraft and sorcery are considered prominent causes of illness, especially in partially Islamized Bambara communities because of the spiritual insecurity caused by the adoption of Islam. Often Moslem clerics are unable to satisfy communal needs in countering the believed effects of witches and sorcerers, and so Bambara magicians and cult leaders are required to quiet people's fears. As Islamization deepens and people feel spiritually more secure, Moslem clerics counter the effects of sorcerers and witches. They also assume the functions of the Bambara diviner, using Islamic methods of divination, especially that of using dreams.

At the present time, in many Bambara communities there is a breakdown of the established religion and an imperfect assimilation of Islam. The elements of both religions are present in the belief patterns of many. Even where organized communal cults no longer exist, individual and family cults often persist.

Individual and communal beliefs about disease causation, treatment and prevention logically reflect the spiritual dualism of these communities. If the Bambara religion cannot provide an acceptable reason for the cause of an illness then the reason as well as the remedial measures will be sought in Islam. It is difficult to quantify the proportions which are present in spiritual dualism of this kind and we can only guess what they might be from certain visible parameters; but even with deepening Islamization, the phenomenon of reciprocal culture contact leaves its mark on the ultimate religious and social character of society. The Bambara religion is still visible through the cover of the universal religion, Islam.

References

Boyer, G. 1953. *Un Peuple de l'Ouest Africain, Les Diawara.* Dakar: IFAN.
Delafosse, M. 1922. L'Islam et Les Sociétés de l'Afrique, *Bulletin du Comité de l'Afrique Francaise et Renseignements Coloniaux*, 321-333.

Dieterlen, G. 1951. *Essai Sur La Religion Bambara.* Paris: Presses Universitaires de France.

Henry, J. 1910. *L'Ame d'Un Peuple Africain, Les Bambara,* Paris: Picard.

Imperato, P.J. 1970. The Dance of The Tyi Wara, *African Arts* IV(1) 8-13, 71-80.

Imperato, P.J. 1975. Last Dances of The Bambara, *Natural History* 94(4): 62-71.

Levtzion, N. 1968. *Muslims and Chiefs in West Africa: A Study of Islam in the Middle Volta Basin in the Pre-Colonial Period.* Oxford: Clarendon Press.

Lewis, I.M., ed. 1966. *Islam in Tropical Africa.* London: Oxford University Press.

Marty, P. 1920. *Etudes sur L'Islam et Les Tribus du Soudan,* 4 vols. Paris: Lerous.

Paques, V. 1954. *Les Bambara.* Paris: Presses Universitaires de France.

Tauxier, L. 1927. *La Religion Bambara.* Paris: Librairie Orientaliste Paul Geuthner.

Trimingham, J.S. 1959. *Islam in West Africa.* Oxford: Oxford University Press.

Zahan, D. 1960. *Les Sociétés d'Initiation Bambara.* Paris: Mouton.

Zahan, D. 1963. *La Dialectique du Verbe Chez Les Bambara.* Paris: Mouton.

Zahan, D. 1974. *The Bambara.* Leiden: E. J. Brill.

5

Folk Medicine among Rural Bambara

Traditional systems of medical care in Africa reflect the perceived taxonomy of disease causation. Thus, there are methods for dealing with both naturally- and supernaturally-caused illness. In many African societies there was, and often still is, a complex institutionalization of medical practitioners. There are generalists and specialists, diagnosticians and therapists. The analogies to Western medicine are obvious, but the contrasts are even more obvious.

Some will argue that there is little difference in the structure of traditional medical practice in rural and urban areas in Africa. They state that many urban people were raised and educated in a traditional rural setting and therefore retain faith in the system. Although this may be true to a certain extent, it must be remembered that Africans in urban environments are more exposed to influences which erode this faith than their rural counterparts. Also, Western medicine is more available to them then to those in rural areas; there are in urban areas hospitals, dispensaries, well-baby clinics, and preventive services. It has been frequently shown that accessibility to Western medicine significantly determines whether or not it is utilized. By accessibility is meant nearness in distance. If a dispensary or hospital is more than a few miles away, a rural African may be unwilling to walk with a sick child on her back or a husband may be unwilling to pedal a bicycle with his sick wife on it (Zeller 1975). In such instances a traditional practitioner will be sought out if for no other reason than that he is nearby.

In large urban centers, Western medicine is generally accessible, usually within walking distance. Also, it tends to be of higher quality because of the concentration of diagnostic and treatment resources and personnel. It is a strong competitor to the traditional system. There are exceptions to these generalizations; but it can safely be said that in much of

Africa traditional medical systems of health care have survived best in rural areas in the form in which they were first met by Europeans. Changes have occurred in rural areas, too, and some of these have been quite dramatic. Colonial administrations often made a concerted effort to abolish certain segments of the traditional health care system, as in Zaire, the former Belgian Congo (Janzen 1975). But, in spite of this, traditional medical practice still flourishes in much of rural Africa, albeit occasionally modified from what it once was.

Traditional Practitioners .

Traditional medical practice among the Bambara typifies the structure of a system that is found in many African societies. Naturally there are differences in the folk medicine practices and beliefs among the various African societies, and in detail these are often encyclopedic. But, in general most societies possess practitioners who deal with either naturally- or supernaturally-caused illnesses. The latter group often consist of an elaborate hierarchy of specialists or a spectrum of specialists not integrated into an organization matrix.

As has been already stated, diseases thought to have a natural causation are treated at home with known remedies. The Bambara possess a pharmacopeia of well-known herbal remedies for diarrhea, skin ulcerations, cuts and bruises, headaches, joint pains, etc. In most Bambara villages there are herbalists, *furatigui* (master of the leaf), and they are often consulted when a tried remedy does not work. They supply the herbs, advise how they are to be prepared, and sometimes administer them themselves. In the past they did not often charge a fee for their services, but today they do.

Traditional midwives and bonesetters are two categories of practitioners who deal with the non-supernatural. The latter may be either men or women, and often they are quite skilled. The former are elderly women who have acquired a reputation for skill in aiding at births. In several areas of Africa, attempts have been made to teach traditional midwives some basic concepts of antisepsis, to diagnose potentially dangerous complications, and to improve their techniques (Namboze 1964). Some of these programs have been quite successful.

Bonesetters often enjoy much esteem because of their success (Zeller 1975). In Western medicine the successful management of fractures requires reduction, that is the realignment of the broken ends of the bone and the healing of these pieces in such a way that function is restored to normal. In Tanzania and West Africa, where I have observed bonesetters, success is not measured in these terms. Often, they do not achieve good reduction and as a consequence the patient does not regain normal function. But clients are satisfied with the results obtained by their native bonesetters, results, it should be added, which if achieved by a surgeon in the United States would result in a malpractice suit. But in the traditional context, client expectations are met and therefore the patient is satisfied. Working in favor of bonesetters in Africa — and of surgeons in the Western world — is the reality that many fractures are not complete, that is the bone is not broken all the way through and even when it is, often the pieces are not displaced, but well aligned. Consequently, no reduction is necessary. All that is required is that the bone be immobilized in a splint.

As previously described, members of various societies believe that there are several supernatural causes of disease, and in response to this belief there is a variety of practitioners who deal with these causes. In some societies there is a sharply defined role for each category of practitioner; but in others, the demarcation between the various categories is often blurred and there is overlap of function.

Herbalists

In a sense, herbalists bridge the gap between the two broad categories of disease, those with a natural cause and those with a supernatural cause. They are often involved in the management of both. They are available with their extensive pharmacopeia to provide herbs for the management of diseases believed to have a natural cause; but they often also practice divination, attempting to uncover the supernatural cause of a patient's illness. Among the Bambara there is much blurring of role function in this regard in that most herbalists also practice divination. In other societies this is not the case, herbalists restricting themselves to diagnosis and treatment of naturally-caused diseases. In Botswana, for example, the herbalists, known as *dingaka tsa dichochwa*, are essentially dealers in herbal medicines. They consult, prescribe and treat and are analagous to the itinerant medicine men who once peddled patent medicines in the United States. In addition, the Botswana possess diviner-healers, *dingaka tsa dinaka*, who are not only herbalists, but also diviners who practice bone divination (Ulin 1975). These practitioners are similar to the Bambara herbalists.

Knowledge of herbs and their use is often passed from father to son or mother to daughter, and in some families both men and women are knowledgeable herbalists. There is sometimes specialization among herbalists, either by choice or because they have earned a particularly good reputation for success in treating a specific disease. If herbalists fail at treating a disease, the patient, on his own or on the advice of the treating herbalist, will assume the causation to be supernatural and seek out the help of an appropriate practitioner. Bambara herbalists divine and so they can diagnose the cause, either on the first encounter, or as is preferably done, when initial therapies fail. At that point they will divine a supernatural cause and refer the patient to another category of healer.

There is much collegiality among Bambara herbalists; often patients are referred by an herbalist to a colleague thought to be more skilled in treating a particular illness. There is also a considerable exchange of knowledge about the preparation and use of herbs, although sometimes herbalists carefully guard as secret some of their more sought-after treatments.

While herbalists are usually cast in the role of benevolent practitioners, their extensive knowledge of plants also qualifies them for malevolent activities. Poisonous plants abound in Africa and such poisons can be obtained from herbalists and slipped into the food of an intended victim. Among the Bambara, the providing of plant poisons by herbalists is not rare.

Divination, Oracles, and Spirit Mediumship

Divination is a function which several categories of traditional practitioners carry out, but it is unusual to find a category of practitioner whose sole role is divination. As already mentioned, Bambara herbalists practice divination; but more frequently it is done by two other types of practitioners, the *basitigui*, who are in a sense diviner-healers, and the *soma* who are diviners and spirit mediums. The Bambara diviner-healers employ herbal preparations for treating the sick, but in addition they prepare amulets and talismans. Many of them are hunters, who wear scores of talismans made of animal hair, teeth, claws, and skin. They are often suspected of practicing sorcery on the side.

The divination methods used by Bambara herbalists and diviner-healers are the same. Three methods are used. *Belee* are small stones thrown on the ground and their relative positions interpreted; kola nuts are widely used in place of stones. *Golongise* are cowrie shells that are also thrown on the ground and their positions interpreted. *N'kenyede* is a system of sand reading in which marks are made in the sand with one's fingers.

When used by a herbalist or diviner-healer, these three systems of divination reveal the type of supernatural cause involved in the patient's illness. It may be spirits, ghosts, witchcraft or sorcery. Once the cause is revealed, the appropriate therapeutic measures are implemented and if witchcraft is involved, the appropriate social measures implemented.

The cause of illness may also be uncovered through the use of oracles. Among the Bambara, the *sirikoun* is an oracle or fetish which when consulted reveals the supernatural causation of illness. These fetishes

Golongise (cowrie shells) being read by a basitigui *(diviner-healer).*

which contain the tail of a bull also contain the animal's *nyama* (ghost) which can be used to inflict harm as well. The *sirikoun* is said to speak, but only those possessing special powers can hear what is said.

The ghosts of dead ancestors and animals, as well as the spirits of inanimate objects, can affect the living and cause illness. The Bambara call these ghosts and spirits *nyama* (see chapter 3). They may inflict harm exteriorly, but more often they do so through possession.

Spirit mediumship is an activity whereby an individual known as a *spirit medium* serves as an intermediary between certain spirits and men. Among the Bambara there are three types of practitioners who are capable of communicating with spirits, that is, three types of spirit mediums. The *soma* are individuals who from the time of their birth are identified as being spirit mediums (Dieterlen 1951). They are thought capable of communicating with spirits for a variety of purposes. They also practice divination. *Soma* possess harps containing cords that are played for specific purposes. Thus, the cord called *fade* is plucked when the *soma* conducts a seance dealing with health matters. As he does so, he sings a repetitive song. While *soma* do go into mild trances during their seances, these seances are quite different from the spectacular and often wild public trances found in other areas of Africa. The *soma* communicates to the patient the cause of his illness and what must be done to appease the offending spirit. Patients are never invited by a *soma* to enter into a mediumistic relationship with a spirit (see below).

    Quinnekilia are not born spirit mediums, but learn the art. They are fortune tellers primarily, who practice spirit mediumship on the side, and they are believed to control a number of spirits which they can use for

A spirit medium (quinnekilila) *from eastern Bambara country.*

malevolent purposes if they so wish. These practitioners divine by using one of the three methods outlined above.

    Nya-bouin or *gnefla* are individuals who can identify sorcerers and witches through divination. But they can also function as spirit mediums.

In many parts of Africa spirit medium cults exist in order to maintain good relations between men and the ghosts of deceased ancestors. Those who are capable of communicating with such spirits do so when in a trance. At such times, the spirit or ghost is believed to reveal what is vexing it and what must be done to appease it. Often diviners will advise a patient that the cause of his illness is neglect of an ancestral or other spirit. The solution lies in permitting the spirit to express itself through mediumship and make its wishes known. A spirit medium is then consulted and, while in an induced trance, he communicates with the spirit or ghost that is causing the patient's illness. The spirit will state what it wants and this in turn will be passed on to the patient.

Sometimes a patient does not go to a diviner first, but directly to a spirit medium who, while in his trance, determines the cause of the patient's illness and tells him what has to be done to placate the spirit. Mediums frequently relate that spirits require the resumption of neglected sacrifices to them. Often a patient is told that the long-term solution to his problem lies in his becoming a spirit medium himself, thereby entering into a permanent relationship, as a medium, with the spirit or ghost which caused his illness. Becoming a spirit medium is usually a long and expensive process, but by giving such advice mediums keep a steady flow of new adepts coming into their cults.

TRADITIONAL BAMBARA MEDICAL PRACTITIONERS

Practitioner	Function
Furatigui	Herbalists who provide herbal remedies and confer supernatural powers on them.
Soma	Spirit mediums and diviners who uncover the supernatural causes of illness and who use supernatural therapeutic methods.
Nya bouin (Gnefla)	Anti-sorcerers (diviners and spirit mediums) who can identify sorcerers.
Basitigui	Diviners whose role is either benevolent or malevolent or both. They identify supernatural causes of illness and treat with magical formulas and charms. Produce amulets.
Moriba (Marabout)	Koranic teachers who diagnose and treat illness by supernatural means.

Possession usually takes place to the accompaniment of music and rhythmic movements. Some reports indicate that during the supposed possession, true dissociation does not occur; there is evidence that mediums simply act the part; but whether they do or not has no bearing on the final results. People believe that mediums are possessed and they react accordingly. The trance, or dissociated state, into which the medium enters, lasts for an hour or so and on rare occasions for several hours. It is a dramatic presentation, with the medium dressed in unusual attire and his or her body colored with kaolin or ochre. Bambara *soma* do not go into trances of this kind. Whatever a medium says while in a trance is in effect the pronouncement of the possessing spirit, and hence the words are treated with great respect.

Spirit medium cults are rare among the Bambara and their cousins, the Malinke. But in the western Bambara country a spirit medium cult known as the *Dyidé* was once fairly widespread (Cheron 1931). As with similar cults in many other parts of Africa, individuals were initiated as a means of curing them of a serious disease. Initiation was costly, in that initiates had to donate chickens, goats, cereal and other material items. The *Dyidé* cult was headed by a chief medium known as the *dyidé-kountigui* and had two levels of initiates, the higher *tondemi na yelena* and a lower level, the *tonde mi ma layele*. The upper level consisted of individuals who had already entered into a mediumistic relationship with the spirit that was causing their illness. Those in the lower level had not yet achieved this relationship. The passage from the first to the second level was achieved by the payment of two kola nuts, a goat, two chickens, milk, and small items such as soap. The initiate was given a drink made from the leaves of *Mitragyne africana*, known as *dyou* in Bambara, and known for its hallucinogenic effects. He was then isolated in a hut alone and made to lie down on a white sheet while the other members of the cult danced outside. (Initiation into the first level was also accompanied by drinking this same infusion.)

The purpose of the *Dyidé* was to cure individuals of severe illness. In many areas, such as in the towns of Kita and Toukoto, the local chiefs of the cult were individuals who had recovered from paralysis. The cult gained many members during the 1930's and 1940's and held regular public ceremonies in most localities where it was present. It became extremely popular and like many spirit medium cults assumed an important political role. Because of this, the French administration eventually took measures to curtail the activities of the cult. The *Dyidé* is now virtually extinct in most of the Bambara country.

Witchcraft

Witchcraft is often suspected when an illness is serious and protracted, and these suspicions are confirmed through divination. Although patients can be protected somewhat from further attacks from witches, in most societies the ultimate solution lay in the destruction of witches. Because this solution to witchcraft was so drastic, it is obvious that the accusation was made when social relations had become so strained that rupture was the only way out (Marwick 1950).

The Lele of the Kasai of Zaire, possessed witchfinding cults and poison ordeals in order to deal with witches. Poison ordeals were both oracular and punitive in function — oracular because they provided a final verdict which divination cannot provide, and punitive because witches were dealt with severely (Douglas 1963). Although poison ordeals were common throughout Africa as a means of detecting and punishing witches, they were especially common in Central Africa in Zaire. In 1924, the colonial administration of the Belgian Congo (now Zaire) suppressed these ordeals by law, but it was not until the 1930's that they disappeared from most of the territory.

The concept basic to the poison ordeal is that a witch dies on drinking a poison beverage because the witchcraft substance within him absorbs the poison. On the other hand, the stomach of a non-witch rejects the poison and vomits it. Those who died were proven to be what their accusers said they were. Those who survived confounded their accusers (Douglas 1963). It is impossible to say what proportion of those who drank ordeal poisons died, but interviews with those who witnessed such rites indicate the the proportion who died was high.

Among the Bambara, witches were dealt with very severely. They were usually burned to death after being tortured, and frequently were killed by having only their heads burned. Thick mats of straw were tied around their heads and then ignited, the individuals dying of suffocation and smoke inhalation. Poison ordeals among the Bambara were abolished during the Moslem Tukulor occupation of the Bambara country a century ago. Likewise, execution of so-called witches was stopped.

Although there is still a strong belief in witches in much of Africa, the traditional means of dealing with suspected witches have been banned. Instead, individuals accused of being witches are banished from their villages in certain areas, for in the absence of the poison ordeal, social ostracism is the only recourse. Among the Bambara witchcraft may be suspected, but specific accusations are not made. This has been compensated for by an increase in a belief in sorcery as a cause of disease. Also, traditional practitioners now concentrate on providing their patients with those devices which will protect them from further harm from witchcraft.

Sorcery

Sorcery is effectively dealt with by countermeasures of which there are many. Among the Bambara, the *nya-bouin* (see p. 59) are experts at identifying sorcerers. They and a number of other practitioners provide patients with anti-sorcery amulets and give warning to those who are suspected of the practice.

Talismans and Amulets

Modern laws, promulgated either by colonial governments or by the governments of independent nations have effectively outlawed witchfinding and poison ordeals, and have provided some punishment for sorcery and spirit mediumship; but anti-sorcery efforts have not been effectively implemented.[1] These laws made spirit mediumship a clandestine activity in many parts of Africa. For people who still believe in sorcery and witchcraft and the influence of spirits and ghosts this has meant a disappearance of the usual lines of defense against these forces. In their place, African societies have elaborated upon the use of amulets as devices to protect against witchcraft and sorcery. Also where witchcraft has been legally regulated out of existence, sorcery has filled the vacuum. Thus among the Bambara, more people now believe in sorcery than before.

By definition, *talismans* are small objects worn on the body which bring good fortune. *Amulets* are similar objects employed to protect against evil. Neither are necessarily material objects. Either can consist of a verbal pronouncement which confers protection or good fortune, as the case may be. In some instances, secret formulas are used in conjunction with a material support. These points will now be illustrated by describing Bambara practices.

Bambara herbalists usually pronounce a verbal formula over their herbal preparations. Such formulas are believed to have supernatural powers. Even individuals who prepare their own herbal medicines at home pronounce these formulas, which are called *kilisi*. The formulas are physically implanted into herbal preparations as one of three ways. The herbalist may spit into the preparation as he speaks; a chicken may be bled from its neck over the herbs and the words pronounced as the blood drips in; or finally the words may simply be pronounced.

The Bambara believe that the first two techniques are more effective. They also believe that the *ni* (soul) which is present in plants is essential to curing the patient and that such formulas must be recited for these souls to become operative. They have no concept of pharmacologi-

---

[1]Witchfinding was a palpable nefarious public activity that resulted in the death of innocent people, and the governments took a hard stand and stamped it out. Sorcery, on the other hand, is an alleged activity done supposedly in private. Thus, it is difficult to suppress it, because it is hard to see it and to prove its existence from the Westerner's perspective.

A hunter-healer from southerh Bambara country wearing around his left wrist a tafo *amulet consisting of a cord with knots.*

cally active ingredients in plants: in a sense the *ni* of plants represent these unseen chemical compounds in the Bambara culture.

Tafo are verbal formulas which are materialized. They are made by herbalists in some areas, by Moslem clerics (*marabouts*), and by diviner-healers (*basitigui*). *Tafo* may consist of a cotton cord with knots tied at various intervals. The practitioner preparing them spits on the knots as they are tied, reciting the verbal formula at the same time. *Tafo* sometimes consist of bits of herbs or bones sealed in tiny leather pacs which are then worn around the affected part of the body. Marabouts write verses from the Koran or cryptic Arabic words on small bits of paper and sew these into small leather pacs, and these preparations are also referred to as *tafo* and are considered amulets. *Moson* are *tafo* that consist of a ball of mud made from a termite hill or a ball of shea butter (fat from the seeds of the shea tree, *Butyrospermum parkii*). The shea butterball is called *kana*. The practitioner preparing these pronounces the formula over them and instills his words by one of the three methods described above. At given intervals, the patient or a member of his family rubs the surface of the ball and then coats the skin of his body with the mud or shea butter. That part of the anatomy which is symptomatic is covered first and at other times the mud or shea butter is painted all over, although sometimes no other part of the body may be coated.

Islamic Practices

Moslem clerics—marabouts or moriba—are found throughout Islamized areas of Africa. Among the Bambara they now fulfill roles played

A Bambara hunter in typical garb from Beledougou in northern Bambara country. Hunters such as this are often also herbalists (furatigui) *or diviner-healers* (basitigui). *This hunter, who is non-Moslem, is wearing three* tafo *in leather sacs around his neck and a protective amulet on his arm.*

at one time by diviner-healers and spirit mediums. Their religious, magical, and healing roles are not neatly separated. They uncover the cause of illness by reading the Koran and treat illness through the use of Koranic amulets. Often, the bulk of a marabout's income comes from the making of Koranic charms for curing illness, preventing illness, and bringing good fortune. In making these amulets and talismans, marabouts consult standard Islamic magic manuals. These charms are called *barah* by the Bambara, a derivation from the Arabic *dabbara* which means "magic making."

There are two general types of charms made by Moslem clerics, those written on paper and worn in a leather sac on the body or as a belt, arm band or necklace, and those which are written on paper or on a wooden slate and washed off with water which is either drunk or else rubbed on the body. These amulets and talismans contain passages from the Koran or else the names of angels or of *jinn*, and mysterious formulas. Personal charms are carried on the body and are called *sewei*. Marabouts produce a

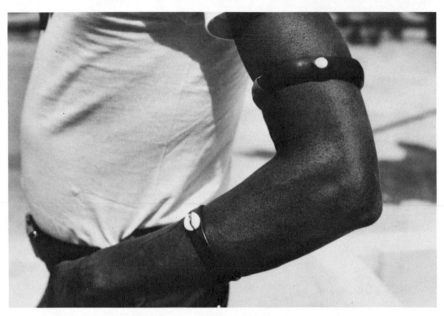

Two types of amulets employed by Moslem Bambara. The one near the wrist is a katemi, *used to prevent illness; and the one on the arm, called* mandara-ba, *is believed to protect the wearer from knives.*

popular form of charm called *mandara-ba* which is thought to protect the wearer from assault with knives. In times of communicable disease epidemics, they make written Koranic amulets called *katemi* which are buried beneath the ground at the doorway of a compound.

   Some marabouts possess a reputation for their ability to invoke genies. The invocation of benevolent genies requires several weeks of intense meditation and such genies are often invoked for good health.

References

Cheron, G. 1931. Le Dyidé. *Journal de la Société des Africanistes* 1:285-289.
Dieterlen, G. 1951. *Essai sur la Religion Bambara.* Paris: Presses Universitaires de France.
Douglas, M. 1963. Techniques of Sorcery Control in Central Africa, in *Witchcraft and Sorcery in East Africa,* edited by J. Middleton and E. H. Winter. London: Routledge and Kegan Paul.

Janzen, J.M. 1975. Pluralistic Legitimation of Therapy Systems in Contemporary Zaire. *Rural Africana* 26:105-122.

Marwick, M. 1950. Another Modern Anti-Witchcraft Movement in East Central Africa. *Africa* 20(2):100-112.

Namboze, J. 1964. General Infection in the Newborn with Special Reference to East Africa. *Journal of Tropical Medicine And Hygiene*, 67:131-132.

Ulin, P.R. 1975. The Traditional Healer of Botswana in a Changing Society. *Rural Africana* 26:123-130.

Zeller, D.L. 1975. Traditional and Western Medicine in Buganda: Coexistence and Complement. *Rural Africana* 26:91-103.

6

Folk Medicine and Modern Health Care among Urban Bambara

Urban centers in Africa vary considerably in their developmental history, size, population composition, economic base, and degree of westernization. Many came into being during the late 19th century and early 20th century as administrative centers for the colonial powers. Often these centers were implanted at the site of an existing village, chosen because of either its strategic geographical location, proximity to easy means of transportation and communication such as rivers, or for political or commercial reasons. National capitals which developed this way include Bamako (Mali), Dakar (Senegal), Conakry (Guinea), Abidjan (Ivory Coast), Niamey (Niger), Lomé (Togo), and Kinshasa (Zaire). In some, the impetus for development was primarily commercial, and European trading companies installed themselves long before their respective governments established a presence. Then the excuse often given for annexing territory was the protection of existing commercial interests. Many of the port cities along the West African coast developed in this fashion.

Other cities were created out in the wilderness where no village or town previously existed. Nairobi, the capital of Kenya, is an example of this. It developed from a railroad work camp during the construction of the Uganda Railroad (Imperato 1964). In contrast to cities like Nairobi are cities which developed long before European colonial rule, which were centers of commerce or capitals of African political states or confederations. Some of the oldest cities of this type are found in West Africa and include Djenné in Mali, founded in about 800 A.D.; Timbuctoo, also in Mali, established in the 11th century A.D.; Kano in northern Nigeria; and Ouagadougou, the

Parts of this chapter were previously published in *Tropical and Geographical Medicine*, 1974, 26:429-440. I acknowledge with thanks the permission of the editors to use this material here.

capital of Upper Volta. In East Africa, the present day capital of Uganda, Kampala, developed around Mengo, the capital of the Buganda Kingdom.

The dynamics of urban development, both past and present, have a strong influence upon the cultural reference of present-day urban populations and their traditional medical beliefs and practices. In old cities such as Djenné and Timbuctoo, little change has occurred since the inception of the colonial period. These cities, once important trading centers, began to fall into decline when the gold and slave trade shifted from a predominantly trans-Saharan direction to the West African coast. Lacking great strategic value, peripheral to the economic life of present day Mali and geographically somewhat isolated, these cities have remained rather insulated from the changes generated by Western technology in other large African cities. Traditional medical beliefs and practices in these cities have tended to remain static, whereas in the still expanding larger urban centers, the traditional system has adapted newer values and attitudes.

Folk medicine has survived in modern urban centers in Africa not only because large numbers of people have faith in it, but also because as a system of medical care it has not remained rigid. It has adapted itself to the new urban scene. The availability of modern medical facilities in these cities has somewhat lessened, but not abolished, dependence on the traditional system. In Ibadan, Nigeria, for example where a world renowned medical school and University College Hospital exist, traditional Yorùba medicine still flourishes. According to Una Maclean, there are some 50 stalls devoted to the sale of medicinal materials alone in one of eight recognized Ibadan markets. In 1963, Dr. Maclean surveyed one of the city's wards containing 5,790 inhabitants living in 528 roofed buildings. Ibadan, which is one of the largest cities in Africa, had a population of 479,000 at that time. Thirteen percent of those interviewed said their families always used traditional medicines, 59 percent responded that they sometimes did, and 28 percent denied any use. The highest proportion of non-users was in the youngest age group (Maclean 1971).

Maclean also found that none of those who had received a secondary school education reported complete reliance on traditional medicines. Twelve percent of illiterate respondents used traditional medicines entirely. But irrespective of levels of education, 60 percent of those interviewed said that they used traditional medicines. In a survey done among outpatients in the hospital, only 30 percent admitted using traditional medicines. Ninety-three percent of all those interviewed said that they used modern Western medicines such as anti-malarials, analgesics and others. Fifty-one percent indicated that family members consulted traditional healers. There were twelve traditional healers in the quarter. Seven percent were members of prayer-healing sects, now common in Ibadan (Maclean 1971).

Among the Yoruba, a West African coastal group, there are two broad categories of practitioners. The *babalawo* are diviners who belong to the *Ifa* (fate) cult and who provide a form of psychotherapy. The *onishegun* are herbalists who hold the god of herbalism, *Osanyin*, in great respect. There is some overlap of function in that herbalists also practice divination and the diviners practice herbalism. In the Ibadan survey Maclean (1971) interviewed 100 practitioners, including diviners and herbalists. Three said they performed both roles. One was a hunter whose knowledge of herbs was great and four were Moslem practitioners. All of these individuals had gained their extensive knowledge through years of apprenticeship and experience. The herbalists generally possessed an extensive knowledge of herbal drugs and of their pharmacologic actions and effects. An important point which emerged from this survey was the existence of vast differences between individuals in the same healing category in procedures practiced. These differences extend through concepts of disease causation and treatment, and illustrate that generalizations about traditional practitioners, even from one ethnic group, in one town, are difficult to make, as Maclean has pointed out. There are no well-established standards for training and no self-regulating mechanism within these groups that produce quality care. This is one of the arguments frequently presented by those who argue against the use of traditional practitioners in a modern health care delivery system.

In the previous chapter, folk medicine as it exists among the rural Bambara of the Republic of Mali was examined in some detail. Bambara folk medicine also thrives in Bamako, the capital of Mali, but folk medicine there differs in many respects from the system found in rural areas.

Folk Medicine in the City of Bamako

Bamako stands on the left bank of the Niger River at the foot of the Manding Hills. Originally a small fishing village and trading center, it became a French military outpost in 1883 and then an administrative center. In 1908, the capital of the territory of the Haut-Senegal Niger, as Mali was then known, was transferred from the town of Kayes to Bamako (Villien-Rossi 1966). The town gradually grew under the influence of the French administration and became an important entrepôt and trading center with links by rail with Dakar, with the Ivory Coast by road, and with the great inland delta of the Niger by river. The population of the city is about 300,000 (Annuaire Statistique 1973). The Bambara constitute about 30 percent of the city's population and the Bambara language is the lingua franca, along with French.

Social Structure of Bamako

Bamako society is composed of two large groups, an upper stratum and a larger lower one. The former is composed of two distinct elite groups, the civil servants and the merchants. The latter are wealthy, but generally illiterate or only semi-literate in Arabic. They are Moslems for the most part, belonging to either the Tidjanist, Quadrya, or Wahabia sects. Their culture is Arabic. Although the merchants avail themselves of modern medical facilities, their basic notions about disease and treatment remain strongly traditional and Moslem (Mellassoux 1968).

The civil servants, of which there are about 10,000 in Bamako, comprise the second elite segment of Bamako's upper social level. They are well-educated, literate, European-oriented and religiously tolerant, with a strong tendency towards atheism. In matters of sickness, they utilize the modern medical care system more frequently than the merchants.

The lower stratum of Bamako consists of uneducated and semi-educated wage earners, apprentices, small tradesmen, and seasonal workers. The majority of these people profess to be Moslem, but retain many animist beliefs and practices. They tend to rely more heavily on the traditional medical care system, although not to the exclusion of the modern sector.

Traditional Medical Practices

The traditional Bambara medical care system described in the previous chapter is modified in Bamako because of a change in basic notions of disease causation, and also because of the presence and availability of an extensive modern medical care system there. The information presented here was collected in Bamako from 1966 to 1971, and in 1973 and 1974.

Herbalism

Mild and well-known symptoms are treated at the household level with herbs obtained from a herbalist (*furatigui*—master of the leaf). Herbalists sell herbs at most of the principal markets. In the Ouloufobou-gou-Bolibana market in Bamako in 1969, for example, there were 11 herbalists, six men and five women, selling herbal preparations. They work cooperatively and not competitively, and often refer a client to a colleague if they don't have a given herb. Over a period of 24 days of observation, spread out over all months of the year, an average of four persons per hour visited each stall in this market during 1969. The majority were female clients who did not solicit advice nor explain the illness. Rather, they simply stated the herb they wanted by name. Some did explain the illness and solicit advice on which preparation to use and how to use it, but they were in a minority.

In the Medina-Coura market in Bamako there were 18 herbalists. In such large markets, herbs are sold as either dried or freshly-cut preparations and more recently as powdered products, the latter being more expensive since the client has little preparation to do. The average inventory of kinds of leaves, stems, and roots in the Bamako market was twenty-eight.

While in rural areas individuals often go out into the bush and obtain their own herbs and roots, such is not the case in Bamako. The

A herbalist (furatigui) *selling herbs and roots in the Oulofobougou-Bolibana market in Bamako.*

Powdered herbs and roots that are sold by an herbalist (furatigui) *in Bamako; herbs and roots in this form are more expensive than when simply fresh-cut.*

distance to the city's limits and the presence around it of plantations and gardens make it difficult for the average person to collect his own herbs. Also, the region around the city has been, and continues to be, progressively deforested because of the large amounts of wood needed everyday for cooking fires.

Herbalists in Bamako act as medicine men, selling herbs and prepared herbal preparations in a retail manner. This represents a departure from their rural counterparts who gather herbs upon client demand. Some herbalists in Bamako also practice divination, but not with the frequency of their rural counterparts.

Thus in urban areas, many herbalists simply sell their herbs. A few, like their counterparts in rural areas also consult, diagnose, prescribe, and confer on the product a verbal formula considered by many to be indispensable in treatment. These formulas (*kilisi*) are thought to confer a supernatural power on the herbal preparation. *Kilisi* are known to many people who use them in treating illness at the household level. Besides those employed by herbalists, many *kilisi* are known to ordinary people, and the words are pronounced when massaging the affected part of the body or when spitting on the affected part of the body. In Bamako, however, *kilisi* are infrequently employed in association with herbal preparations. Individuals purchase herbs because of their proven efficacy and for the most part do not request that a magical formula be imparted to them.

Amulets consisting of a cotton cord of knots or a small leather sac filled with herbal preparations are still frequently made by herbalists, but with less frequency than in rural areas. In Bamako, they have been displaced by Islamic amulets consisting of small leather sacs containing bits of paper on which are written verses from the Koran or cryptic Arabic script. Balls of mud and shea butter (respectively, *moson* and *kana*) are commonly used amulets made by herbalists in rural areas, but they are infrequently used in Bamako.

Divination, Oracles and Spirit Mediumship

Divination in Bamako is more frequently performed by marabouts than by either herbalists or diviner-healers (*basitigui*). Very few diviner healers remain in Bamako at present. The divination methods employed by herbalists and marabouts often are the same as those employed in rural areas, namely cowrie shells which are thrown on the ground, sand reading, and throwing kola nuts or stones; but the more orthodox marabouts do not use these methods in Bamako. They divine by reading passages from the Koran. The more orthodox Moslems view the three animist methods of divination as incompatible with Islam.

The use of the *sirikoun*, an oracular fetish, while common in rural areas, is rare in the city. Equally rare are the *soma*, individuals who are spirit mediums and diviners. Belief in their powers is limited to those who are illiterate or semi-literate and with a strong animist orientation. The *quinnekilila*, who are also spirit mediums and controllers of spirits, are not found practicing in the city. The *nya-bouin* or *gne-fla*, as they are also known, are diviners who identify sorcerers and witches; there are very few in Bamako, their roles being assumed by Moslem marabouts. There are no spirit-medium cults in the city at present.

In general, the animist practitioners who function as diviners, spirit mediums and anti-sorcery agents have to a large extent been supplanted in the city by the Moslem marabouts who combine all of these functions in modes acceptable to people whose cultural and religious reference is now Moslem.

Witchcraft

The firm distinction which exists in the minds of many rural folk between witches and sorcerers is blurred among people in Bamako. Belief in witchcraft has declined markedly among both the rural and urban Bambara, but especially among the latter. For people in Bamako, the characteristics of both witches and sorcerers are combined in the same individuals (Imperato 1970). The actions attributed to individuals and their dominating characteristics are those of sorcerers, but the name applied to such people is witch (*souba*). (These *souba* have been described in detail in Chapter 3.) Belief in sorcery is not condemned by Islam, whereas belief in witchcraft is, and this accounts for the survival of sorcery beliefs in Bamako. In addition, the former colonial administration and the present government of Mali suppressed witchcraft beliefs through a number of strong administrative actions, indirectly increasing beliefs in sorcery for people whose need for belief in a supernatural cause of illness is still strong.

Islamic Practices

Islam is very strong in Bamako among the Bambara and most profess to be Moslems. But Islam accommodates animism, and syncretic beliefs are the usual result for the individual. Marabouts are found in large numbers in all of the quarters of the city, and for many of them the manufacture of Koranic charms and medical care constitute the principal source of income. Islamic medical practices in Bamako are essentially the same as those already described in the previous chapter. However, they are not as securely established as in old cities like Timbuctoo, and they face competition from a system of modern medicine which is competing for patients who are gradually abandoning their animist beliefs.

Other Medical Practitioners

There are a number of Hausa medicine men from northern Nigeria who visit Bamako seasonally, selling medicines for a variety of illnesses. They walk through the dirt streets of the city with their medicines, charms and amulets stored in large leather sacs which are carried over one shoulder. This, plus their distinctive Hausa dress, makes them immediately identifiable to most people. These practitioners only sell medicines. They do not diagnose nor directly treat patients.

Hausa barber-surgeons on straw mats in front of the great mosque in Bamako. Their horns, used in cupping, are in the foreground.

Distinct ˉfrom the Hausa medicine men who are viewed with suspicion by many, are the generally respected Hausa barber-surgeons who are principally found in three locations in the city: around the great mosque, in the main market, and in some of the smaller markets. These surgeons remain in Bamako for limited periods. Some return every year or every few years and only a few are permanently installed in the city. They perform three types of surgical procedures which are essentially derived from early Arabic medicine. Sitting on straw mats, they practice in the shade of a tree or wall, usually with a row of their cupping horns inverted and set on a wooden slab in front of them. Their razors and knives are kept in small leather bags next to them.

They practice their surgery in full view of everyone, with the patient sitting or lying in front of them on the same mat. The commonest procedure performed is that of bloodletting and cupping. It is used for muscle aches, joint pains, sprains, and any type of body pain. Several small cuts are made over the affected part of the body and a horn of suitable size placed over the area. The barber-surgeon sucks on the tip of the horn through a small hole, creating a vacuum which is sealed in by the plugging of the hole with a piece of bees' wax which is first softened in the mouth. A horn is left in place for about ten minutes. Often, the barber-surgeons only scarify and do not apply horns.

A less frequent procedure performed by them is uvulectomy, the removal of the uvula, the rounded piece of tissue which hangs down from the back of the soft palate. This is removed by a long instrument with a hook-shaped knife at the end. Patients seek this treatment for any illness affecting the throat, including hoarseness, pharyngitis, stuttering, and acute or chronic laryngitis. Complications of bleeding and/or infection are common.

When not performing these surgical procedures, the Hausa barber-surgeons shave men's heads with razors and trim beards.

Modern Medical Services in Bamako

Bamako has two large hospitals, Gabriel Toure with 465 beds and Point-G with 625 beds. In addition, there are seven dispensaries in the city, five maternal and child health centers, a school health service, a hygiene service, and a preventive medical service. In addition there is a leprosy treatment and rehabilitation institute (Institut Marchoux) which, while regional in nature, in practice serves the population of Bamako. There is also a well-equipped ophthalmologic institute (IOTA) which was designed to serve all of the people of French-speaking West Africa but which in reality serves primarily the people of Bamako. There are several pharmacies in the city, operated by the state-owned Pharmacie Populaire, selling a broad spectrum of modern drugs and surgical supplies. In addition there are two privately-owned pharmacies. There is an excellent biological laboratory which performs a variety of tests.

Modern medical care is at its best in Mali in Bamako because of the concentration there of resources such as hospitals and dispensaries with their diagnostic and treatment capabilities and the large number of medical personnel found in the city. By U.S. or European standards, the medical care provided by the two major hospitals is mediocre and highly variable, depending on the physicians and paramedical personnel handling a given case. There is also much variability of quality in care from service to service and little depth in terms of staffing with well-trained personnel. But, in spite of these deficiencies, an acceptable level of modern medical care is available to the city's population and this has had an impact in reducing reliance on the traditional medical system.

This process involves a patient population which is gradually being Islamized, abandoning animism or parts of it. The people of Bamako are not yet thoroughly imbued with a reliance on Islamic practices as are people in Timbuctoo. In a sense, then, modern medical services in Bamako are competing at an advantage with Islamic practices which are not yet firmly established among many. In Timbuctoo, modern medical services are competing with Islamic practices, but at a disadvantage since the latter have been long established and are highly respected.

Modern Medical Practitioners in Bamako

The cadre of modern medical practitioners in Mali is at present quite small compared to neighboring African states. The table below shows the numbers of the major categories of medical professionals in the country. The ratio of the numbers in any category to the population is extremely small. Fifty-five of the 108 physicians (50.9 percent) are in the capital city of Bamako and 82 of the 108 (76.1 percent) in major towns and cities. This means that the majority of the rural population is not served by physicians; but a large proportion of Bamako's population is. The 65 Malian physicians in the country are a heterogeneous group composed of a small number of individuals possessing an M.D. degree from universities in France and other countries of western Europe and a larger number who either received degrees as *Médecin Africain* in Dakar in the 1930's and 1940's or M.D. equivalents in the U.S.S.R., Poland, Czechoslovakia, and East Germany.

Modern Western medicine, therefore, is represented to the bulk of the rural population by *infirmiers* (male nurses) of whom there are two

MEDICAL AND PARAMEDICAL PERSONNEL
IN MALI, 1972*

Category	Malians		Foreigners		Total	
	Male	Female	Male	Female	Male	Female
Physicians	60	5	32	11	92	16
Infirmiers	1204	322	0	0	1204	322
Medical Aides	563	583	0	0	563	583
Mid Wives	0	163	0	5	0	168
Mid Wife Aides	0	178	0	0	0	178

*Source: *Infrastructure Sanitaire du Mali, 1972.*

categories, the first possessing a level of education equivalent to a high
school diploma in the United States, and the second the equivalent of a
junior-college degree. Individuals in both of these categories receive their
basic training in government schools. The training is mostly theoretical,
with little experience provided. Upon graduation a certificate is conferred.
There is no licensing. Virtually all *infirmiers* work for the government.
There are also medical aides, individuals who may at most possess a few
years of education, but in many rural areas they are illiterate. Midwives
possess the equivalent of a grade-school education, and their assistants
considerably less education.

Attitudes of Modern and Traditional Practitioners Towards One Another

Data collected among modern and traditional medical practitioners
in the Bambara country in 1967-1974 show that most physicians (78.0
percent) express a willingness to cooperate with herbalists, but with none
of the other types of practitioners. Male nurses (*infirmiers*) also expressed
a willingness to cooperate with herbalists (95.2 percent of those ques-
tioned). Likewise, 94.3 percent of medical aides, 100 percent of mid-wives
and 100 percent of mid-wife assistants expressed a desire to cooperate with
herbalists.

Whereas none of the physicians offered cooperation with traditional
practitioners other than herbalists, almost one-fifth of the *infirmiers* did.
More than half of the medical aides recommended cooperation with *soma,*
basitigui, and *moriba*. This is not surprising since most are attached to a
traditional culture base and use the services of such practitioners
themselves. Most mid-wives did not support cooperation with *soma* nor
with *basitigui*, but they did with marabouts. Mid-wife assistants (*matrones*)
are similar to medical aides in educational background and expressed
similar views.

ATTITUDES OF TRADITIONAL MEDICAL PRACTITIONERS TOWARDS MODERN MEDICAL PRACTITIONERS

Would Support Cooperation With

Category	No. Interviewed	Physicians No.	%	Infirmiers No	%	Midwives and Midwife Assistants No.	%
Furatigui (herbalists)	35	32	92.8	32	92.8	35	100.0
Soma (Spirit mediums-diviners)	8	1	12.5	1	12.5	6	75.0
Basitigui (diviners-healers)	14	0	0	0	0	8	57.1
Moriba (Koranic teachers)	47	21	44.6	21	44.6	47	100.0

ATTITUDES OF MODERN MEDICAL PRACTITIONERS TOWARDS TRADITIONAL MEDICAL PRACTITIONERS

Would Support Cooperation With

Category	No. Interviewed	Furatigui (herbalists) No.	%	Soma (spirit mediums-diviners) No.	%	Basitigui (diviners-healers) No.	%	Moriba (Koranic teachers) No.	%
Physicians (M.D.)	16	12	78.0	0	0	0	0	0	0
Infirmiers	42	40	95.2	10	23.8	8	19.1	8	19.1
Medical Aides	64	60	94.3	36	56.2	38	59.4	58	91.2
Midwives	20	20	100.0	5	25.0	5	25.0	17	85.0
Midwife Assistants	9	9	100.0	6	66.6	5	55.5	9	100.0

In summary the highest degree of unwillingness in cooperation was expressed with regards to *soma* and *basitigui*. Low levels of cooperation support were expressed towards marabouts by physicians and *infirmiers* but not by medical aides, mid-wives and mid-wife assistants.

Herbalists expressed the greatest degree of willingness to cooperate with all professionals and paraprofessionals. *Soma* and *basitigui* expressed willingness to cooperate with mid-wives and mid-wife assistants but not with either physicians or *infirmiers*. Only 44.6 percent of the marabouts expressed willingness to cooperate with physicians or *infirmiers*, but all were willing to cooperate with mid-wives and mid-wife assistants.

The Role of Traditional Practitioners in the Health Care Delivery System

No one will argue with the fact that traditional medical practitioners by and large perform useful functions in most African societies (Weisz 1972). Nor would many take exception to the statement that there are within the system a proportion of crafty charlatans who effect more harm than good. But the important question that must be asked and that has been asked in the past is what should be their place, if any, in the modern health care delivery system. If quality medical care is understood to mean the delivery of services which meet quality standards established by learned consensus on the basis of proven scientific facts, and delivery by personnel who also meet high standards of training, experience, and performance, then it would be hard to envisage a role for the traditional practitioner. Thus in the developed countries of the world, it would be the minority view which would advocate the delivery of health services by folk healers.

The realities of the Bambara country include few or no physicians, a few infirmiers and other medical workers who have at their disposal virtually none of the diagnostic resources available in developed countries and few of the treatment resources. The choice for the rural Bambara then is not between a modern clinic with a laboratory and a well-stocked pharmacy on one hand and a traditional practitioner on the other, but between the traditional healer and a small bush dispensary devoid of diagnostic resources save those of the medical personnel and possessing at most a handful of medications. In such a setting it would be difficult to cast aside the traditional practitioners because in reality it is they who service most of the population most of the time.

That certain categories of them are unwilling to cooperate with modern medical practitioners should arouse reflection, as should the unwillingness of modern Malian practitioners to cooperate with them. The data collected in this study clearly show a cooperative spirit between modern medical practitioners and herbalists. Each has confidence in the abilities of the other, each respects the usefulness of the other in the health care delivery system.

The mutually negative view expressed by *soma* and *basitigui* and modern medical workers is not really surprising. *Soma* and *basitigui* enjoyed great prestige, power, and wealth in the traditional animist setting. Recent decades have witnessed an erosion of all these advantages under the influence of Islam and modern technology. This is especially so in large urban centers. They see themselves as a group being gradually disadvantaged and are viewed by modern medical workers, who are Moslem for the most part, as charlatans from the animist past.

It is noteworthy that modern medical workers, physicians excluded, are more willing to cooperate with marabouts than marabouts with them. It is rather common knowledge in the Bambara country that many marabouts are arrested upon client complaint for charlatanism and often marabouts comprise the bulk of inmates in local jails. Those marabouts inclined towards charlatanism would be uncooperative in joining hands in any delivery system for fear the association would lead to their being uncovered. Medical workers, on the other hand, being Moslem, tend to assign more credibility to marabouts than objective facts suggest.

If progress in medical care in Africa means the advancement towards higher quality medical services and a reduction of morbidity and mortality rates, then such goals lie in the upgrading of professional personnel and material resources such as hospitals and clinics. Professional recognition of traditional practitioner categories with a long history and high incidence of charlatanism would be a step in the wrong direction. On the other hand, much can be said for the legitimatization of those categories whose records are good. In Mali, herbalists in Bamako are licensed by the central pharmacy, a procedure which does not give them any great advantage. It would certainly be worthwhile to analyze herbal preparations for their active constituent. Mere impressions and intuitions about their efficacy will always be open to question unless such facts are presented.

Among the Bambara, traditional medical practitioners presently are pre-eminent in rural areas and are holding their own in cities. Attainment of better health care in this part of Africa lies in the development of a quality health services infrastructure and not in the support and conferring of official status on traditional practitioner categories whose training, intentions and methods raise questioning doubts among consumers themselves. For the present there is no other option for some consumers. Once options do become available, those practitioners viewed as delivering poor quality service will gradually be phased out by consumer rejection of them and what they are offering.

References

Annuaire Statistique 1971. Bamako: Direction Nationale du Plan et de la Statistique, 1973.

Imperato, P.J. 1964. *Doctor in the Land of the Lion.* New York: Vantage Press.

Imperato, P.J. 1970. Indigenous Medical Beliefs and Practices in Bamako, a Moslem African City, *Tropical and Geographical Medicine* 22(2):211-220, 1970.

Maclean, U. 1971. *Magical Medicine.* London: Penguin Press.

Meillassoux, C. 1968. *Urbanization of an African Community, Voluntary Associations in Bamako.* Seattle: University of Washington Press.

Villien-Rossi, M.L. 1966. Bamako, Capitale du Mali, *Bulletin de L'Institut Fondamental D'Afrique Noire*, 28 (Series B)(1-2):249-380.

7

Folk Medicine in Timbuctoo

Islam is now strongly modifying traditional Bambara medical beliefs and practices. One of the oldest islands of Islam close to the Bambara is the city of Timbuctoo. The Bambara historically have had close commercial and political ties with Timbuctoo and, indeed, conquered and ruled the city at the end of the 18th century (Imperato 1976). Traditional medical beliefs and practices in Timbuctoo are essentially Islamic. A brief examination of these beliefs shows both similarities and differences relative to those of the Bambara. As Islam becomes stronger and more widespread among the Bambara, the similarities will become stronger.

Traditional medical beliefs and practices among the Bambara have never been static. Rather, they have been in a state of constant change, reflecting the incorporation of new concepts, the modification of existing ones and the abandonment of others. Islam has influenced traditional medicine. Although islands of Islam have existed among the Bambara for several centuries, the steady and widespread adoption of Islam by the Bambara did not begin until the advent of the twentieth century. Bambara Islam as we know it today has certain unique characteristics, reflecting the traditional religious heritage upon which it is being built.

Islamic practices constitute the core of folk medicine in Timbuctoo, but not to the exclusion of those derived from an animist culture base. Timbuctoo is an old city and unlike its newer counterparts in West Africa possesses a conservative and tradition-bound population. The population is a stable one and has remained somewhat insulated from those influences currently causing profound social changes in urban Africa. The presence in the city of a well-equipped and well-staffed hospital has somewhat lessened dependence on the traditional medical care system.

Parts of this chapter were previously published in *The Bulletin of the New York Academy of Medicine*, 1976, 52(2):214-252. I acknowledge with thanks the permission of the editor to use this material here.

The city of Timbuctoo stands on the northern banks of the Niger River in Mali. It had its origins as a seasonal camp for the Tuareg nomads in the 11th century A.D. During this period, the camp and its wells were entrusted to a woman whose name was Buctoo. The name, Timbuctoo, is derived from the two Tuareg words, "Tin," meaning "that belonging to" and "Buctoo" (Miner 1965). By the 14th century A.D., Timbuctoo was a thriving caravan center handling most of the gold travelling to North Africa from mines in Bambouk and Wangara to the south. As a consequence of its

A panoramic view of Timbuctoo, a city of mud-brick structures.

intimate contacts with the Moslem world of North Africa, the city eventually developed into a center of Moslem scholarship. Its contacts with animist peoples living to the south were also a consequence of its commercial role in this part of Africa. Salt mined in the Sahara was and still is shipped southward through Timbuctoo, and slaves from the south were shipped northwards through the city.

The city never enjoyed long periods of political stability and it fell under the dominance of several diverse ethnic groups including the Tuareg, Peul, Maure, Songhoi, Bambara, and the Moroccans. As a consequence, the city is ethnically extremely heterogeneous. But Islam, which is professed by most, serves to unite these diverse peoples.

The existence of Timbuctoo was well known in Europe for many centuries. The lack of direct European observation of the city until the 19th century, and its location across a then hostile Moslem world and miles of desert, generated an aura of mystery about it and encouraged the notion that it was at the end of the world. This latter idea has been carried through in popular language usage, especially in the United States, where the word Timbuctoo is used in the sense of a far away or an imaginary place. Many are astonished to learn that Timbuctoo is a real place.

The first written detailed description of the city was provided to the western world by René Caillie who visited Timbuctoo in 1828 (Caillie 1830). Heinrich Barth, the scholarly German explorer, resided in the city for eight months in 1853-1854 and furnished the finest detailed description of Timbuctoo and its peoples (Barth 1857-1859). The city fell to the French under Joffre in 1893 and became part of the French Sudan (Joffre 1915).

The People of Timbuctoo

The present-day population of Timbuctoo is 12,000 (Annuaire Statistique, 1973). However, during the early months of the year the population swells by a few thousand more due to the influx of Tuareg nomads and the individuals arriving with salt caravans.

The Songhoi, who are agriculturists, form approximately three-quarters of the population. They are divided into two classes, the Arma, who are nobles, and the Gabibi who were until fairly recently their serfs. The Gabibi are reputed for their ability to control genies and to perform sorcery. The Arabs, or Maures as they are frequently called, are divided into three classes, the nobles, descendants of former slaves, and the Berabich nomads. The Tuareg are nomads for the most part. Only their former slaves, the Bela, are fixed inhabitants of the town. The Tuareg nobles and their former serfs come into the city on a seasonal basis (Imperato 1975). In addition to these groups are considerably smaller numbers of Bambara and Peul.

The Position of Islam

In Timbuctoo, Islam is not only a religion but also a way of life. It provides the essentials of custom as accepted by all and furnishes the civil and criminal codes of law. While Islam plays a varying role in the lives of different individuals, it lays the foundation for mutual understanding and unites people across ethnic and class lines. Dogma is interpreted by the clerics, the marabouts, also known as *alfa*, individuals who are able to read the Koran. Marabouts also dispense charms and talismans and treat illnesses believed to have a supernatural cause. Marabouts are considered not only to be learned men, but also individuals who possess *baraka*, supernatural powers. There are no fixed standards governing the training of marabouts. The longer a man studies, the more learned he is considered to be. However, his general reputation is contingent upon a number of factors, not the least of which is an empirical assessment of his success in treating illness. These characteristics of marabouts are not unique to Timbuctoo, but are found throughout Moslem West Africa (Trimingham 1959).

There is no religious hierarchy in Timbuctoo. Marabouts tend to attach themselves to the mosque situated in their quarter of the city. Any male in theory can become a marabout, but to do so he must learn Arabic, which is considered to be not only the language of Islam but also the language of supernatural power. In practice, the Arma and Gabibi rarely become marabouts, but in recent years this long-established pattern has changed. The most respected marabouts have traditionally been found among the Arabs (Maures) and the certain clans of Tuareg nobles (Miner 1965).

The Cause of Illness

Serious illness in general is believed to be due to supernatural causes. Consequently, people do not ask how they become ill; rather they ask *why* (see also chapter 2). Recognized disease syndromes are not consistently attributed to the same supernatural cause; rather, each case is considered individually and the specific supernatural cause determined. An exception to this are epidemics in which all cases are attributed to one supernatural cause. Minor illnesses are most often attributed to natural causes and are managed at the household level.

In Timbuctoo several supernatural causes are most commonly incriminated. These are genies, witches, magicians and sorcerers. The latter two inflict illness either directly or through the medium of special charms and fetishes.

Genies

There is a very strong belief in genies in Timbuctoo and they are often held responsible for sudden death and serious illness. Genies are believed to roam about at night and are only rarely encountered during the day. Although a few genies are considered to be benevolent, most are believed to be extremely evil spirits who assume a number of terrifying physical forms. It is believed that some masquerade at night as dogs and cats and for this reason people avoid these stray animals after sundown. They are believed to be especially numerous in certain areas of the city (Miner 1965). Genies rarely enter people's homes.

It is strongly believed that the Gabibi exert control over many evil genies. Knowledge of such control is passed on from father to son within the framework of the artisan guilds (butchers, masons, and blacksmiths) which are for the most part composed of Gabibi. The Bela and certain marabouts are also thought capable of controlling evil genies. Genies are controlled through the pronouncement of magical formulas consisting of words in both Arabic and Songhoi (Miner 1965).

Witches

Witches in Tumbuctoo are known as *tyerkow*. In many ways, they are more comparable to the Western concept of a vampire than to that of a witch. They assume the form of a bat and attack their victims by drinking blood from their necks. It is believed that a witch attacks the same victim on successive nights rendering him weak, cachectic, and febrile. Prolonged febrile illnesses and bouts of malaria are most often thought to be the work of a witch. Witches are also said to be capable of attacking people during the day by touching them or by putting something into their food or drink. Thus, most cases of acute gastroenteritis are attributed to witches.

Those suspected of being witches are usually strangers in the town. Some Gabibi and Bela are also believed to be witches. The non-Arab peoples of Timbuctoo believe that witches are grouped under a leader in a given locale and hold regular nightly meetings at which victims are selected. A few areas of the city and around its perimeter are thought to be meeting places of witches (Miner 1965).

Sorcerers and Magicians

Sorcerers are believed to be individuals who possess those supernatural powers capable of inflicting illness or some other harm on their intended victims. They are known as *dabarey futu koy*, which literally translated means "master of evil." Belief in sorcerers is largely restricted to the Songhoi population of the city; the Arabs and the Tuaregs do not believe in their power. Most sorcerers are said to be Bambara or Peul and in general are strangers in the city. However, some Gabibi guild artisans and Bela are believed to be sorcerers.

Sorcerers inflict illness through two principal mechanisms. The first of these is the *korte*. The *korte* is a magical charm which may consist of a grain of cereal, a stone, a piece of metal or some other small physical object. It is believed that these small objects can be sent through the air over great distances to their intended victims and cause the desired illness by passing through the skin. Sorcerers must impart certain magical qualities to these objects to make them effective *korte*. Either magical formulas are pronounced over them or herbal preparations sprinkled over them. Sorcerers who use *korte* to cause illness are often called *korte koni* by the Songhoi which means, "he who makes charms" (Rouch 1960).

Other sorcerers are said to cause illness through the use of a fetish known as *kambu*. Literally translated, *kambu* means "tweezers." *Kambu* are in fact metal tweezers composed of copper, silver, or iron. Charms composed of cryptic Arabic script are attached to these tweezers as well as pieces of red, white, black, and yellow cords. During the preparation of a *kambu*, the sorcerer recites incantations over the pieces of cord and ties several knots into each of them. At the same time, cowrie shells are also attached to the fetish (Miner 1965).

In order to make a *kambu* effective, the sorcerer conducts a chicken sacrifice over it accompanied by a lengthy ritual. In addition, macerated kola nuts are rubbed over the kambu; it is believed that supernatural qualities are thus imparted. In order to employ this fetish for nefarious ends, the sorcerer takes one of the cords, ties it around the body of the fetish while reciting what it is he wishes. The cord used during this recitation depends upon the color of the intended victim, black for Negroes, red for Arabs, and yellow for whites. The powers of *kambu* can be neutralized if the intended victim wears protective charms (Miner 1965).

Treatment of Illness

The treatment of minor illnesses in Timbuctoo is handled at the level of the household through home remedies. These illnesses, such as mild respiratory infections, conjunctivitis, and mild dermatitis are believed to have natural causes. Herbal remedies abound and are used widely for treating these diseases. While some of these herbs are gathered by individuals in the surrounding rural areas outside this city, many are sold by herbalists. In general, individuals simply inform the herbalist of the preparation they need, for the specificity of given herbs is well known; but occasionally, the client will inform the herbalist of the disease problem and he in turn will recommend a given herb.

Most herbal preparations consist of leaves and stems and occasionally of roots. Usually, they must be pounded into powdered form in a mortar with a pestle and then mixed with water so that a solution results. Herbalists provide clients with directions for preparing these remedies; but, often, individuals are familiar with their preparation through frequent use.

Severe illnesses are treated by either Moslem clerics, the marabouts, or by Gabibi magicians known as *tynibibi koy* (master of black talk). These same practitioners are also believed to prevent illness through the use of charms.

Marabouts

Some marabouts make use of standard Islamic magic manuals. However, others do not; instead they learn the art of making amulets and charms from their teachers. The marabouts' charms for preventing and treating illness are similar to those discussed in Chapter 5. The first are written charms, known as *tira*. These are composed of small pieces of paper on which verses from the Koran are written along with magical Arabic formulas. These charms are sewn into small rectangular leather satchets and usually worn around the neck. The Arabs in Timbuctoo do not wear many *tira*, but the Tuareg nobles often wear a half dozen or more at a time. These charms are used for treatment, and also for the prevention of illness.

More commonly, marabouts treat illness through ritual charms — writing passages from the Koran on wooden slates with either ink or charcoal and then washing off the writings with water. The solution is either drunk by the patient or else rubbed over that part of the anatomy considered ill. During this process of washing the words off the slate, the marabout repeats ritualistic prayers which transfer his *baraka* (supernatural power) to the solution. Some marabouts spit on the patient and rub their saliva into the affected part of the anatomy, reciting cryptic formulas as they do so. Marabouts often provide patients with myrrh to which their *baraka* has been transferred. The patient burns the myrrh every day, thus being exposed to the *baraka*.

Miner reported that at the time of his studies in Timbuctoo, in 1941, there were a few powerful marabouts who possessed good genies who did their bidding. The marabouts used these genies to cure illness, including insanity. However, at the time of my studies in 1967-1974, there was little belief in the cure of illness through the medium of genies controlled by powerful marabouts (Imperato 1976).

Marabouts are not judged harshly by their patients if they fail to achieve a cure. The overriding fatalism inherent to Islam explains away these failures as God's will. Seriously ill individuals may consult several marabouts if the cause of their illness is not altered by maraboutic intervention. However, most individuals adhere to the treatments of their family marabout.

Marabouts do not provide their services free of charge and often-times charge relatively exhorbitant fees for their charms. Certain charms, such as those worn by women to prevent miscarriages, cost the equivalent of ten U.S. dollars, and this corresponds to the bi-monthly wage of an average civil servant in Timbuctoo.

Magician-Healers

The Arabs in Timbuctoo do not believe in supernatural causes of illness which are outside the context of the Koran; the other ethnic groups in the city do, however. The magician-healers who deal with these supernatural causes of illness are known as *tynibibi koy*. In Songhoi this means "master of black language." The majority of magician-healers are Gabibi. Belief in the *tynibibi koy* has considerably diminished over the past decade, due in part to the rising levels of literacy and the gradual Westernization of the city's population.

Magician-healers make a variety of charms whose purposes range from the prevention of illness to acquisition of wealth. These charms, known as *gulli*, are composed of braided or knotted pieces of string of different colors. The magician-healer pronounces secret incantations as he ties a knot in the string. The magical formula is then believed to reside in the knot.

At one time, magician-healers were frequently called in to treat people believed to be suffering from the attack of a witch (Miner 1965). This is less so today since with a deeper Islamization of the non-Arab segments of the population, there is a decline in the belief in witches. Magician-healers usually treat their patients by pronouncing magical formulas over some edible sustance such as milk, porridge, or butter. The substance is then eaten by the patient and a portion of it rubbed over his body. This treatment is often repeated on successive days. Magician-healers were once often called upon to exorcise suspected witches during an elaborate ritual. This is infrequently done today.

Modern Medical Facilities

Modern medical services, while present in Timbuctoo to some degree since the turn of the century, have not generally been available to the general population until the last two decades. There is a 30-bed hospital built since Mali became independent in 1960. The hospital has a modern operating room, reserved for the most part for life-threatening emergencies, and modern x-ray equipment.

There is also a hygiene service attached to the hospital, responsible for environmental sanitation in the city and a unit of the national preventive medical service, the Service des Grandes Endemies, responsible for mass immunization campaigns.

Medical services are supervised by one Malian physician who received his training in Europe. There are no ex-patriate physicians in the town. There are six nurses and one mid-wife attached to the hospital. In general, the quality of medical care provided at the hospital is above the average for rural Mali.

Although the hospital and its satellite dispensaries provide relatively good quality medical care, they have not made a significant inroad into the treatment sphere of many marabouts in certain parts of the city. Among traditionalists, the basic belief in a supernatural cause of disease precludes treatment at the hospital. Others view the results obtained at the hospital as less satisfactory than those obtained through marabouts. Cure for the traditionalist in Timbuctoo has two components, the disappearance of symptoms and psychologic reassurance. Even if the marabout fails at the first, he almost never fails at the second.

Attitudes towards modern medical services are slowly changing. More and more traditionalists are seeking care at the hospital, but not necessarily to the exclusion of maraboutic care. Often they will seek care in the outpatient dispensary and then seek out the advice of a marabout, or the sequence may be reversed. Equally common is the habit of inpatients to have their marabouts treat them on the ward in the hospital. The proportion of the population which utilizes the hospital to the exclusion of the marabouts is quite small, consisting mostly of government officials and the educated elite.

Coexistence of Modern and Traditional Medicine

Confidence in marabouts and magician-healers generally runs high, and they function in an Islamic community that readily accepts treatment failure as God's will. Unlike nurses at the Timbuctoo Hospital, they can donate a great deal of time to individual patients and in so doing provide them with the psychological assurances they need.

The medical services provided by the Timbuctoo Hospital are not perceived by many of the town's inhabitants as superior to traditional treatments. Attitudinal factors aside, the hospital personnel are often less successful than they should be because of a lack of diagnostic aids and specific therapeutic agents. A diagnosis of amoebic dysentery may be made, but if the hospital pharmacy has no amebicides, medical personnel cannot properly treat the patient. This is not an uncommon dilemma in Timbuctoo. There is widespread recognition, however, that acute surgical emergencies are best handled at the hospital.

In Timbuctoo, traditional practitioners practice side by side with the modern health care delivery system, a phenomenon observed elsewhere in Africa. There is rarely any conflict or confrontation generated by the traditional system. Confrontation, when it does occur, is usually generated by personnel at the hospital. They are understandably angered by receiving a patient whose outcome has been compromised by days or weeks of delay due to treatment by the traditional sector. Even if the hospital personnel are successful in treating the illness, credit for cure may not go to them but to the traditional healers, a common phenomenon in many areas of Africa (Imperato 1967). Marabouts often visit their patients in the hospital, impart their ritual cures and advise the patient to continue his hospital treatment. In so doing, they participate in whatever success may result.

The traditional system of medical practice in Timbuctoo will continue to thrive in spite of the progressive Westernization and the raising of educational levels of the population, for the concepts of disease causation and the accepted methods for dealing with disease lie deep in the socio-religious convictions of the Timbuctoo population. This is in sharp contrast to the situation prevailing in Bamako. This enduring power of the traditional system is bound to its ability to provide the patient with what he really wants to know, namely, why—not how—he became ill (Maclean 1971).

References

Annuaire Statistique. 1971. Direction Nationale du Plan et de la Statistique. Bamako.

Barth, Heinrich. 1857–1859. *Travels and Discoveries in North and Central Africa.* New York: Harper and Brothers.

Caillie, Rene. 1830. *Travels through Central Africa to Timbuctoo.* London: Colburn and Bentley.

Imperato, P.J. 1967. *Bwana Doctor.* London: Jarrolds.

Imperato, P.J. 1970. Indigenous Medical Beliefs and Practices in Bamako, A Moslem African City, *Tropical and Geographical Medicine* 29:211-220.

Imperato, P.J. 1975. *A Wind in Africa.* St. Louis: Warren H. Green.

Imperato, P.J. 1976. Traditional Medical Beliefs and Practices in the City of Timbuctoo, *Bulletin of the New York Academy of Medicine* 52:(2)241-252.

Imperato, P.J. 1977. *Historical Dictionary of Mali.* Metuchen, New Jersey; Scarecrow Press-Grolier.

Joffre, J. 1915. *My March to Timbuctoo.* New York: Duffield.

Maclean, M. 1971. *Magical Medicine.* London: Penguin.

Miner, H. 1965. *The Primitive City of Timbuctoo.* New York: Doubleday.

Pefontan, C. 1922. Histoire de Tombuctoo de Sa Fondation à L'Occupation Francaise, *Bulletin du Comité d'Etudes Historiques et Scientifiques de l'A.O.F.* 7:81-113.

Rouch, J. 1960. *La Religion et La Magie Songhay.* Paris: Presses Universitaires de France.

Trimingham, J.S. 1959. *Islam in West Africa.* London: Oxford.

8

Mental Illness

Of all the disease states present in Africa, mental illness has received perhaps more attention than most in recent years in the medical literature. Within this broad area, several foci of interest exist. A number of published papers and symposia have emphasized the nature of mental illness in Africa drawing attention to both the similarities and differences between these disorders among Africans and among individuals in Western cultures (Carothers 1953; Edgerton 1966; Orley 1970; Collomb 1973). Others have focused on the social implications of mental illness, emphasizing how traditional societies perceive the mentally ill and how they manage them in a sociologic sense (Edgerton 1966; Ortigues et al. 1966; Lambo 1965). An extremely large area of interest is that of the use of traditional means and healers to treat mental illness (Lambo 1965; Zempleni 1969; Collomb 1972; Renauld 1974). Finally, a number of studies have been published dealing with the management of mental disorders through modern inpatient units and ambulatory care programs (Dia 1973; Thebaud 1974; Hazera 1974; Boussat et al. 1974; Fellous 1973).

The emphasis in this chapter is on the management of mental illness by traditional medical systems. Many of these traditional systems for treating mental illness have been studied and described in detail elsewhere. They often bear strong similarities to one another. A general overview of the traditional management of mental illness is given here. More detailed information on the treatment of mental illness in several African groups is presented in two fine works by Dr. Ari Kiev, *Transcultural Psychiatry* and *Magic, Faith And Healing*.

Psychotic Disorders

Mental illness is present in Africa in all those forms recognized in the developed countries of the world. Schizophrenia and its clinical variants comprise the most common group of psychoses found in Africa. It has been observed, however, that the symptom complex among non-literate Africans tends to be quite different from that usually observed in developed countries and among literate Africans. Delusions of grandeur are rare in non-literate rural Africans, whereas they are common in Western cultures and among literate Africans who are tied into a Western culture base. Delusions among non-literate rural Africans tend to focus on ancestral cults and the supernatural world. Hallucinations are usually auditory in nature which Lambo (1965) ascribes to cultural determination. Spoken language is the major form of communication among non-literate Africans and thus Lambo reasons that most of the hallucinations are auditory.

The other characteristics of schizophrenia among non-literate Africans include episodic confusional states, emotional lability, and incoherence. Mental confusion is the most prominent feature of schizophrenic psychosis among non-literate Africans. However, because the usual classic symptoms of this disorder are modified by the cultural environment of the non-literate African, they often do not surface, rendering the diagnosis difficult. Lambo and his colleagues have found that schizophrenia among the Yoruba in Nigeria tends to be found in near relatives of schizophrenic patients. The disease also tends to be episodic, with episodes lasting from a few hours to a few days. Also, the African schizophrenic disorders are less prone to chronicity than those in the West or among the Chinese (Lambo 1965).

Grossly aberrant behavior is quickly recognized in Africa and persons manifesting it are considered mentally ill. However, certain forms of mental illness recognized in the Western world are not recognized in many African societies (Leighton et al. 1963). Two examples are psychopathic personalities and senility. Both entities are recognized but they are not considered to represent mental illness. In a study of four East African groups, the Hehe, Kamba, Sehei, and Pokot, it was found that bizzare behavior was only considered to be psychotic if it occurred without an apparent reason (Edgerton 1966). It was also found that this bizzare behavior did not have to be severely disruptive to be considered psychotic. Even mildly disruptive behavior such as going around naked and hiding or sleeping in the bush were considered psychotic if they occurred without apparent cause.

Miner and DeVos (1960) have reported that in some areas of Algeria communal recognition of the existence of psychosis in an individual very much depends on the individual's symptoms. A psychotic patient who becomes a religious zealot is not considered psychotic, whereas if he paraded nude in public he is declared crazy. Communal diagnosis of psychotic behavior is therefore subjective, dependent on the types of symptoms manifested. Depressive states are extremely common in Africa.

Earlier writings suggest that depression was rare in Africa, but this may have been because the syndrome was looked for and not the individual composite symptoms. Leighton (1963) found a sizeable number of depressive patents among the Yoruba of Nigeria. Yet, the Yóruba whom he interviewed did not have a name for the syndrome of depression. They did recognize the various components of the syndrome — crying, feeling blue, and loss of appetite — but these did not form a single syndrome in their minds. Disease syndromes composed of several symptoms are often not recognized in Africa as forming a single entity (Imperato 1971).

It is rather difficult to determine the incidence and prevalence rates for the psychotic disorders for most African countries for a variety of reasons. Most of the pertinent data has come from established mental hospitals in the larger urban areas. Strongly affecting these data are such factors as the number of available places in these hospitals, their admitting policies, the referral system for getting patients to the hospital, and wide variation in diagnostic criteria. In many African societies, there is often a very high tolerance for unusual mental states and for psychiatric symptoms. As a consequence, many psychiatric disorders never find their way to national mental hospitals. Certain disorders may be underrepresented in national mental hospitals, while others may be overrepresented. Thus, studies of mental illness in Africa based upon hospital admission data are somewhat misleading and generally inconclusive (Kiev 1972). They have served a useful function, however, in pointing out the need for long term epidemiologic research to define the scope of the problem. A number of this type of study have been undertaken in Africa and, taking into account as they do the cultural content in which psychiatric illness occurs, they have provided clearer insight into the magnitude of the problem (Carothers 1953; Tooth 1950; Leighton et al 1963; Kiev 1964).

Psychoneurotic Disorders

Incidence and prevalence data for the psychoneurotic disorders, such as anxiety and depressive states,[1] are even more difficult to come by in Africa than those for the psychotic disorders. Many of these disorders may not be so severe as to even require treatment within the framework of the traditional system. A smaller proportion of them than the psychotic disorders probably comes to the attention of the modern medical sector.

A number of special surveys have been conducted in various parts of Africa to determine the kinds of psychoneurotic disorders present and to

---

[1]Two types of depressive states are distinguished. The psychoneurotic depressive states are less severe and are easier to treat than the psychotic depressive states.

characterize their distribution in the population. Some of these have been undertaken in urban areas where technological advances and cultural changes have placed considerable stress both on individuals and on the traditional societies from which they come. They have often focused on how various social groups compensate for the difficulties of adjustment in urban areas (Dawson 1964). Ethnic groups vary considerably in their general psychological susceptibility to the process of social change in an urban environment. These variations are due to differences in established traditional values and cultural patterns, according to Dawson (1964). Unfortunately, it is often not possible to come up with firm data about the prevalence and incidence of psychoneurotic disorders in urban areas, even during the course of such studies. (It must be pointed out that it is often difficult to obtain such data even in the developed countries of the world.) It would be incorrect to assume that urbanization and industrialization have led to a higher prevalence of psychiatric illness in Africa. Valid comparative data for pre-industrialized rural groups is lacking.

The Treatment of Mental Illness

There are several methods for treating the mentally ill in Africa that can be found in use in most tribal groups. Considerable variations in a given method are present, but in general they do not constitute a sharp departure from the generic nature of African therapeutic methods. As described in a previous chapter, the causes of illness (mental illness included) as perceived in African cultures are many. Sorcery, witchcraft, and spirit possession are viewed as common causes of mental illness. Among the Bambara, sorcery is often ascribed as the cause, working through a system of contagious magic in which strands of the victim's hair are obtained and a spell worked over them. Dr. Raymond Prince (1964) in studying indigenous Yoruba psychiatry investigated 101 cases treated by traditional healers. The causes of mental illness in the opinion of these healers were 20 percent natural, such as heredity, bad blood and hemp smoking, 18 percent supernatural, and 45 percent preternatural. The supernatural causes were spirits and the Shopona spirit, the god of smallpox. Among the preternatural causes were witchcraft, sorcery and curses. The remaining cases were ascribed to miscellaneous causes or else were unknown.

The principal approaches to the treatment of mental illness are the use of drugs, treatment through cult rituals, spirit mediumship rituals, and the performance of appeasing sacrifices of various types. It should be appreciated that these approaches are implemented within the matrix of the society of which the patient is a part. Great importance is attached to the interrelationship of the patient, the therapist, and the family in the therapeutic process. Thus, for example, among the Yoruba, a patient is first seen by a priest-diviner, the *babalawo* who diagnoses his condition after performing divination. In a series of divination ceremonies, the patient is advised to make appeasing sacrifices to a number of possible causative supernatural agents, to take certain herbal medicines, to employ charms protective against witches, sorcerers and spirits, to change his place of residence, and even to change his usual manner of behavior. In addition to this, the priest-diviner may suggest that the patient join one of the *Orisha* cults, cults dedicated to various minor deities. If all of these measures fail, the patient will then be referred by the priest-diviner to a healer who specializes in the treatment of mental illness (Prince 1964). At the treatment centers operated by these healers, a number of methods and techniques are employed in treating patients. Drugs are given to the patient, animals sacrificed to appease offended spirits, and rituals conducted to remove the cause of the disorder.

Throughout this process, a number of therapeutic techniques are employed. These include suggestion, command, simile, the use of illustrative stories, rituals, and magical gestures. The patient's environment may be manipulated by his being told to move to a new compound. The ego is strengthened and an attempt made to prevent relapses by advising the patient to enter an *Orisha* cult. By so doing, he enters into contact with a supportive environment of new friends who are joined together by initiation and the possession of secret esoteric knowledge. These cults are either masquerade cults, generally for males, or possession cults, usually for women. Through them the patient is drawn into a sort of group therapy. He obtains high status, acts out aggressive and sexual behavior, reverses sexual roles often and has temporary freedom of responsibility for his actions (Prince 1964).

It is noteworthy that indigenous psychiatric therapy in Africa does not include attempts to give patients insights into their own motives and in so doing to develop self-awareness and personality maturation.

Drug Therapies

There are a wide variety of herbs in Africa for treating mental illness. Among these are several hundred species of plants with alkaloidal narcotic properties. There are stimulants, sedatives, and hallucinogens which respectively increase, decrease and alter awareness. Cocoa, opium, tobacco, hemp and coffee are five of these alkaloids which are used widely on a commercial scale. In addition to this category of drugs, there are others such as the *Rauwolfia* alkaloids which have been widely used as tranquilizers.

Bambara Drug Therapies

There is considerable variation in the herbal drugs used for treating psychiatric illness from one area to another. For the most part, they are used in conjunction with a broader program of therapy involving regimens that address the presumed supernatural cause of the illness. What now follows is a description of some of the herbal preparations used by the Bambara. These remedies are used for patients who are psychotic.

The Bambara refer to psychotic states as *fa*. Medicinal therapies of various kinds are often used successively when prompt results are not obtained, which is often the case. A striking characteristic of these remedies is that many of them are applied externally only, either to the head or to the entire body. In a certain sense, then, they are used to ritually cleanse the patient. They are usually applied in conjunction with the recitation of magical formulas. Others are inhaled and only a few are ingested. Also, virtually all of these remedies are administered over a very short period of time ranging from a day to a week, three days being the average. Most remedies consist of using a mixture of two or more plants, rarely one. Often, a salve made from one or more plants is rubbed on the head and then washed off with a solution made from one or several plants. The urine and feces of certain sacred animals such as the vulture, lion, or hyena are often mixed into the topical remedies.

A common treatment consists of shaving the head and of rubbing over it the powder obtained from pulverizing the branches of *gongo-sira* (*Sterculia setigera*). After this, the patient's head is bent over smoldering embers over which the leaves of *Cymbopogon giganteus* have been spread. This treatment is repeated once a day for several days.

The head is often washed with a solution containing the roots of *Borassus aethiopum* mixed with the roots of *suruku ntomo* (*Zizyphus mucronata*) and occasionally with other roots. Another common treatment involves covering the head with a salve made from the charred roots of *n'tama* (*Parinari curatellifolia*). After being on for a few hours, the patient's head is then washed with a solution made with the leaves of the same plant. Often, the feces of animals such as lions, vultures and certain antelopes are added to these two typical treatments.

Psychotic patients are often washed with cow urine and then struck on the back with a fresh branch from *Calotropis procera*. Another bathing remedy employs a solution made from the bark of sacred village trees which are the residence of village protective spirits. The symbolism of this treatment is apparent in that these trees are normally never touched and their barks are considered to be especially sacred.

Ingestion remedies are proportionally few among the Bambara and Malinke. The commonest ones are as follows. A powder made from the pulverized leaves of *Lannea acida* (*m'peku*), *Vitex cienkowskii* (*koro ba*) and *Guiera senegalensis* (*kune*) is mixed with fresh milk. This is given to the patient who is then asked to breathe in the fumes created from burning the powdered leaves of *Heteropogon contortus* over smoking embers. Another remedy requires the use of three plants which are mixed in water, *sebeke* (*Borassus aethiopium*), *ndanga* (*Annona senegalensis*) and *suruku n'domo* (*Zizyphus mucronata*). The patient is given this mixture for several days. Herbalists often administer a solution of *Rauwolfia vomitoria* which has strong tranquilizing properties (Traoré 1965).

It is difficult to accurately assess the pharmacologic efficacy of these remedies, but my impressions from field observations are that they are not very effective.

Cult Rituals

The Bambara and Malinke possess six initiation cults which have the same psychotherapeutic value as the *Orisha* cults among the Yoruba of Nigeria. These six Bambara and Malinke cults are known as the *Dyow*. They hold regularly scheduled ceremonies throughout the year. Behavior that is normally considered deviant is permitted during these ceremonies and individuals are able to act out aggressions and sexual impulses. For example, during the annual festival of the *Komo* cult, the men do not wash themselves for several weeks, an aberrant state under normal circumstances. During the ceremonies, which may last from a week to several weeks, the women and children are required to remain in their houses and defecate in these houses, which is highly aberrant under normal circumstances. The *Kwore* cult, the most complex in terms of structure, has as its principal aim the conferring of advanced knowledge about man on its initiates. Self-flagellation and flagellation of one another occurs during the rituals, and initiates often enter into dissociated states. The *Kwore Duga* class within the cult, through which initiates pass, permits its members to utter every known obsenity, make obscene gestures and dress in absurd costumes. Its members gather together all manner of rubbish, as do many psychotic patients, and carry it around with them. In many ways, the *Kwore Duga* imitate the behavior of the psychotic patient.

The *Dyow* of the Bambara and Malinke differ from the *Orishas* of the Yoruba in that they are virtually obligatory for all males. The women also have their cults, but they are of lesser social significance than the *Dyow* (Henry 1910).

Prince (1964), mentioned above, describes how psychiatrically-disturbed individuals are initiated into the *Orisha* cults as a means of therapy. Cults are not employed in this sense among the Bambara and

Malinke, but they do serve as a prophylaxis against the development of mental illness in the ways outlined above.

Spirit Medium Cults

These cults, which have been described in a previous chapter, are often used to treat psychiatric patients. Initiation into these cults is viewed as a form of therapy in that the patient fulfills the wishes of the offended spirit by becoming a devotee of the cult. The Bambara and other groups believe that recurrences are also prevented when the patient is a devotee of the cult.

The *Shopana* cult of the Yoruba is an example of a spirit medium cult. The spirits of this cult are believed responsible for a variety of illnesses including smallpox and the psychoses. Although the cult was prohibited by the British administration because it was believed responsible for spreading smallpox, it still exists in a clandestine form in Nigeria (Prince 1964). Initiation into Shopana requires 21 days. Prince recorded the dramatic improvement in a psychotic woman after she had been initiated. Follow-up study was not recorded so the long-term results are not known.

In the 1920's and 1930's a spirit medium cult, the *Dyidé*, developed in the western Bambara country (see chapter 4, above). Many psychiatrically ill individuals were initiated as a means of therapy and as prophylaxis against recurrence. The initiates were given a drink made from the leaves of *Mitragyna africana*, which has a strong hallucinogenic effect. The cult was disbanded by the French because of its political activities which were viewed as detrimental to the colonial administration. Unfortunately the therapeutic success of this cult in managing psychiatric patients was never assessed.

Healers

While spirit medium cults and the rituals of other types of cults play a significant role in the treatment of mentally ill persons, the majority of such patients are treated by healers when home remedies fail. Which categories of healers take on this responsibility is variable, depending on the ethnic group in question. The treatment of mental illness by such healers has been studied in considerable depth among certain ethnic groups such as the Yoruba of Nigeria and the Wolof of Senegal (Prince 1964; Zempleni 1969).

The treatment successes of traditional healers are difficult to evaluate. As Maclean (1971) points out, the margins of insanity among the Yoruba are obscure and shifting. Many of the problems brought to the attention of Yoruba priest-diviners are neurotic disorders, the outcome of which with even minimal therapy is often excellent. The Yoruba priest-diviners employ herbs and use their own powers of insight which, coupled to their knowledge of the *Ifa* oracular system, enables them to be excellent psychotherapists. According to Maclean many of the remedies recommended by the Yoruba priest-diviners have to do with reordering the patient's relationships with his family and friends and especially with the spiritual world. Patients are obliged to participate in a treatment plan which consists of rituals performed to appease spirits of different kinds and taboos which must be observed for varying periods, such as not eating certain foods or not having sexual intercourse. The implementation of this treatment program brings the patient's family into active participation. Since the restoration of social order and the re-establishment of normal interpersonal relationships are the goal of the healer, communal participation in the treatment process is essential.

Yoruba priest-diviners traditionally provided residential care to psychiatric patients, but they have gradually relinquished this proficiency to other types of healers (Maclean 1971). Psychotic patients who are violent must first be subdued since they may harm themselves or others around them. In most African societies this is accomplished by tying the patient in chains. Among the Luo of Tanzania I often observed psychotic patients chained to a log or tree (Imperato 1966). In Mali, most ethnic groups restrain violent psychotic patients by shackling them. The process of applying chains to a psychotic patient is not undertaken lightly. In Islamized areas in Mali, Koranic charms that are meant to confer on them the ability to subdue the patient and protect them from harm are supplied to the men who must physically get hold of the patient. Comparable charms are often used in animist areas.

Maclean reports that charms and medicines are often applied to the padlock of the chain whose purpose is to prevent the patient from escaping. Among the Yoruba, she states that *Senecio abyssinicus* is often compounded with other ingredients and applied to the padlock.

Among the Bambara and Malinke of Mali, once the patient is secured, his head is shaved and the remedies described above are applied. In addition, an animal such as a chicken, sheep, or goat may be sacrificed and offered at the ancestral altar of the family or the village altar, the *dasiri*. Essentially then, the first phase of treatment involves ritual cleansing and sacrifices. The initial phases of therapy among the Yoruba are quite similar (Maclean 1971).

In Yoruba country, there are treatment centers where psychiatric patients are treated by healers. Nowadays, patients are referred to such centers by priest-diviners (Prince 1964). He has vividly described these centers as consisting of the healer's large family compound behind which are houses for the patients and a kitchen where herbal preparations are continuously being made over open fires. The houses for the patients contain isolation rooms for violent patients who are shackled around the neck with chains hung from the ceiling. Non-violent patients mingle in with the healer's extended family in the main courtyard where their own families also come. The healers keep a garden of medicinal plants near their houses.

Prince observed that psychotic patients were intitially given *Rauwolfia* to tranquilize them and sometimes prior to this a purgative-emetic mixture to weaken them. Initial treatment at these Yoruba centers includes blood sacrifices of various animals aimed at appeasing spirits. If witchcraft or sorcery are suspected, their effects are countered by the introduction of various medicines into the skin of patients through small cuts made in the skin. Patients are placed on doses of tranquilizers and other medicines for three or four months (Prince 1964). The use of *Rauwolfia* is common among these healers. Although *Rauwolfia vomitoria* is used by healers among the Bambara, who call it *kolidohi*, it is not given in regularly scheduled doses as among the Yoruba, nor is it given for such long periods of time.

At Yoruba treatment centers, relatives of the patients are always on hand, a practice which also prevails in modern hospital settings in Africa. An attempt is made early in therapy to re-integrate the patient into normal life pattern and for this reason he is allowed to work in the healer's fields or do other chores. The patient's long term therapy at these centers consists of rituals, magical recitations, and pharmacotherapy. An important aspect of therapy is the elaborate discharge ceremony which healers undertake (Maclean 1971). These ceremonies are conducted to insure against relapse, which is quite frequent (as it is among patients in the developed countries).

Prince has given a very vivid description of a discharge ceremony which he witnessed at Ife. In this ceremony the healer, two assistants and the patient waded into the middle of a stream where the water was waist deep. There the patient's head was shaved and three doves were used in a complex ritual sacrifice, the blood of two of the doves being spattered over the patient's head and body. The third dove was drowned and its body used along with a piece of soap to wash the patient's head. The killed birds were allowed to flow downstream along with a white robe the patient was wearing. Prince likens this ceremony to a *rite de passage*, the patient passing from a sick form of life to a healthy form of life.

Yoruba healers are well paid for their services and often they complain that they would be more successful if patients' families paid what they requested. I observed in 1967 in Ibadan that many of these Yoruba healers raised this matter with such frequency that one suspects that it is a means of explaining treatment failures.

Zempleni (1969) has described in great detail the traditional management of mental illness in Senegal among the Wolof and the Lebou. He points out that these two groups view mental illness as a form of exterior aggression from supernatural forces such as ancestor spirits, witchcraft, sorcery, or Islamic spirits. There are four types of healers among the Wolof and the Lebou — antisorcerers (*bilejo*), ancestral spirit priests (*n'dopkat*), Islamic healers, the *marabouts*, and their animist counterparts, the *jabarkat*.

I have observed that among the Wolof, as among the Bambara, the family often arrives at a consensus about the cause of the patient's illness. Once this is done the patient is taken to the appropriate healer. Quite often there are considerable differences of opinion about the cause, and the consensus opinion is arrived at only after much heated discussion. A Wolof healer does not interrogate the patient as a Western psychiatrist would. In fact he demonstrates little or no interest in what the patient has to say. He focuses on things which can pinpoint the causative agent for him. Thus, the time of onset of illness, the place of onset, and such types of related information are obtained from the family. Divination is conducted and the healer determines the cause of the illness. The patient has no participating role in this process. Once this is done, the healer seeks to have the family confirm this diagnosis by involving them in a complex interrogation procedure which ends in their formulating a consensus opinion identical to his (Zempleni 1969). Spirit mediums, the *n'dopkat*, are prominent in the treatment of Wolof patients. Through rites of possession, called *n'dop*, the will of offended ancestral spirits is made known and the patient obliged to perform the requested rituals and observances.

In highly Islamized areas of Mali, Senegal, and Guinea, the Koranic teachers, the marabouts, also known as *alfas* and *karamokos*, play the most prominent role in the management of psychotic patients. Patients are often brought to the homes of these priest-healers where they are kept for long periods. Some of these practitioners are renowned for their therapeutic abilities and keep several patients at a time in their compounds. Their approach to treatment is fairly standard, consisting of the use of Koranic methods such as prayers, incantations, and washing the patient's head with water that has been poured over a wooden board inscribed with passages from the Koran. Some of these healers use herbal preparations which they give to patients by mouth. In central Mali I observed one such healer who used *Rauwolfia vomitoria* with excellent results.

Dawson (1964) studied the therapeutic activities of Moslem clerics in Sierra Leone, and found that some of them tried to induce pyrexia in patients. The patient was seated on the ground with a pot of steaming boiled water between his legs and a blanket placed over him. The water is changed from time to time to insure a high temperature in the enclosed environment that the patient occupies. Dawson raises the possibility that these Moslem healers might have observed the psychiatric improvement in some patients who had tertiary syphilis after they had a bout of malaria.

This is certainly possible and hyperpyrexia secondary to malaria might have cured a certain number of patients with tertiary syphilis in this part of Africa. Dawson found that the Koranic healers in Kabala, a town some 250 miles from Freetown, the capital of Sierra Leone, enjoyed a greater reputation for treating psychiatric patients than the healers in the capital itself.

In my experience, Koranic healers in Mali did not have much success in treating psychotic patients. The spectre of psychotic patients roaming the streets of the towns or the bush tracks of rural areas, in rags, their hair long and matted and their arms full of bags of refuse, is all too common. Although precise information is lacking, the incidence and prevalence of psychotic disorders is highest in Mali in the northern regions of Mopti and Gao where syphilis is also endemic. It is in these two regions where Islam is strongest, having been present for over 500 years. Traditional medical treatment, therefore, is purely Islamic. Many patients are brought to Bamako from these areas by their relatives for treatment after Moslem clerics have not succeeded. They are treated on the psychiatric ward of the Point-G Hospital, Mali's national hospital in Bamako. Often after discharge they remain in the capital and do not return home. They often relapse and do not re-enter the hospital, but spend their time roaming the streets.

Koranic healers in the sahelian and desert zones of West Africa are disadvantaged from the lack of abundant flora in the environments where they live. Most of the herbal remedies they use must come from latitudes farther to the south. Consequently, whenever they use them, they do so sparingly.

Conclusions

Traditional medical systems in Africa have addressed themselves to the management of mental illness for a long time. They have had their successes and failures, as has modern western medicine. There is often a tendency on the part of some observers to express the qualitative judgement that the traditional system is superior to the modern medical approach. Such a judgement is made without full knowledge of the facts. If the traditional system were so successful there would not be so many psychotic patients roaming the streets and roadways of Africa. Routinely they are rounded up by the police or army whenever an important conference is held in a capital or a visiting dignitary arrives. They are trucked out into the bush and let go, only to find their way back to the streets of the capital in a few days. That this occurs with such regularity reveals that both the traditional and modern systems of psychiatric care in these countries are not fully successful. When the recent cholera epidemic swept through West Africa many psychotic patients died from it since they lived in such unhygienic conditions and did not receive treatment for cholera (Imperato 1974). Again, this was symptomatic of the inadequacies of both systems.

Certainly, the traditional medical systems have much to offer in the management of mental illness, but the development of quality psychiatric services lies in the establishment of community-oriented clinics staffed by paraprofessionals and professionals who can be responsive to local needs with what modern scientific medicine has to offer. Cooperation with local healers is a hotly disputed matter in most circles. Most would agree that traditional healers have an important contribution to make in the management of borderline neurotic patients. The prevalence of charlatinism among traditional practitioners and the absence of any quality control of their activities makes most modern psychiatric specialists wary of formalizing relationships with them.

The subsistence economies of most of the countries of modern Africa will undoubtedly impair the establishment of ideal models of modern community-based psychiatric care for a long time to come. Consequently, traditional approaches will continue to flourish.

References

Boussat, M. Feller, L. and Hladik, M. 1974. Le Champ Psychiatrique Infantile Au Sénégal. *Afrique Médicale* 13(124):913-920.

Carothers, J.C. 1953. *The African Mind in Health and Disease, A Study in Ethnopsychiatry.* Geneva: World Health Organization, Monograph Series No. 17.

Collomb, H. 1972. Psychiatrie Sans Psychiatres, *Etudes Médicales* 4:295-311.

Collomb, H. 1973. La Schizophrenie dans Les Sociétés Africaines, Brussels: *Symposium of the World Psychiatric Association.*

Dawson, J. 1964. Urbanization and Mental Health in a West African Community, in *Magic, Faith and Healing*, edited by Ari Kiev. New York: The Free Press, pp. 305-342.

Dia, M. 1973. *Une Communauté Therapeutique: Le Pinth de Fann*, Memoire Pour Le Certificat d'Education Speciales de Psychiatrie. Dakar.

Edgerton, R. 1966. Conceptions of Psychosis in Four East African Societies. *American Anthropologist* 68:408-425.

Fellous, M. 1973. Une Année de Psychologie Clinque à Bamako. *Etudes Maliennes,* 7:54-69.

Field, M.J. 1960. *Search for Security: An Ethno-Psychiatric Study of Ghana.* London: Faber and Faber.

Hazera, M. 1974. Assistance Psychiatrique Extra-Hospitalière dans La Région D'Abidjan, *Afrique Médicale*, 13:881-888.

Imperato, P.J. 1966. Witchcraft and Traditional Medicine among the Luo of Tanzania, *Tanzania Notes and Records* 66:193-201.

Imperato, P.J. and Sow, O. 1971. Incidence and Local Beliefs about Onchocerciasis in the Senegal River Basin, *Tropical and Geographical Medicine* 23(4): 385-389.

Imperato, P.J. 1974. Cholera in Mali and Popular Reactions to Its First Appearance, *Journal of Tropical Medicine and Hygiene* 77:290-296.

Kiev, A. 1974. *Magic, Faith and Healing*, New York: The Free Press.

Kiev, A. 1972. *Transcultural Psychiatry*. New York: The Free Press.

Lambo, T.A. 1965. Schizophrenic and Borderline States, in *Transcultural Psychiatry*, edited by A.V.S. de Reuck and Ruth Porter. Boston: Little, Brown and Co.

Leighton, A.H., Lambo, T.A., Hughes, C.C., Leighton, D.C., Murphy, J.M. and Macklin, D.B. 1963. *Psychiatric Disorder among the Yoruba*. New York: Cornell University Press.

Maclean, U. 1971. *Magical Medicine*. London: Penguin Press.

Miner, H. and DeVos, G. 1960. *Oasis and Casbah: Algerian Culture and Personality Change*. Ann Arbor: University of Michigan Press.

Orley, J. 1970. *Culture and Mental Illness: A Study from Uganda*. Kampala: East African Publishing House.

Ortigues, M.C. and Ortigues, E. 1966. *Oedipe Africain*. Paris: Plon.

Prince, R. 1964. Indigenous Yoruba Psychiatry, in *Magic, Faith and Healing*, edited by Ari Kiev. New York: The Free Press.

Renauld, J.L. 1974. La Psychiatrie à Bobo-Dioulasso-1973. *Afrique Médicale* 13:124, 891-900.

Thebaud, E.E. 1974. Ouelques Aspects De La Psychiatrie Au Liberia. *Afrique Médicale* 13:124, 875-878.

Tooth, G. 1950. *Studies in Mental Illness in the Gold Coast*. London: H.M. Stationary Office, No. 6.

Traore, D. 1965. *Médecine et Magie Africaines*. Paris: Présence Africaine.

Zempleni, A. 1969. La Thérapie Traditionnelle des Troubles Mentaux Chez Les Wolof et Les Lebou (Sénégal). *Social Science And Medicine* 3:191-205.

9

Fertility and Reproduction

There are about 300 million people living in sub-Sahara Africa. They constitute 75 percent of the entire continent's population and eight percent of the world's population. (*World Health Statistics Annual*, 1974). The most populous countries are Nigeria with 60 million inhabitants, Ethiopia with 23 million and Zaire with 16 million. There are wide variations in population densities in Africa, ranging from a low of six per square kilometer in Central Africa to a high of 16 per square kilometer in West Africa. The average density for the continent is 11 per square kilometer, compared to the world average of 25 per square kilometer. Population density ratios of this kind can be misleading since such vast areas of Africa are non-arable. The average number of inhabitants per square kilometer of arable land in Africa is 135, compared to the world wide figure of 212.

Demographic Trends

Between 1930 and 1950, the average annual rate of population growth in Africa was 1.5 percent. During the 1960's however, the average annual rate rose to 2.3 percent. This high rate of growth is second only to that of Latin America which is now 2.8 percent per year. The world wide rate is about 1.9 percent per year and that for North America 1.5 percent (Som 1974).

The African population is one which is overwhelmingly young. Forty percent of the population is below 15 years of age. The age pyramid for most sub-Saharan countries is one with a large base and a rapidly narrowing top. The vast majority of the population lives in rural settings. Approximately 13 percent of the population lives in towns and cities with

Parts of this chapter were previously published in *African Arts* Volume VIII, No. 4, 1975. I acknowledge with thanks permission to use this material here.

populations above 20,000 (Som 1974). There is a steady trend towards urbanization, and many African states are currently experiencing the problems associated with this phenomenon.

Birth rates in Africa are generally very high, averaging 45 per 1,000 inhabitants per year. The lowest rate is present in Gabon, 35 per 1,000, and the highest in Guinea, 62 per 1,000 (Som 1974). There are a number of cultural forces which engender early marriage for women and large numbers of offspring. Fecundity for African women is usually high and the societal rewards of having many children are extremely attractive. Children provide the nuclear family with an economic asset when they reach a certain age. They can draw water from the well, tend the herds, gather firewood, and work in the fields. Social ties can be extended through the marriage of children, bringing with them considerable advantages. Finally, children, particularly males, provide parents with a source of support in their declining years.

Polygamy

One of the key distinctions between African and Western marriage is the polygamy in the former and the monogamy in the latter. In a survey of 154 ethnic groups in Africa it was found that 88 percent thought polygamy to be ideal (Goode 1963). There are many rationalizations put forward in support of polygamy, especially by the Africans themselves who have become increasingly proud and chauvinistic about such typically African institutions. It is said that polygamy appeals to a man's vanity and satisfies his sexual drives. It tends to reduce extramarital contacts on the part of males during their wives' post-partum. In many societies a man cannot have intercourse for months or even for two or so years after the birth of a child. It is believed that the semen will enter the mother's body and adversely affect the milk. Polygamy greatly increases the prospects for many children. Polygamy in Africa is rationalized by such arguments. It is very strong in Africa, but is being influenced by encroaching Westernization.

The progressive Westernization of many African states has proceeded with an accelerated pace during the past decade. With it has come a mass migration to the cities of men seeking employment. Their entry into the cash economy, and the expenses of living that they face in the cities, make polygamy difficult to sustain. Whereas several wives and many children are an economic asset in rural areas, they are a liability in the cities. Food, water, and lodging must be purchased at high prices, school fees for children paid, and women and children dressed with clothing which is more expensive than they would have in rural areas. In east, central, and south Africa and along the coast of west Africa where

Christianity is a strong influence, polygamy has been downgraded. However, in the interior of West Africa, where Islam is very strong, polygamy still prevails, in spite of the economic hardships it imposes on those living in the cities.

Two surveys conducted among students in Ghana and Sierra Leone showed that 73 percent and 93 percent respectively of respondants favored monogamy (Omari 1960; Little 1966). Surveys such as these can be misleading as to the attitudes of most people since they represent a sampling of a very small group of educated elite.

In Bamako, the capital of Mali, polygamous marriages have flourished against a background of Islam which encourages such marriages. Many men have overcome the economic hardships of polygamy by having one or more of their wives work at a cash-paying job; they have thereby succeeded in extracting economic return from a wife's labor, one of the traditional advantages of polygamy.

Infertility

The failure of a man and wife to have children is generally ascribed in Africa to a defect in the wife, unless the man is impotent. Efforts to correct infertility are therefore directed towards the wife. Such efforts are pursued with great zeal by societies which esteem children so much. The women themselves urgently desire children since their status in society very much depends upon their having many. In most African societies a female cannot become a woman in a cultural sense until she has borne a child. A female who is barren is always considered to be a girl. Among the Hausa of Niger she is called *karwwa*, a term which means prostitute, divorcee, and an individual of low esteem all at the same time (Faulkingham and Thorbahn 1974). In this part of Africa, the rights and privileges of manhood are not accorded until a wife has borne a man a child. An unmarried adult male is accorded little prestige. A year or two after childless marriages divorces are common. The woman is considered to be sterile and suffers the greater disapprobation (Faulkingham and Thorbahn 1974).

While there is generally a basic knowledge of the facts of reproduction among Africans, there is little or no knowledge of the variations in fecundity at different points in the menstrual cycle. In many societies there is an awareness of decreased fecundity among lactating women and there are taboos against men having sexual relations with girls who have not yet menstruated, and with pregnant women and post-menopausal women.

Although there is an almost universal tendency to attribute infertility to women, among the Lobi of Upper Volta both man and wife are equally suspect in a childless marriage. Before divorce proceedings are begun, a trial is conducted to determine which member is sterile. Two pots are filled with mud taken from a termite mound. Into each of these a handful of beans are placed and then each partner is asked to urinate into one of the pots. These pots are guarded for several days by a notable of the village and then brought out in public. If the beans have germinated in both pots, neither is considered sterile, but they are deemed incompatible. If germination does not occur in either pot, both are considered sterile and if it occurs in just one, then the other is considered a reflection of sterility in the partner.

The common pattern is that a man generally marries a second wife if the first marriage is childless. If this second marriage is also childless, then serious questions about sterility in the man will be raised. This will be virtually confirmed if he married a third time and the result is the same.

Remedies for Infertility among the Bambara

There are a number of traditional remedies for presumed female infertility. These are sometimes used directly by women without the advice of a traditional practitioner; but where a supernatural cause is suspected, such as witchcraft or sorcery, these remedies will form but a part of the overall approach. Given the nature of infertility, most women meet with failure on using a given treatment. The usual pattern then is for them to employ a succession of treatments until they eventually resign themselves to the fact that they are sterile.

A wide variety of remedies are employed which are either ingested or applied externally to the body. Some are inserted into the vagina. As with many remedies used in Africa, treatment success is believed to depend on the remedies being taken on certain days and at certain hours of the day. Some of the infertility remedies recorded among the Bambara of Mali are as follows:

1. The bark and fruit of *Ficus capensis* (*toro*) are mixed with a porridge made from millet and drunk daily for a period of four days.
2. The roots of *Annona senegalensis* (*ndanga*) are crushed with the unripe fruit of *Ficus capensis* (*toro*). The powder is dried in the sun. A pinch of this powder is then added to porridge which is taken every day.
3. The dried placenta of sheep is crushed and the powder mixed with the crushed bark of *Fagara xanthoxyloides* (*goro ngua*). This is added in small quantities to a porridge of millet and taken daily.

4. A hank of wool is dipped in peanut oil and then wrapped around two small pieces of garlic. This is introduced into the vagina with the fingers and left in place for one or two days.
5. The leaves of *Smilax kraussiana* (*ka gunam*) are boiled along with the leaves of *Combretum racemosum* (*nánaka*). A woman must wash before nightfall with this solution for a week. The solution itself must be boiled up on a Thursday or Sunday. On Thursday and Friday nights the liquid is also drunk. This regime is followed for several months. Along with it, the woman must observe certain prohibitions such as not sitting at the doorway of her house and not sleeping with her back away from the doorway (Traore 1965).

In Islamized areas, Koranic charms are provided to women to make them fertile, and in animist areas sacrifices are often made over ancestral altars. Among the animist Bambara, infertile women often made sacrificial offerings to the fetishes of the *Komo, Kono* and *Nama* secret societies. Woman also make offerings of kola nuts, millet porridge, and chicken blood to the village protector spirits (*dassiri*). Often they swear before the *dassiri* to name the child after the fetish or to make a great offering to the *dassiri* if they conceive and give birth.

Impotence

One of the most frequent medical complaints of adult married males in Africa is impotence or diminished potency. During my years of treating such patients I found that complaints of impotency were generally most prevalent among polygamous males with three or more wives. On further inquiry, it usually turned out that the patient was not impotent, but was suffering from diminished potency.

Polygamous males rotate on a regular schedule between the rooms or houses of their various wives. If a man has three wives he will spend two successive nights per week with each wife. Often he will have coitus each night, which is in a sense a minimally acceptable frequency for each wife since it amounts to twice a week for each of them. As a man becomes older it is difficult for him to maintain this frequency, and as a corollary he becomes a ready client for remedies to increase his potency. There is often an unfounded fear that the wives will seek extramarital relations if the husband does not have sexual relations with them frequently enough.

Among the Hausa of Northern Nigeria, impotence in a male is confirmed or excluded in the following manner. The individual is stripped and placed on a mat lying on his back. A pin or thorn is then lightly rubbed over the inside of his thigh. If the scrotum or testicles do not move, the individual is considered impotent (Traoré 1965). There is a physiologic basis for this procedure. The maneuver in effect tests the cremasteric reflexes. The cremaster muscle contracts and pulls the testical upward on stimulation of the inside of the thigh.

Remedies for Impotence

A large number of remedies are employed for impotence and aphrodisiacs for increasing potency. It is difficult to evaluate the success of these since psychological factors play such a strong role. I have personally treated many African males suffering from decreased potency with multivitamin tablets, telling them that they were powerful aphrodisiacs. The level of success was amazing, due no doubt to suggestion.

The following are a few of the many remedies used for impotence by the Bambara of Mali.

1. The bark of an old tamarind tree, *Tamarindus indica* (*tomi*) is mixed with salt and pulverized. The powder is added to a meat soup made from the testicles of a ram and the kidneys of an old rooster. The soup is eaten at night.
2. The roots of the following plants are pulverized and added to a porridge of millet: *Simlax kraussiana* (*ka gunam*), *Strychnos spinosa* (*gangora*) and *Annona senegalensis* (*ndanga*). The head of an old rooster is boiled in water along with the testicles of an old ram and added to the porridge. The porridge is then eaten in the early morning and at night.
3. The flowers of *Heliotropium indicum* (*nangi ku*) are mixed with kola nuts, *Cola acuminata* (*ouoro*), which have been pulverized. To this is added a soup made from the boiled head of a black rooster. This soup is eaten for two days.
4. A solution of water containing the powdered roots of *Cassia sieberiana* (*sinjan*) and *Xylopia aethiopica* (*kani fin*) is taken at night for five days (Traoré 1969).

Among the Islamized Bambara, Koranic charms enclosed in leather sachets are worn around the waist to counteract impotence. Often impotence is ascribed to a supernatural cause and the necessary Islamic rituals are conducted to cure it. Remedies, such as those detailed above, are usually prepared and taken with the recitation of magical formulas. Often, they form only part of a treatment regimen which includes ritual sacrifices to ancestor shrines and village protector spirits.

When impotence or sterility are found to exist in a male among the Luo of Tanzania, his brother will secretly have sexual relations with the wife. Thus, the matter is never made public provided this arrangement is satisfactory to the wife.

Pregnancy

Pregnancy is not viewed lightly in most African societies, there being serious concern throughout for its outcome. Miscarriages are extremely common in many areas because of the presence in mothers of infections such as syphilis and malaria and marginal states of nutrition. In the pre-antibiotic era, female syphilitic infections were a major cause of many pregnancies not going to term. There are wide variations in the specific practices undertaken during pregnancy by different ethnic groups. Their ultimate goal is to insure the safe delivery of a healthy and live infant. Both the mother and fetus must be protected from witchcraft and sorcery and other malevolent forces. Miscarriages due to syphilis and other infectious diseases or to a blighted fetus are usually ascribed to the malevolence of a supernatural force.

A widespread practice is the cessation of sexual relations between husband and wife as soon as the wife is known to be pregnant. Often the woman is sent home to the care of her mother or some older female relative for the duration of the pregnancy and for delivery of the child. Among the Bambara, women are excused from labor in the fields during the third month of pregnancy but continue to perform their household chores up until the time of delivery. At about this time, husbands often consult a diviner to find out what types of sacrificial offerings should be made to the ancestor and village protector spirits. At the same time, the diviner also prognosticates the sex of the child. Bambara men also loosen the cord which holds up their trousers, it being believed that a tight belt impedes the development of a fetus in the mother's womb. This cord is sometimes tied around the woman's abdomen during labor.

Many ethnic groups employ herbal infusions which are taken by women during their pregnancies to insure safe delivery at term. These are sometimes taken daily as among the Bahanda (Roscoe 1911), or they may be taken periodically as among the Bambara of Mali.

In order to safeguard the pregnancy, Bambara women employ a number of herbal remedies which are either drunk, bathed with, or both. Traditionally, their use was more frequent during the first five months of pregnancy, the period when miscarriages secondary to syphilitic infections were quite common. Their primary purpose is the prevention of miscarriage. But they are also used to confer certain desirable attributes on the unborn child such as wealth, wisdom, or political power. Some are used to determine the sex of the child, male or female, as desired by the parents.

A few of these remedies are as follows:

1. An infusion made from the leaves of *Annona senegalensis* (*ndanga*) is taken periodically during the first five months of pregnancy.
2. The roots of *Imperata cylindrica* (*ndole*) are boiled together with the fruit of the sycamore tree, *Ficus capensis* (*toro*), and the liquid drunk from time to time.

3. The roots of *Annona senegalensis* (*ndanga*) are pulverized and mixed with peanut sauce and eaten.
4. A daily bath is taken with a solution made from the leaves of *Trema guineensis.*
5. A daily bath is taken with a solution made from the leaves of *Ipomoea rubens* (*bugu mugu*) (Traoré 1965).

Prolonged Pregnancies

It is not traditionally taken for granted in African cultures that the duration of pregnancy is nine months. The reasons for this are that women often miscalculate the approximate time of conception by a wide margin and that they often claim to be pregnant when in fact they are not. Although custom dictates a cessation of sexual relations as soon as pregnancy begins, behavior does not often follow suit. As a result women often become pregnant long after they have announced that they are pregnant. Gestation productive of a live infant can then appear to last anywhere from seven months to a few years.

The Bambara call prolonged pregnancy *konon-dale* and use a number of herbal preparations to hasten it along. The Luo of Tanzania likewise believe in this condition and employ herbal preparations and rituals to speed up the pregnancy (Imperato 1964). Both groups attribute it to malevolent forces. The remedies used by both these ethnic groups are either drunk as a beverage, used as a bathing solution, or both. Their use is often accompanied by the pronouncement of magical formulas, and the hour and day of use carry ritual significance. Traoré (1965) found that the Hausa of Northern Nigeria also believed in prolonged pregnancies and employed a variety of remedies to speed them up.

Complications of Pregnancy

In African societies primarily symptoms and not syndromes are recognized except when the latter are dominated by one symptom. Two of the major complications recognized by the Bambara are toxemia of pregnancy and hydramnios (excessive fluid in the uterus). The former syndrome is also known as eclampsia and as pre-eclampsia in its earlier phases. The Bambara call it *oulloko-banan*. The later condition is called *jinoro* or *ji*. Pre-eclampsia and eclampsia are conditions marked by hypertension, pathologic changes in the kidneys and liver, and the accumulation of body fluids leading to edema. Untreated serious cases can go on to the death of both the mother and child. The disease manifests itself primarily in the last trimester of pregnancy when severe edema can occur along with convulsions and death.

The cornerstones of modern therapy are bed rest, restriction of salt in the diet, prevention of excessive weight gain during pregnancy and the use of supportive measures to prevent and treat convulsions. While the Bambara recognize the symptom of edema, they are, of course, unaware of the hypertension usually present and of the other pathologic changes. Their therapeutic efforts are directed, therefore, towards reducing the edema. Many of their remedies are used externally and are for the most part ineffective. Because the birth of the child terminates the syndrome as they observe it, these remedies are erroneously ascribed great effectiveness. The Bambara do not restrict salt intake during pregnancy nor among women with pre-eclampsia.

Some of their remedies for pre-eclampsia and eclampsia are as follows:

1. The leaves of *Annona senegalensis* are boiled and the solution used to bathe with. Some of it is also drunk.
2. The roots of *Cassia tora* (*bani gono ka tiga*) are boiled and the solution drunk and some of it applied to the swollen parts of the body.
3. The stems of *Ipomoea rubens* (*bugu mugu*) are boiled and the solution used as a bath liquid and as a drink.
4. The leaves of *Eugenia owariensis* are boiled. The patient then bends over the steaming pot and inhales the steam. Once the liquid has cooled off the patient drinks it and applies it to the swollen parts of the body (Traoré 1969).
5. The western Bambara and the Malinke of Kita scrape off moss from rocks and trees and boil it in water. The solution is then applied externally to the body.

The diagnosis of hydramnios is not made unless it is a severe case. Otherwise it goes unnoticed. The following are some remedies used for treating this condition:

1. The leaves of *Crossopteryx febrifuga* (*balimbo*) are boiled. The boiling pot is removed from the fire and the patient made to bend over it with a blanket over her head. The steam is then inhaled. Later, when the solution has cooled it is drunk and also applied externally to the body. This plant is a strong diuretic but it does not affect the hydramnios. In the eyes of the Bambara it is effective because of the impressive diuresis produced (Traoré 1969).
2. Cooked millet is mixed with the stems of *Nymphaea lotus* (*ngoku*) and eaten daily for five days.

Childbirth

The customs surrounding childbirth are diverse and they govern such things as the place of delivery, the mode of delivery, immediate ante-partum care, the role of traditional midwives, the management of prolonged or obstructed labor, and the immediate post-partum care of both the infant and mother. Placental retention is especially feared among the Bambara and there are many remedies for dealing with it. In terms of numbers these customs are encyclopedic and are described in a number of anthropological works about specific ethnic groups. Harley (1941) has summarized a number of the earliest observations made by both travelers and scholars in West and East Africa.

Complications of childbirth such as post-partum hemorrhage, placenta praevia, post-partum sepsis, uterine rupture, vaginal and perineal lacerations, and obstructed labor are not generally handled well by traditional practitioners. This accounts for such cases being brought to the attention of modern facilities with great frequency nowadays. These complications are by no means limited to women experiencing their first pregnancy. Often they occur among women who have had several uneventful pregnancies. These women, as a result of their success in getting through a number of pregnancies without difficulty, tend to become overconfident and often develop complications. The following three case histories are illustrative of some of the problems mentioned above and how they arc managed. I observed one of these cases in Kenya and one in Tanzania in 1961 and the last in Mali in 1970.

> Case 1. M.W. was a 19-year-old Kikuyu female from Nyeri, Kenya, who I saw after she had been in labor for two days. Several herbal preparations had been applied to her abdomen by the old women of her family who had also tried to push the child out by placing their heels against the top of the uterus, a widespread technique. The patient was febrile with a fever of 104°F. On questioning I also learned that the old women had placed their fingers in the girl's vagina in an attempt to pull the child out, a possible reason for the septicemia that was now present. I had the woman taken to the hospital at Nyeri where an immediate Cesarean section was performed. The infant was dead and macerated and grossly decomposed. I later learned that the woman had been in labor for five days. She died during the procedure.
>
> Case 2. G.W. was a 40-year-old Luo woman who had previously delivered nine live and healthy infants. I happened to come upon her quite by accident while on a bush trek in northern Tanzania. She had been in labor for two days. An old woman was pounding on her abdomen, trying to force the child out when I walked into the compound. I took the woman back to the hospital where on examination I found that she was obstructed, the baby's head being too big to come down the birth canal. A Cesarean section was performed immediately and a live infant boy delivered. Both the mother and child did well afterwards.
>
> Case 3. H.S. was a 17-year-old Bambara girl from the Segou region of Mali in her seventh month of pregnancy. I saw her in a rural village, Boussin, where she complained of having some bleeding and cramps. Suspecting a possible premature delivery, I

recommended that she be taken to a nearby hospital, 20 miles away. This was eventually done a week later, after labor began. Her family placed her on a two wheeled donkey cart and set off for the hospital. En route she delivered a baby boy and hemorrhaged to death. The child died two days later.

Such occurrences as those just described above are not rare in the harsh world of rural Africa. In all three instances the traditional system could not effectively respond to the problems presented, primarily because they were of a nature requiring surgical intervention.

Delivery and Post-Partum Care among the Bambara

Among the Bambara, traditional mid-wives, *maniamaga mousso*, often deliver children. For this service they are given a sum equal to two U.S. dollars plus all of the mother's old clothing. (A woman in the post-partum period is presented with new clothes by her husband.)

Women give birth in a semi-recumbant position with the legs bent at the knees and the feet flat on the ground. One woman supports the mother from behind while the mid-wife receives the child. The Bambara do not manipulate the abdomen as a rule. The umbilical cord often is not cut until after the placenta is delivered. It is cut by the midwife with her teeth, a knife, or a razor, and tetanus and other infections of this newborn often result. The placenta is immediately buried.

Immediately after giving birth, the mother is given a broth to drink made from dried fish, whose purpose is to speed up the expulsion of the afterbirth. The woman is then washed with warm water and later with a solution made from boiling the bark of *Ipomoea rubens*.

The child is washed with warm water and then completely covered with a cloth and placed on a mat next to the mother. Before the child is permitted to nurse, its genitals, nose and mouth are washed with millet beer (*dolo*). It is believed that if maternal milk touches these areas before they are ritually protected, they will decay. Dr. Hewat (1906) reported that Basuto children were forced to drink cow's milk before breast feeding. The Basuto believed that the mother's milk would corrode the infant's stomach and cause it to decay unless it was protected by cow's milk.

Bambara women rest indoors for eight days after giving birth. Among the Moslems, the child is given a name a week after birth. Once the child is named, women reappear in public and resume their chores.

Delivery and Post-Partum Care among other Ethnic Groups

Women give birth in a separate hut among the Bakongo of Equatorial Africa. The woman is supported from behind in a semi-reclining position by two other women, while a third receives the child. The child is laid between the mother's legs until the placenta is delivered. The mother herself cuts the umbilical cord with a piece of sharp wood and ties the stump to a string placed around the infant's waist (Cureau 1915).

Among the Kababish of the Sudan, the child is delivered in the mother's tent by a midwife. The father is called to witness the cutting of the umbilical cord. The cord is tied and then cut, blood from the stump being rubbed on the infant's gums (Seligman and Seligman 1932). The placenta is buried outside the tent where the woman remains confined for 40 days. A sheep is killed after the child is born and the midwife given the liver and kidneys.

Yao women of Malawi traditionally went into the bush near their huts to deliver. Lying in a semi-reclining position supported by another woman, the mother delivers with her legs bent at the knees and her feet flat on the ground. The umbilical cord is not cut until the placenta is delivered. A long length of cord is left attached to the child and is tied with a piece of bark string. It is then cut with a piece of maize stalk (Stannus 1922).

Among the Banyankole of Uganda, the mother-in-law acted as the midwife. The woman sat on a carpet of freshly gathered grass while holding onto a strong cord.net hung from the rafters above. The midwife squatted behind the mother. The umbilical cord was cut with a knife or strip of reed and the mother then placed it on a cow skin. A fire was kept burning in her hut and everyone prohibited from taking a light from it. If anyone did, it was believed that the umbilical cord would never fall off the child. The mother remained secluded in her hut for eight days, but both she and the midwife were permitted to leave by a back door made expressly for them. Around it a small courtyard was constructed. On the eighth day, the mother was washed and her husband was permitted to visit her and remain with her (Roscoe 1923).

Midwives delivered children among the Banyoro of Uganda. The umbilical cord was not cut until the placenta was delivered. The placenta was buried on the right side of the doorway if the child were a boy and on the left if a girl (Roscoe 1915). The mother was kept in seclusion for four days if the child were a boy and three days if a girl.

Among the Hausa and Fulani of Northern Nigeria the umbilical cord is cut with a razor blade. It is not ligated. The infant is bathed several times with medicated water and the cord washed until it looks clean and white. On the third day after birth the child's uvula is excised by a traditional barber surgeon using a sickle shaped knife. It is believed that the uvula will swell and rupture and cause the child to suffocate if it is left in place (Fleischer 1975). In a two year study of 5,650 children admitted to the R.C. Mission Hospital in Jos, Northern Nigeria, Fleischer found that most of those under six months of age were anemic. His studies indicated that this anemia was due to significant blood loss because of the way the umbilical cord is treated and to blood loss secondary to uvulectomy. He found that 96.2 percent of Hausa and Fulani children had had uvulectomies. He also observed that the operation was accompanied by significant blood loss which is ignored by the parents who consider it to be altogether normal.

Twin Births

Twins are regarded as either a blessing or a curse in African societies. The Bakuria of Kenya consider them a curse and used to kill twins at birth. They likewise used to kill children born with the legs or arms first, considering this to be an evil omen. The Yoruba of Nigeria and the Bambara of Mali consider twins to be a blessing and have established cults to honor them. Among the Yoruba this cult is called *Ibeji* and among the Bambara and Malinke *Sinzin*.

There are still Bambara and Malinke villages where every Friday the mothers of twins or the twins themselves walk down the alleys and into the courtyards carrying small calabashes (gourds) and solicit offerings. If the twins are more than a few months old, the mother will carry one and have a young girl from the family carry the other. And once a few years old, the twins will walk with their mother as she makes her rounds of the village. When old enough they will go along, until the age of puberty, when the weekly ritual is abandoned. Offerings are presented in equal amounts for each child with the hope of receiving special blessings from the twins who are believed to be extraordinary beings with special powers and the direct offspring of *Faro*, a principal Bambara and Malinke deity. Gifts presented to twins are in effect offerings to *Faro* himself.

The gradual Islamization of both the Bambara and Malinke is reflected in changes which have occurred and which are still occurring in the *sinzin* twin cult. Where Islam has been the family religion for a few generations, the cult has generally been abandoned, for people no longer embrace the fundamental beliefs of the *sinzin*. In areas where Islamization has been more recent, the twin cult still persists but is in gradual decline, manifesting syncretic elements reflective of a blending of the old animist religion with Islam. It is only in a few localities where the impact of Islam has been slight that the twin cult exists much as it was originally described by Abbé Joseph Henry in 1910.

Although the *sinzin* cult has been briefly described by a few writers in addition to Abbe Henry, very little has been written about the wooden sculptures which are sculpted by blacksmiths when twins die in childhood (Tauxier 1927; Travele 1931; Dieterlen 1951; Zahan 1960; Paques 1954; Imperato 1975). The information presented here is based on my field investigations conducted in Bambara and Malinke country between 1968 and 1974.

Twin births are extremely common among the Bambara and Malinke. In 1968 there was a total of 761 twin births out of a total of 34,780 births recorded in fifty-two maternity centers in Mali. These 34,780 births represented approximately one-quarter of all live births in Mali (Keita 1968). In the 24 maternity centers which service most of the Bambara and Malinke country there was a total of 22,261 births of which 399 were twin births. Based on these data, the incidence of twin births for Mali as a whole is 21.8/1,000 births and for the Bamana and Maninka, 17.9/1,000 births. Both of these rates are considerably higher than the U.S. mean of 9.9/1,000 births and that for American blacks which is 14/1,000 births (Imperato 1971). The incidence of twin births among the Yoruba of Nigeria is the highest known in the world—45.1 per 1,000 (Nylander 1969).

Because twins are regarded among the Bambara and the Malinke as a blessing bestowed by the supreme being, their birth is received with great rejoicing. They are referred to as *flani*, meaning "two little ones," and are considered to be the direct offspring of *Faro*. Because they are *Faro*'s offspring, it is believed that they do not inherit either the *ni* (soul) of a deceased person or their *dya* (double), as is the case in single births. Rather, it is held that twins receive new souls directly from *Faro*.

An article of Bambara and Malinke animism is the belief in the duality of the human soul. (See Chapter 4, above.) Both the *ni* and the *dya* are inherited by a newborn from a person who dies immediately before their birth. The *dya*, or spiritual double of the *ni*, is represented by one's shadow or reflection in water or a mirror. It is believed capable of separating from the *ni* and moving about on its own and of disappearing at night and on cloudy days. It is thought to be especially vulnerable to the mischief of sorcerers and other malevolent personalities. The *dya* of twins, unlike that of ordinary persons, is guarded beneath the water by *Faro* and consequently, twins are less vulnerable to harm inflicted by sorcerers and others. Twins are external to the cycle of soul re-incarnation and, further, have their *dya* specifically guarded and protected by *Faro*, who himself is believed to inhabit rivers, streams, ponds, and wells. Each twin is considered to be the *dya* of the other.

Although a pregnant woman and/or her female relatives and friends may have suspected a multiple pregnancy, traditionally these suspicions were never discussed. Even when twins were born, the news was never announced verbally to the village or town quarter. A member of the family informed people by holding up the index fingers of both hands. Those women assisting in the delivery informed the father that twins have been born before informing anyone else. If he was not available they informed his oldest brother. It was once common practice for the father, or in his absence his oldest brother, to come before the house where the newborn twins were with his hands tied loosely behind his back (Travele 1931). He knelt down on one knee before the doorway and offered up prayers to the twins, asking their protection and blessings for all his family. Once these prayers had been said, his wrists were untied. This rite has virtually disappeared except from a few scattered areas in the western Bambara country and the Gangaran and Bambouk regions of the Malinke country.

Newborn twins were ritually washed by the first wife of the oldest living village blacksmith within the first hour after delivery. Neither parent was permitted to touch the children until this washing had been completed. The twins were washed with a solution of tepid water to which a solution made from the leaves of the *nama ba* (*Piliostigma thonningii*) was added. This ritual washing has for the most part been abandoned. In only two villages, out of 74 surveyed, was there a history of this ritual having been performed in the past decade.

Once the ritual prayers and washing were completed, the father of the twins or one of his brothers went to the village blacksmith to order the twin cult fetish, known as *sinzin*. The literal translation of *sinzin* is "support." During the present study considerable regional variation was found in the physical form of the *sinzin* fetish. Three principal types were observed, two of which were most frequently seen in the eastern Bambara country and one in the western Bambara country and among the Malinke. It must be mentioned that many of these fetishes were made many years ago and were in the possession of Islamized families who, while not actively sacrificing to them, were reluctant to discard them. Among the Bambara living in the *cercles* of San and Segou, close to the banks of either the Niger or Bani rivers, it was the custom to have the fetish fashioned by one of the Bozo people, and usually by a Bozo blacksmith. Most of the Bozo are migratory fishermen who live along the Niger or the Bani. They are believed to be the descendants of two female twins created by *Faro* after he created the seven heavens and descended on earth in the form of water. Thus, from their origins, the Bozo have been closely associated with twins.

Bozo blacksmiths sculpted two small wooden cups in a variety of shapes, but often in the form of funnels. These were attached at their apices, giving the composite shape of an hourglass. The Bambara in this eastern region most often fashioned two cups of woven straw and likewise attached their bottoms together so that the whole looked like an hourglass. In most, but not in all, the openings of the cups had very large diameters and the bottoms came to an almost narrow point. At the point where the two cups were joined, a small piece of wood or of iron was suspended, around which pieces of the umbilical cords were intertwined. The maker of the *sinzin* fetish was called *sinzin d'la tigui*, "master maker of the sinzin." Dieterlen observed fetishes made from wooden cups in the Segou region in the 1940's. Abbe Henry observed fetishes made of woven grass cups in the same area around the turn of the century. Both of these forms were placed inside of a large calabash which was then hung upside down from the roof of the vestibule leading to the house of the mother of the twins. Abbé Henry reported in 1910 that the cost to the father of the twins of this fetish varied from 820 to 1200 cowrie shells (Henry 1910).

Another form of the fetish which I observed most frequently in the western Bambara country and among the Malinke consists of two sticks with forked ends, measuring two inches in length. These sticks were attached at their forked ends by cotton thread spun by the mother of the twins and suspended in a calabash. The sticks were fashioned by blacksmiths from the *sunsun* tree, *Diospyros mespiliformis*. Pieces of the umbilical cords were wrapped around the two sticks. As in the eastern Bamana country, the calabash containing the fetish was suspended from the roof of the house of the mother of the twins, and sacrifices were made to it. Over the years, the two suspended sticks became impregnated with dried sacrificial blood and in the case of very old fetishes, the entire gourd is almost completely filled.

The parents of twins are called *kunandi*, that is "privileged ones." Soon after delivery, the mother of twins tied a band of white cotton, which was called *dyala*, around her forehead. The *dyala* headband symbolized the presence of the *dya* of the twins in the care of *Faro*. On the day of the birth relatives and neighbors offer gifts to the twins. As already mentioned, such gifts are looked upon as gifts to *Faro* and it is believed that his blessings and protection are given in return.

Prior to Islamization, it was the custom to confer names on the twins during a ritual held on the banks of the Niger, one of its affluents, or along the shores of a lake or pond. It is at these sites where *Faro* is believed to reside. While this practice is still current in a few localities, it has been completely abandoned in Islamized areas. The mother and father each carried one of the twins accompanied by a retinue of relatives and neighbors. Often, but not always, the naming ceremony was conducted by a blacksmith and was always held on the eighth day after the birth. The twins were washed in the water of the river or pond and their heads shaved, the hair being thrown into the water.

Dieterlen recorded the following ritual prayer said during this part of the ceremony, *Ba faro i wolo dew kansi ye nin ye*, "Mother faro, your children are born, here is their hair" (Dieterlen 1951). The dyala headband was then removed from the mother's head, rubbed across the foreheads of the twins and the following words pronounced, *Nin ma fla ka koro u ma, u cua dali nyama ka ta fini disa few dyala fe*, "These two beings are older than I, may the *nyama* of the names about to be given them part with the *dyala*." After this a special name was given to each twin as the *dyala* was rubbed across their foreheads. (The *nyama* is man's character which moves about freely after his death. During life, when the character or conscience has a material support; namely, the human body, it is called *tere* [Paques 1954].)

Certain names were reserved for twins and even today among Islamized Bambara and Malinke, certain Moslem names are reserved for them. There were regional variations in the animist names employed. Abbe Henry (1910) states that the commonest names used in the eastern Bambara country were Sinna, Mafene, Gno, and Wassa. Dieterlen recorded that among animists, Seni and Sine were the common names for male twins and Bintou and Wassa for female twins. Among the Moslems she reports that Alassan and Fouseni were the commonest names employed, which she states are deformations of Arab names given to twins in Morocco (Dieterlen 1951). During the present study it was found that Seni and variations of it were given to the male of a mixed twin birth and Sine and variations of it to the female twin. For two female twins, the names Sama and Kafeune are used and for two males, Seni and Gno. In place of these names, the Moslems have substituted Arab names. For two male twins the names Lassana and Fouseni are employed, and for two females either Adama and Haoua, or Bintou and Wassa. If the twins are of mixed sexes, Lassana is given to the male twin and Stafine to the female. The child born to a woman after a twin birth is called Sadio, a practice followed by both animists and Moslems.

Twins traditionally always remained physically together, even when grown to adulthood. They wore the same types of clothing and ate the same food. They were simultaneously scarified at the age of four months if the parents decided to have them scarified. Not all children were routinely scarified among the Bambara and Malinke. Males who were not, had their ear lobes pierced. In general, three parallel scarification marks were made, extending down the face from the temple to the chin. In the Baninko, the area around the Bani River, more extensive scarifications were made over the abdomen and on the flexor surfaces of the arms among women. These scarifications were performed every seven years and were the occasion for a week-long festival during which sacrifices were made to family and community fetishes, including the *sinzin*. Scarification practices had already been abandoned by and large in much of the eastern Bambara country by the turn of the century. Abbé Henry reports that the practice was rare in the Segou area due to Islamization and the specific prohibition of it in the latter half of the 19th century by the Moslem Tukulor rulers of the area (Henry 1910). The practice has for the most part now disappeared except for a few areas in the northern Bambara country, specifically the Beledougou and in the south in Massigi and Beleco.

Twins were and still are circumcised at the same time. The second twin born is always circumcised first because he is considered to be the oldest. It is believed that the first twin born is sent out into the world by the second in order to examine it and convey his impressions of it.

In the eastern Bambara country a pair of male twins married the same woman, this being one of the few examples of polyandry in this part of Africa. Dieterlen (1951) also reports this practice in the Segou region. However, in most areas two male twins were engaged simultaneously to two different women who entered their respectives houses the same day. Both male twins, however, were permitted to have sexual relations with one another's wives. The children of male twins were never referred to as the offspring of a specific twin, but as "the children of twins." Two female twins were similarly engaged and married simultaneously. Their prospective husbands were required to pay a double bride price to their father. The husbands of female twins were likewise permitted to have sexual relations with both women. Travele (1931) reports that while the marriages took place at about the same time they did not necessarily occur on the same day. Thus, both female twins entered the first husband's house on the marriage night, he having sexual relations with both, starting with the oldest (the second born), regardless of whether this was his wife or not (Travele 1931). Whenever twins were of mixed sexes, that is one male and one female, the brother generally had sexual relations with his sister before she was taken to her new husband's house.

Infant mortality rates being extremely high in this part of the world, it was not and is not uncommon for one or both twins to die in childhood. It should be noted, however, that twins have traditionally been given a margin of advantage over other children in that they are the recipients of gifts of food and clothing and money. Thus, the health and nutritional status of twins is better than that of their peers, which enables them to better survive the rigors of infancy and childhood in a marginal subsistence society. Even when twins purchased something in the marketplace, it was the custom for merchants to give them twice the quantity. Because of these practices, twins often acquired great wealth. But, often, merchants tried to avoid doing business with them since any sale resulted in a considerable loss for the merchant.

In spite of their advantages, many twins die, an event which evokes great sadness in the entire village. Whenever a twin died in either infancy or childhood, the father had a wooden figure sculpted by the village blacksmith. This figure was sculpted in the sex of the deceased twin and was given the name of the deceased twin. It was kept by the mother of the twins in her room and carried by her beneath her robes whenever she went out with the surviving twin. Because of the strong belief in the inseparability of twins, the figure was always kept physically close to the surviving twin. It served as a material support for the *nyama* of the deceased twin. When the surviving twin reached puberty and was circumcised, responsibility for the care of the figure was transferred from the mother to him or her. If a twin died after circumcision, which traditionally took place between twelve and fifteen years of age, a figure also was sculpted. A figure was not sculpted, however, if a twin died after being married.

Figures representing dead twins are referred to by the name *flanitokele* which means "twin which remains," or "double which remains." In Malinke country, the figures are often referred to as *sinzin*,

Twin doll (flanitokele). *These are sculptered by the Bambara upon the death of a twin.*

the term usually employed for the twin cult fetish. However, the general appellation among both the Bambara and Malinke is *flanitokele*.

Twin figures are carried by the surviving twins at the time of circumcision and excision. During the period immediately following these ceremonies, the statues are placed next to the surviving twins on their sleeping mats at night. Following this period, the figures are returned to the house of the father of the twins where they remain. There is considerable variation in this practice. In some areas, the surviving twin keeps custody of the statue for the remainder of his life. In other areas, the statue is placed in the house of the father of the twins and is not removed, unless the surviving twin be a female. She takes the statue with her when she marries. If the surviving twin is a male, the statue remains in his father's house since upon marriage he will continue to live in close physical proximity to his father. In terms of custody of the statues, depending upon the sex of the surviving twin and local custom, statues potentially can pass from the mother to the surviving twin and then to the father.

Flanitokele are often dressed and decorated with jewelry and are usually offered gifts identical to those presented to the surviving twins. There is considerable variation in this practice also. Abbé Henry reported that in the Segou region, the statues were generally given five cowrie shells whenever a gift was presented to the surviving twin. At that time cowrie shells were used as currency in the Western Sudan.

Currently, it is rare that *flanitokele* are sculpted when a twin dies. It is not uncommon, however, to find surviving adult twins who still continue to care for their *flanitokele* even though the *sinzin* cult may have been abandoned and people's attitudes towards twins changed.

Whenever a surviving twin married, another statue, opposite in sex from the deceased twin was sculpted and placed alongside the *flanitokele* representing the dead twin. If it were a male statue, it was called *flanitokele tye*, "husband of flanitokele," and if a female statue, *flanitokele mousso*, "wife of flanitokele." From then on, the two statues were kept together, side by side. In effect then, it is impossible to identify a given figure as a *flanitokele* or as a *flanitokele spouse* figure unless one is aware of the provenance and the statue's history. In many areas male statues were not made for female statues when the surviving twin married. Thus there are many more female statues than male ones. The two types of statues did not and do not receive equivalent levels of attention and care, no specific offerings nor decorations being given to the spouse figures. In many areas it was customary for the statues to be stood on the ground in a corner of the room where they were stored. This resulted in termite damage of the feet and thus it is a common characteristic of both the *flanitokele* and the spouse figures to have eroded and broken feet.

Information concerning the frequency of observance of the *sinzin* cult must be weighed in light of local variations in twinning incidence, influences such as Islam favoring decline and abandonment of the cult, and pre-Islamic observance patterns. One might expect that the *sinzin* was more widely observed in pre-Islamic times in areas of high twinning incidence compared to areas of low twinning incidence, but this may not be necessarily so. Information provided by older knowledgeable informants has provided a perception of sixty years and has enabled me to form a loose matrix of cult observance patterns and twinning incidence patterns. This aspect of the study is still in progress, but thus far the data reveal that the incidence of twinning was higher in certain circumscribed geographic areas where the *sinzin* cult was also more widely observed.

The traditional role of twins in Bambara and Malinke societies was essentially benevolent, unlike the situation among the Yoruba where twins are both benevolent and malevolent (Hammersley-Houlberg 1973). No one needs to be protected from twins in Bambara and Malinke society. According to the Ibeji cult of the Yoruba, twins can inflict such misfortunes as death and illness. Hammersley-Houlberg makes a very cogent remark that neither Islam nor Christianity offer any positive alternatives to existing rituals for placating Yoruba twins. And from this follows that the Ibeji twin cult, rituals, and images may continue to survive and evolve among the Yoruba for some time. Because Bambara and Malinke twins are purely benevolent, no rituals were ever required to placate them. Those blessings once sought from *Faro* through the *sinzin* are now provided through the rituals of Islam which have in effect become attractive and competitive alternatives. The existence of such a strong positive alternative to the *sinzin* ritual has, in contrast to the situation in Yoruba land, resulted in the gradual decline and disappearance of the *sinzin* and *flanitokele*. As for *Faro*, he has been smoothly assimilated into Bambara and Malinke Islam as a benevolent water genie who resides at the bottom of the Niger River and in ponds, lakes, and wells.

References

Cureau, A.L. 1915. *Savage Man In Central Africa*. London: Unwin.
Dieterlen, Germaine. 1951. *Essai sur La Religion Bambara*. Paris: Presses Universitaires de France.
Faulkingham, R.H. and Thorbahn, P.F. 1974. The Demographic Impact of the Drought, An Ecosystem Study of a Village in Niger. Paper presented at the Chicago Meeting of the African Studies Association.
Fleischer, N.K.F. 1975. A Study of Traditional Practices and Early Childhood Anemia in Northern Nigeria. *Transactions of the Royal Society of Tropical Medicine and Hygiene* 69(2):198-200.
Fortes, M. 1969. A Demographic Field Study In Ashanti, in *Culture And Human Fertility*, edited by Frank Lorimer. New York: Greenwood Press.
Goode, W.J. 1963. *World Revolution And Family Patterns*, Glencoe, Illinois: Free Press.

Hammersley-Houlberg, Marilyn. 1973. Ibeji Images of the Yoruba. *African Arts* 7(1):27.

Harley, G.W. 1941. *Native African Medicine with Special Reference to its Practice in the Mano Tribe of Liberia.* Cambridge, Massachusetts: Peabody Museum.

Henry, Joseph. 1910. *L'Ame d'un Peuple Africain, Les Bambara,* Munster: Bibliothèque Anthropos.

Imperato, P.J. 1964. *Doctor in the Land of the Lion.* New York: Vantage Press.

Imperato, P.J. 1971. Twins among the Bambara and Malinke of Mali, *Journal of Tropical Medicine and Hygiene* 74(7):154-159.

Imperato, P.J. 1975. Bamana and Maninka Twin Figures. *African Arts* VIII(4): 52-60.

Keita, Daouda. 1968. *Rapport Annuel de Service de Santé.* Bamako.

Little, K. 1966. Attitudes towards Marriage and the Family among Educated Sierra Leoneans, in *The New Elites of Tropical Africa.* London: Oxford University Press.

Nylander, P.P.S. 1969. The Frequency of Twinning in a Rural Community in Western Nigeria. *Annals of Human Genetics* 33:41-44.

Omari, T.P. 1960. Changing Attitudes of Students in West African Society Towards Marriage and Family Relationships. *British Journal of Sociology* 11:197-210.

Paques, Viviana. 1954. *Les Bambara.* Paris: Presses Universitaires de France.

Roscoe, J. 1911. *The Baganda.* London: Macmillan.

Roscoe, J. 1915. *The Northern Bantu.* Cambridge: The University Press.

Roscoe, J. 1923. *The Banyankole.* Cambridge: The University Press.

Seligman, C.G. and Seligman, B.Z. 1932. *Pagan Tribes of the Nilotic Sudan.* London: G. Routledge and Sons.

Som, R.K. 1974. Perspectives Démographiques en Afrique, in *L'Accroissement de la Population et L'Avenir Economique de L'Afrique,* edited by S.H. Ominde and C.N. Ejiogu. New York: The Population Council.

Stannus, H.S. 1922. *The Waejao of Nyasaland.* Cambridge, Massachusetts: Harvard African Studies.

Tauxier, Louis. 1927. *La Religion Bambara.* Paris: Librairie Orientaliste Paul Geuthner.

Traore, D. 1965. *Medecine et Magie Africaines.* Paris: Présénce Africaine.

Traore, D. 1969. Personal Communication.

Travele, Moussa. 1931. Usages Relatifs Aux Jumeaux en Pays Bambara. *Outre Mer*: 3:99-102.

World Health Statistics Annual 1971, Geneva: WHO. 1974.

Zahan, Dominique. 1960. *Sociétés d'Initiation Bambara, Le N'Domo, Le Kore.* Paris: Mouton.

10

Childhood Diseases

The principal disease problems among children in Africa are communicable diseases on the one hand and malnutrition syndromes on the other. Among the former, malaria, measles, gastroenteritis, and broncho-pulmonary disorders rank highest as the major causes of morbidity and mortality. Measles is by far the greatest killer of children in Africa and because of its importance it will be dealt with in detail in the following chapter.

In the normal course of events, African children are breast fed for the first 18 months at the end of which time they are abruptly weaned. Among the Bambara and Dogon, the child is carried on its mother's back during this period and consequently is always in close touch with her. Weaning is accomplished in 24 hours, the child being placed on the ground and given a high carbohydrate diet of millet, corn, and rice. Psychologically, this is an extremely traumatic period for children, but in general they appear to adapt to their new mode of existence within a few days. If a woman should become pregnant before the suckling period runs its normal course, the child will be abruptly weaned.[1] This may occur therefore when the child is but a few months old. The Bambara commonly believe that the mother's milk becomes poisonous for the child when she is pregnant. (This erroneous belief is also held in many other areas of the world.)

A number of remedies given to newborn children with the finest of intentions often cause serious illness or else complicate an already existing illness. Children who nurse from mothers found to be pregnant are given remedies to protect them from the supposed ill effects of the mother's milk. Remedies are given for infantile diarrhea, dentition, fevers, convulsions, colic, vitamin deficiency syndromes, umbilical tetanus, coughing, ricketts,

---

[1] Menstruation usually does not resume after childbirth until a woman stops suckling her infant. There is much variation in this, however. During this period, women are infertile because ovulation is suppressed by the pituitary hormone, prolactin.

as well as treatments to make a child fat, intelligent, talkative, or to prevent excessive crying, stuttering, enuresis, or to guard against the development of umbilical hernia. In addition, there exist a large number of remedies for recognized childhood disease syndromes—whooping cough, chickenpox, tetanus, measles, diphtheria, poliomyelitis, hepatitis, pneumonia, and the parasitic infections.

The classification of diseases among Africans only occasionally corresponds to that used in modern medicine. Malaria for example is known to many Africans as a fever, not separated from other fever-producing diseases, although the Bambara of Mali do distinguish malaria from other fevers. Monosymptomatic diseases such as whooping cough, or polysymptomatic diseases such as yaws and leprosy with dominating dramatic symptoms, are recognized as distinct diseases as in modern medicine. Otherwise, the disease classification used by the Bambara tends to be based primarily on symptoms such as cough, diarrhea, fever, vomiting, skin eruption, headache, abdominal pain, etc. The multiple symptoms of some diseases such as onchocerciasis (river blindness) are viewed and treated as separate entities. These symptoms are not regarded as part of the same disease process (Imperato 1971).

Whether or not children are ill, they are given herbal preparations believed to be either curative, preventive, or both, or to impart to the child a desirable characteristic. That many of these remedies, and the customs which are practiced with them, do considerable harm goes unnoticed. The herbal preparations used in Africa for these purposes are encyclopedic in number. No attempt is made here to be comprehensive; rather illustrative examples are given for some of the more prevalent and important disease states.

Nutritional Disorders

The principal nutritional disorders present in children in Africa are protein malnutrition known as *kwashiorkor*, and protein-calorie malnutrition known as *marasmus*. Both are common among children two years of age and slightly older who have just been weaned. There is often a seasonal fluctuation in the prevalence of these disorders, reflecting food supplies which vary. After the annual harvest, food supplies are plentiful but decline to an annual low during the planting season; it is then that marasmus and kwashiorkor become common.

Kwashiorkor

Among the peoples of Mali, kwashiorkor is recognized not as a protein-deficiency syndrome but primarily as a symptom, namely generalized body edema. Since they do not understand the cause of the disease

BAMBARA DISEASES TERMINOLOGY*

Disease or Symptom	*Bambara Name for Disease*
Abdominal cramps	kono dimi
Abscess	soumoni
Acne	gorou
Anasarca	fanu m'ba
Arthritis	kolochi
Conjunctivitis	nye dimi
Constipation	kono dya
Coryza	moura
Deaf-muteness	boboya
Dental caries	soumon
Dracunculiasis	segele
Dysentery	tokotokoni
Earache	klo dimi
Elephantiasis of lower extremities	youmpogolo
Fractures	kolokari
Gonorrhea	damadyala
Headache	kungolo dimi
Hiccups	yegerou
Impotence	kulusi dyala siri
Intestinal parasites	konona toumou
Taenia	n'toro
Pinworm	toumoni
Jaundice	say
Laryngitis	ka sisi
Leprosy	bagi
Low-back pain	koro dimi
Malaise	dyen dye wolofe
Measles	neone
Meningitis	finyabana
Neurologic diseases	
Anxiety	kakili wili
Madness	ya (fa)
Epilepsy	kilikilimacien
Poliomyelitis	n'gara
Prickly heat	klani
Ringworm	kaba
Schistosomiasis	nenkenieblenke
Secondary syphilis	blen boro
Skin ulcers	cyoli
Smallpox	zo
Syphilis	da
Thyroid goiter	folo
Trypanosomiasis	sunoko bana
Yaws	m'soron

*This list presents a few examples only.

they institute no dietary measures to treat it. Although the hair often becomes red and thin, and changes in skin pigmentation and texture often occur, these symptoms are not as consistent as that of body edema; thus they are not considered associated with edema as part of the same syndrome. The following case history is illustrative of how kwashiorkor often occurs and how it is treated.

      Moussa Keita was a two-year-old Malinke boy who I had seen delivered in December, 1970, in Bamako, Mali. He received close medical supervision during the first year of his life and at one year was a healthy robust child. At that time I left Mali and cautioned his parents to be especially careful to prevent his developing kwashiorkor. At 14 months it was discovered that his mother was pregnant again. He was abruptly weaned and sent to live with his grandmother who lived in the town of Kita some 200 miles away. It is a common custom in this part of Africa to send recently weaned children off to live with relatives. In Kita he was fed a carbohydrate diet consisting chiefly of millet and corn. Over a period of several months he became gradually ill and developed edema of the extremities and face. At 21 months he was returned to his parents with a full-blown syndrome of kwashiorkor. His father, who worked as a driver for the Ministry of Health and whom I had cautioned about kwashiorkor, went to an herbalist in Bamako and obtained herbs to apply to the swollen parts of his body, believing that these preparations would reduce the swelling. When I returned to Bamako, M.K. was 23 months old and his father brought him out to the airport with him when he came to meet me. What a shock it was to see this classical textbook case of kwashiorkor standing in the airport lobby. The child was by this time both irritable and lethargic.

      Fortunately, the disease process was arrested and reversed with the implementation of a high protein diet. Within two months, M.K. had recovered. His father, a man with six years of education, frankly said that he didn't have the money to buy the child powdered or even ordinary milk, the foodstuff which is best for treating the disease. Nor am I totally convinced that he would have employed it even if he could have, for the disease in his culture is thought to have a supernatural cause—scarcely a matter for treatment with milk.

This case illustrates several points, not in the least of which is the tenacity of traditional beliefs among urbanized and educated Africans.

    The majority of treatments for kwashiorkor among the Bambara are applied externally to the body as baths or lotions. In many regions whatever meat might be given to a child is withheld in the belief that it will worsen the condition. Thus the traditional system withholds a food which is known to modern physicians to cure the condition.

    A few of the treatments commonly used for treating kwashiorkor among the Bambara are as follows:

    1. The bark of *Sclerocarya birrea* (*mguna*) is boiled in water and the child washed with it (Traoré 1970).

2. The leaves of *Ximenia americana* (*ntonge*) are boiled along with some shea butter. The child is washed with this solution once a day for several days.
3. The roots and leaves of *Waltheria indica* (*kankane tema*) are boiled in water and the child washed with this solution once a day for several days.

Marasmus

Protein-calorie malnutrition (*marasmus*) is believed by the Bambara to be due to a child's nursing from a mother who is pregnant. The Bobo and Dogon peoples claim that it is due to the parents having sexual relations before custom permits. The condition occurs because children are getting neither adequate amounts of calories or of protein in their diet. The following case history illustrates the cogent points concerning the development of marasmus.

M.S. was a year old Marka boy who had been born five years after his mother had given birth to her only other child, a girl. Thus, he was greatly esteemed by his parents. His mother was a thin and poorly nourished woman who did not have a sufficient quantity of milk to satisfy the child's needs. When I saw him he was thin, slightly emaciated, and anemic. His parents had not been giving him any supplemental foods to eat. I instituted a treatment regimen which included powdered milk to supplement his mother's milk. He drank a half liter of this milk per day on the average. Within six weeks his condition was greatly improved.

As with kwashiorkor, marasmus is generally treated by the Bambara with baths and lotions applied externally to the body. The following are some of the Bambara remedies for treating marasmus.

1. The branches and leaves of *Parkia biglobosa* (*nere*) are boiled and the child washed once a day with the solution.
2. The roots of *Ficus capensis* (*toro*) are boiled and the child bathed in the solution.
3. The roots of *Detarium senegalense* (*ndaba*) and *Cussonia barteri* (*bolokouro*) are boiled and the child washed in the solution several times a day (Traoré 1965).

Infantile Diarrhea

Diarrheal syndromes are extremely common among children below four years of age in Africa. Weanling diarrhea is one of the major causes of morbidity and mortality in young children. Its precise cause is still unknown and it may be that a variety of pathogenic viruses and bacteria are responsible for it. This condition does not usually respond to antibiotics, which lends support to the theory that it may be caused by a virus. It occurs primarily among children who are malnourished or marginally nourished.

Besides weanling diarrhea, there are a number of diarrheal syndromes due to specific pathogenic organisms. Among these diseases are amebic dysentery, typhoid and paratyphoid fevers, and bacillary dysentery. Distinctions are not made by most ethnic groups between these various diseases. The symptom of diarrhea is treated without regard to and without knowledge of the disease process of which it may be a part. Exceptions among certain ethnic groups are typhoid fever and cholera which, because of their distinctive clinical symptoms, are recognized as distinct syndromes. In general, a distinction is also made between diarrhea in infants and the disease in older children and adults. The distinction here is made not on the basis of differences in symptoms, but on the basis of the age group among whom the disease occurs.

There are numerous remedies used for infantile diarrhea some of which have been observed by Western-trained health personnel to be quite effective. In Tanzania, I observed that kaolin was frequently used for treating all forms of diarrhea by the Luo and the Basembeti (Imperato 1966). This is an effective product, used also in Western medicine, for reducing the looseness of the stool.

In South Africa, Hewat (1906) found that a distinction was made between ordinary diarrhea, typhoid fever, and diarrhea with abdominal colic. The treatments for the three varied. Ordinary diarrhea is referred to as *uxanxazo* and is treated in one of three ways. The powdered root of *Pelargonium reniforme* is mixed in milk and drunk after being heated. The powdered root of *Solanum capense* is mixed in milk, boiled and then drunk. *Monsonia ovata* is used as a tincture. Hewat (1906) relates that this product was widely used by colonial physicians in Africa for treating cases of typhoid fever.

The Bambara refer to diarrhea as *kono kari*, whether it occurs in infants, children, or adults. Dysentary is called *tokotokoni* and is distinguished as being severe diarrhea accompanied by explosive bowel movements, abdominal cramps, and blood and mucus in the stool.

A common folk remedy used in simple infantile diarrhea is the fruit of the baobab tree (*Adansonia digitata*). The infant is given the sweet white meat of the fruit. This remedy is now routinely used in many child health clinics in Mali since it has been found to be so effective. Many of the anti-diarrheal remedies employed by the Bambara are applied externally to the child's body and are not given by mouth. (A few are given to the mother to eat, leaving one to wonder if the Bambara understand the possibility that these remedies might find their way to the mother's milk.) A few of these remedies are as follows:

1. The child is bathed in a solution made from the boiled leaves of *Terminalia albida* (*voloeide*).

2. The mother is given a gruel of small millet into which pulverized charcoal is added.
3. A solution is made from the leaves of *Parinari curatellifolia* (*ntama*) and this is given as a beverage to the infant.

Dysentery

As mentioned above, dysentery is distinguished from ordinary diarrhea by the Bambara. The remedies for it are generally eaten or drunk, in sharp contrast to those for infantile diarrhea which are often applied as a bath or lotion. Some of the common remedies employed by the Bambara are as follows:

1. Pieces of dried gum arabic, *Acacia arabica* (*bagana*) are pulverized and mixed with rice and eaten several times a day.
2. The root of *Ximenia americana* is pulverized and mixed with a porridge of millet and eaten several times a day (Traore 1965).
3. The root of *Annona senegalensis* is pulverized and mixed with curdled milk and drunk.
4. The leaves of *Combretum glutinosum* (*tangara*) are boiled in water and drunk.

Vomiting

The Bambara refer to vomiting as *fono* and possess a variety of remedies for treating it. Hewat (1906) observed that vomiting was attributed to withcraft or poisoning among the Bantu peoples of South Africa. It was routinely treated with hot water and purgatives. The Bambara have separate treatments for simple vomiting and for vomiting accompanied by diarrhea. These remedies are used for both adults and children. For simple vomiting the following are used:

1. The roots and bark of *Entada africana* (*sama nere*) are boiled and the warm solution given to the patient.
2. The leaves of *Guiera senegalensis* (*n'kudye*) are boiled and the solution mixed with millet gruel. It is then drunk.
3. The leaves of *Scoparia dulcis* (*timitimini*) are pulverized and boiled. The solution is then drunk (Traoré 1965).
4. The seed pods of the baobab tree are eaten along with some gum arabic.

The following are some remedies used by the Bambara for vomiting accompanied by diarrhea.

1. The wood of *Cyperacee sp.* (*madia*) is pulverized and mixed with attar and eaten. *Madia* is also worn as a necklace by women after

they have given birth and is frequently used for morning sickness by pregnant women.

2. The leaves of *Parkia biglobosa* (*nere*) are boiled and drunk.

Constipation

Constipation is called *kono dya* by the Bambara and *uku gunjeliva* by the Bantu of South Africa (Hewat 1906). Constipation is viewed as a serious disease by Africans who conclude that retained feces cause all manner of ill effects.

Hewat recorded the use of a sort of enema in South Africa. The small end of a cowhorn, with the point cut off, was inserted into the anus. The horn was then filled with a herbal liquid and the contents emptied into the bowel. Lastouillas (1974) observed the widespread use of enemas among the Mossi of Upper Volta in the early 1930's. Enemas are also used in many other parts of Africa and their use has occasionally been portrayed in bronze sculptures among the Yoruba of Dahomey.

Purgatives are widely used to relieve constipation. Hewat (1906) observed that the Bantu people of South Africa employed as a powerful cathartic milk from the stem of *Euphorbia pugniformis*, which was drunk. He also noted that they used the bark and roots of *Euclea lanceolata*.

The Bambara employ a variety of purgatives, especially two, boiled salted milk and tamarind juice (*n'tomi*). The latter is the commonest one used. Some other purgatives employed are as follows:

1. The leaves of *Cassia alata* (*ko taba*) are boiled and the solution drunk.
2. The leaves of *Ostryoderris stuhlmannii* (*kongo dugura ni*) are boiled and the solution drunk. The is a very common purgative used for infants and small children (Traoré 1970).
3. The leaves of *Cassia alata* (*ko taba*) are boiled along with its flowers and fruit and mixed with some spices. This is then drunk. *Cassia alata* is one of the most effective cathartics known in western Sudan, used most frequently after the juice of the tamarind tree, *Tamarindus indica*.

Convulsions

Convulsive disorders are frequently encountered among African children. Most often they are febrile convulsions secondary to fevers due to another disease process. Maclean (1971) reports that in Ibadan, Nigeria, a preparation widely used for both treating and preventing seizures is *agbo tutu* (see chap. 18). This herbal medicine's name literally means "cold medicine," because no heating is involved in its preparation. It is made from green tobacco leaves which are marinated for several days in either human or cow urine. A number of other constituents are also present and these vary from place to place. (Gin is occasionally added.) The resulting drug is a strong nicotine preparation which is small doses stimulates the brain, but which in large doses depresses it (Maclean 1971). Many children are brought into hospitals unconscious after having been given this product and it has been responsible for a number of deaths. Studies are in progress in Ibadan on the toxicity of such preparations and on the toxicity of cow urine, which is used in a number of remedies.

The Bambara call epilepsy *kilikilimacien*, a term which is also used for febrile convulsions in children. They employ the same treatments for both conditions. It is difficult to evaluate the efficacy of these remedies in febrile convulsions since the condition is episodic and remits without intervention. The majority of these preparations are either eaten or drunk by the patient. Two common anticonvulsant remedies used by the Bambara are the bark of *Mitragyna inermis* (*dioun*) and *Heliotropium indicum* (*nangi ku*), both of which are drunk as a beverage.

Fevers

The Bambara name for fever is *fari-gouan*. It is applied to any febrile condition except malaria, which is called *souma-koumaou*. The principal anti-pyretic agent used in the savanna of West Africa is *Teclea sudanica*, known in Bambara as *kinkeliba*. The best quality is found growing on the slopes of Kita Mountain in western Mali. Its leaves and stems are boiled and the solution drunk as a hot infusion. *Kinkeliba* is also a strong diuretic. Because of its proven efficacy, it is often used by modern dispensaries in place of aspirin. Another common remedy is to have the child drink an infusion made from the leaves of *Fluggea virosa* (= *Securinega virosa*) (*souroukou-gningnin*). Infusions are also made from the pulverized boiled leaves of *Guiera senegalensis* and *Hymenocardia acida*.

Coughing

Coughing is a symptom of a number of diseases of the respiratory system and is the object of a large number of indigenous remedies. The Bambara call coughing *souasoua*. A few of the antitussives used by Bambara are:

1. The bark of *Anogeissus leiocarpus* (*ngalama*) is boiled in water and the solution drunk. The leaves of this plant are used for dying white cloth a bright yellow color. Thus the plant has more than one use.
2. The bark and roots of *Pergularia daemia* (*fataka*) are boiled in water and then mixed with milk. The mixture is then drunk.
3. The roots and bark of *Scoparia dulcis* (*timitimi*) are boiled in water and drunk as a beverage.

References

Hewat, N.L. 1906. *Bantu Folk Lore.* Capetown: T. Maskew Niller.

Imperato, P.J. 1966. Witchcraft and Traditional Medicine among the Luo of Tanzania. *Tanzania Notes And Records* 66:193-201.

Imperato, P.J. 1971. Incidence of and Local Beliefs about Onchocerciasis in the Senegal River Basin. *Tropical And Geographical Medicine* 23(4):385-389.

Lastouillas, J.P. 1974. Personal Communication.

Maclean, U.C. 1971. *Magical Medicine.* London: Penguin.

Traoré, D.A. 1965. *Médecine et Magie Africaines.* Paris: Présence Africaine.

Traoré, D.A. 1970. Personal Communication.

11

Measles

Measles is a highly contagious disease whose usual symptoms include a high fever, cold, inflamation of the eyes (conjunctivitis), bronchitis and a rash which usually appears three to four days after the onset of the first symptoms. A rash can also develop on the lining of the intestinal tract and small white spots, known as Koplik spots, develop on the mucosa of the mouth. Most deaths from measles are due to pneumonia which occurs as a complication of the disease. Another rarer complication is encephalitis which usually appears after the acute infection is over.

Measles is the most important disease of childhood in Africa. It occurs throughout the continent, the incidence being highest in most areas every third year. Measles epidemics occur at the peak of the dry season in West Africa, from March through May, when stores of food and human nutritional levels are at their lowest. By the time the rains begin in late June, epidemic measles disappears from rural West Africa, probably due to the lack of a remaining susceptible population, and to a decrease in transmission which diminishes during the rainy season because travel is reduced. Children in rural areas are often sent out for the several months of the rainy season to live on their family fields where they are isolated from all children except their own siblings.

From 1958 through 1975, the annual number of measles cases reported in Mali has ranged from 10,000 to 40,000, with case mortalities of 15–20 percent. In the city of Bamako, with a population of 120,000, from March 1963 through October 1967, 2,838 patients with measles were admitted to the central hospital, and 431 died—a case mortality of 15.2

Parts of this chapter were previously published in the *Transactions of the Royal Society of Tropical Medicine and Hygiene*, 1969, 64(6):768-780. I acknowledge with thanks permission of the editor to use this material here.

percent. The overall mortality rate for the city is obviously lower, since only the most severely ill patients are admitted to the hospital. In epidemics that I investigated in Mali in 1967 and 1968, however, mortality rates of 50 percent and more were seen.

Among hospital patients, only 2.7 percent of measles patients were aged 0-5 months whereas 85.4 percent were aged six months to two years. Ninety percent of all deaths among hospitalized patients occurred in patients between the ages of six months and two years.

Though refined statistics for rural Mali are lacking, the results of several individual epidemic investigations have revealed a similar distribution. Measles in Mali, therefore, is a disease of very young children. Morley and MacWilliam have found a similar pattern in Nigeria (1961).

Relationship of Traditional
Practices to the Severity of Measles

The morbidity and high mortality associated with measles in African children has been attributed to its occurrence against a background of poor nutritional status, intercurrent infection, and insanitary environment. In the past few years, however, Morley and MacWilliams (1961) have drawn attention to the important influence of traditional beliefs and practices on measles mortality and their contributing role in complications. Because measles is a highly infectious disease which virtually all non-immune African children get, and a serious disease which carries a frightening mortality, most societies have developed special attitudes and practices unique for it.

In the Mali republic, in every ethnic group, there is no other disease for which there has been developed so impressive an array of nursing care practices, dietary restrictions, and medicinal therapies. The practitioners of modern medicine condemn many of these practices, are indifferent about a few, and support some. Many clinicians who have treated measles in Africa are well aware that traditional practices strongly influence the mortality, the severity, and the kinds of temporary and permanent sequelae that ensue. These factors are often overlooked in considering why measles is such a killing disease in Africa (Imperato and Traore 1969).

Though factors like poor nutrition, superinfection, and poor hygiene are more obvious, traditional attitudes and the practices they generate scarcely catch the eye of those without an anthropological orientation. There are notable exceptions to this, outstanding among which is Morley's (1967) current world-wide study of traditional beliefs about measles.

Clinical and epidemiological experience with measles in Africa over the past several years has demonstrated the tremendous role traditional practices play in affecting the outcome of measles, and a systematic study of these beliefs and practices was therefore undertaken in Mali (Imperato and Traoré) in early 1967, and carried out in the course of epidemic and case investigations among all of Mali's major ethnic groups. A second one was then undertaken in which a questionnaire was mailed to the chief medical officers of each of Mali's 42 districts (cercles). This questionnaire was patterned after one used by the Institute of Child Health, London, in its world-wide survey on traditional practices and beliefs about measles. The medical officers (*médecin chefs*) were instructed to fill in the questionnaire with information obtained from one or two old villagers.

Bambara Names for Measles

The Bambara have several different names for measles. There are some obvious similarities, the differences in spelling reflecting differences of pronunciation. Most names are found among the Bambara, the largest ethnic group in Mali. Because the Bambara are spread over a large geographical area, dialect differences are striking. The most common name for measles among these people is *neone*, which means "little millet," because the macules that occur on the skin of patients are said to resemble the grains of this cereal in size and color. *Messemani* and its variant *missimani* are commonly used in the northern areas of Bambara settlement, their literal translation being "small spots."

Among the Bambara of Segou, a pseudonym, *demba gnouma*, which means "a good mother," is often used to refer to measles, for fear that use of the proper names will cause the disease in one's family. In this area, measles is also called *gnanzani*, "children's illness," and *fin missen*, "small thing." *Gnanzani* is restricted in use to measles and never refers to another childhood disease.

Finyabana in Bambara means "wind illness" and is used not only for measles, but also for smallpox and other eruptions. Because of the widespread anatomical distribution of these eruptions it is believed that their mode of transmission is the wind, for only the wind touches all parts of one's anatomy.

Names among Other Ethnic Groups

The Bozo name *fourou*, the Bobo-Oule *larabokou*, and the Dogon *sadeguere* literally mean "small spots." The Malinke and Kassonke, who live in western Mali, are cousins to the Bambara. Most of the names used for measles among them are linguistic variants of a corresponding

TRIBAL NAMES FOR MEASLES IN MALI

Ethnic Group	Cercle	Name for Measles
Bambara	Banamba	Messenemani
	Segou	Demba Gnouma
		Gnan Zani
		Fin Missen
	Macina	Fin Missima
	Kolokani	Gnoni
		Gnaninsa
		Missimani
	Bamako	Neone
		Finyabana
Bozo	San	Fourou
	Djenné	Fourou
	Mopti	Fourou
Bobo-Oule	Yorosso	Larabokou
	Tominian	Larabokou
Dogon	Bankass	Sadeguere
	Koro	Sadegere
	Bandiagara	Sadegere
Kassonke	Bafoulabe	Finibana
		Nioni
	Kayes	Finibana
		Nioni
		Missinmesinni
Malinke	Kangaba	Niakalesom
	Bafoulabe	Finibana
		Nioni
	Kayes	Messinsene
Marka	San	Misenin
Maure	Timbuctoo	Alhaima
	Nara	Beuridbasseu
Minianka	Koutiala	Mughoro
Peul	Mopti	Dougodie
	Tenenkou	Tieoude
	Djenné	Tieoude
	Douentza	Tieoude

Bambara term. The Kassonke name *missinnesinni*, however, means "appearance of new elements." The Malinke of Kayes employ a pseudonym for measles, *demba niouma*, meaning "good mother," which greatly resembles that of the Bambara of Segou.

Various Tuareg names are dialect variants of *loumatt*, meaning "child's disease," and *talassabatt*, meaning "small spots."

The Cause of Measles in Bambara Folk Beliefs

The Bambara always consider the cause of measles to be spiritual, as do other ethnic groups in Mali. This is not surprising since measles is an epidemic disease with a high mortality. While Moslem Bambara consider God to be the cause of most epidemics, the traditional Bambara ascribe the disease to witchcraft and sorcery. In certain isolated instances, the Moslem Bambara ascribe measles epidemics to evil genies.

Attitudes toward Active Cases among the Bambara

Persons with measles are often hidden in their houses and not even immediate neighbors are made aware of them, although there are differences in this practice. Some Bambara hide their sick children, others speak about them freely. Children with measles are not hidden in their houses as a rule; those still small enough to travel on their mothers' backs may even be taken out of the villages and to markets. Older children, of course, remain at home, being too sick to move. In certain areas of the cercles of Bamako and Macina, however, children are hidden, particularly if they are the first cases in the villages. They are hidden once the rash appears. This stems from a shame and fear of admitting that one's child has been the object of the malevolent work of a witch, sorcerer, marabout, etc.

The hiding of children with measles seems to have been the rule among the Bambara several decades ago, but the practice broke down gradually over the years in urban and administrative centers. In the bush it has broken down under the influence of medical authorities. This form of isolation is not useful in preventing the spread of the disease, since most transmission occurs during the initial stage before the rash appears and before children are hidden. Today, children with measles are often isolated on the edge of the village in temporary shelters, even though this constitutes a physical inconvenience for the parents.

Attitudes towards Active Cases among other Groups in Mali

The Bozo, except for some in Djenne, also hide their measles-infected children, and the same holds true for the Bobo-Oule, Dogon Kassonke and Marka groups in Mali. Unlike the Bambara, these groups

MEASLES AMONG SOME ETHNIC GROUPS

Ethnic Group	Cercle	Cause according to Folk Beliefs	Attitude Toward Active Cases	Attempt to Bring Out Rash	Method Used to Bring Out Rash	Period Unwashed
Bambara	Segou	God Sorcerers Witches	Spoken of or Hidden	Yes	Honey by mouth	During eruption
Bozo	San	God Water genies	Hidden	No	—	During eruption
Bobo-Oule	Yorosso	Sorcerers	Hidden	Yes	Soaks of solution of bark of wild raisin tree	During eruption
Dogon	Bankass	Genies Fetishers	Hidden	Yes	String beans eaten	Weeks
Kassonke	Bafoulabe	Witches God	Hidden	Yes	Body covered with honey	During eruption
Malinke	Kayes	Sorcerers God	Hidden	Yes	Baths of monkey feces solution	Weeks
Marka	San	God	Hidden	No	—	Weeks
Maure	Timbuctoo	God Genies	Spoken of	Yes	Body covered with warm blankets	Weeks
Minianka	Koutiala	Sorcerers Witches Fetishers	Hidden	No	—	Weeks
Peul	Tenenkou	God Sorcerers	Hidden	Yes	Honey by mouth	Weeks
Sarakole	Yelimane	Genies God	Spoken of	No	—	Before eruption appears
Senufo	Sikasso	Sorcerers Witches	Hidden	Yes	Body covered with dirt from termite hill	Weeks
Songhai	Ansongo	God Genies	Hidden	Yes	Child kept out-doors	During eruption
Tuareg	Kidal	Devil God Genies	Hidden	Yes	Body painted with mixture of camel feces and sheep hair	Weeks

believe that exposure of the child to outside air will retard the appearance of the rash, and this retarding of the rash is regarded as undesirable. In addition, the cases are not spoken about outside the family circle for reasons similar to those explained above for the Bambara.

The Maures living in Timbuctoo speak about their cases freely, and readily bring them to local medical authorities. Those, however, who live out in the desert keep them pretty much of a secret, an easy matter, since they move only in small family or clan groups. The patients, however, are placed in a tent down-wind from the rest in the camp. Measles among adult Maure women is not uncommon owing to the fact that they live isolated lives from childhood and rarely go outside their tents; thus often they are not exposed to the measles virus when young and they remain susceptible to the infection into adulthood. As with infants, the adult patients are hidden.

The Songhai of Timbuctoo universally hide their cases from their neighbors and keep them indoors. The Songhai in Gao and Ansongo, however, keep their measles-infected children outdoors for the few days before the rash appears, believing the air beneficial for bringing out the rash. During this period the family does not disclose to their neighbors their suspicions that the child has measles. Once the child's rash starts to come out, he is taken indoors and hidden.

Among the Tuareg nomads of the desert, all patients are kept inside the tents before the rash appears, even if they are spoken about freely. Among this group the general belief is that exposure to the outside air will prevent the rash from developing and cause the fever to rise. The exception to this are the Tuareg of Gourma-Rharous, who take their children outside as soon as the rash appears. Like the Maure, the Tuareg do not let their non-relatives know that one of their children has measles. This attitude is a part of the general reserve of these people who rarely divulge anything but innocuous generalities outside the extended family circle.

Except for the Tuareg, those tribal groups who hide their children also do not divulge the matter to their neighbors. The reasons for physical concealment relate in some way to the outcome of the disease and in certain instances, as among the Bambara, to social fears.

Therapeutic Measures

Bringing the Rash Out

The Bambara make some attempt to bring out the rash as quickly as possible. The almost universal reason for this is the empirical observation that once eruption is complete, the other symptoms such as muscle soreness, coryza, cough, headache, photophobia, and fever improve. They also believe that once the disease becomes localized in the skin it can be dealt with in a more direct and effective fashion.

Other ethnic groups also attempt to bring the rash out. Most methods consist of the topical application of innocuous substances such as honey and goat's milk. Several involve the oral administration of products

MEASLES TREATMENT AMONG SELECTED ETHNIC GROUPS IN MALI

Ethnic Group	Cercle	Purges	Indigenous Ophthalmic Preparations	Reactions Caused By Ophthalmic Preparations	Acceptance of Western Medicines	
					Oral Agents	Injected Agents
Bambara	Banamba	None	Honey Goat's milk Tamarind juice	Mild Mild	Accepted	Accepted
Bozo	Djenné	None	None	—	Avoided	Accepted
Bobo-Oule	Tominian	None	Crushed onions Peanut flour solution	Mild Mild	Avoided	Avoided
Dogon	Koro	Increased	Wild peas solution	Mild	Accepted	Accepted
Kassonke	Kayes	Increased	Human milk Sourwood Goat's milk	Mild Severe Mild	Avoided	Accepted
Malinke	Kangaba	Increased	Human milk Goat's milk Sourwood	Mild Mild Severe	Avoided	Avoided
Marka	San	Increased	Peanut flour solution Goat's milk	Mild Mild	Avoided	Accepted
Maure	Timbuctoo	None	None	—	Accepted	Accepted
Minianka	Koutiala	None	Goat's milk	Mild	Avoided	Avoided
Peul	Djenné	None	Soot from cooking pots	Severe	Accepted	Accepted
Sarakole	Yelimane	Increased	Human milk	Mild	Accepted	Accepted
Senufo	Sikasso	None	Solution of leaves from shea butter tree	Mild	Accepted	Accepted
Songhai	Gao	Increased	Solution of leaves of dom palms	Mild	Avoided	Avoided
Tuareg	Kidal	Increased	Tannin solution Henna solution	Mild Mild	Avoided	Avoided

such as honey and string beans. A few methods used such as application of plasters of camel feces and baths in solutions of monkey feces, may be potentially injurious.

Washing

The Bambara do not wash children who are in the eruptive stage of measles. Other groups cease washing children as soon as the early symptoms appear and do not resume it until desquamation—loss of superficial skin as the rash disappears—is complete. Some stop washing only when the rash begins to appear and resume as soon as the eruptive phase is over. The Tuareg of Gourma-Rharous stop washing exactly seven days after the onset of the early symptoms and they do not reinstitute washing until desquamation begins. In general, this corresponds to the beginning of the eruptive phase.

Washing is avoided because they believe that it prevents the rash from coming out on the skin. This idea is held even by those who make no special efforts to bring out the rash. In essence, therefore, washing is thought to prolong the duration of the eruptive phase and its severe systemic symptoms. The Tuareg believe that washing with water not only prevents the rash from coming out on the skin, but also drives it to come out on the mucous membranes and in the intestinal tract. This, they say, results in severe measles and high mortality. Of interest is the fact that the Tuareg are familiar with Koplik spots (eruptions inside the mouth usually appearing a day or two after the first symptoms).

Purges

Purges of various kinds are often given to children in Mali whether or not they are ill. Among the Bobo-Oule, the Peul and among some of the Bambara, Maure, and Tuareg, purges are withheld during measles because of fear of initiating or worsening a diarrhoeal episode, which is considered an ominous prognostic sign. Other groups, however, increase the normal amounts of purgatives during measles, considering constipation to have a bad effect on the intestinal lesions. The purgative most frequently used is tamarind juice, which in Bambara is called *n'tomi*.

Ophthalmic Treatments

The possibility of a child with measles being left with permanent corneal scarring is well recognized and greatly feared. This scarring mostly results from superficial keratitis or from corneal ulcers which become secondarily infected. The Bambara commonly employ honey, goat's milk and tamarind juice.

Certain groups such as the Malinke of Kayes and the Songhai of Timbuctoo prevent children with measles from sleeping during the day, believing that diurnal sleep causes the appearance of macules on the cornea. Cold water is often thrown in their faces to keep them awake. The Maure and Tuareg of Timbuctoo are the only ethnic groups who do not put some preparation directly into the eyes; they do, however, paint ochre on to the face, believing it to prevent the rash from spreading into the eyes.

Most ophthalmic preparations are innocuous and cause mild reactions or none. Others, however, such as the solution of sourwood (*Parkia biglobosa*) used by the Kassonke and Malinke of Kayes, causes severe chemical conjunctivitis, and severe reactions are also seen among the Peul children who have had a solution of soot from cooking pots put into their eyes. There has not been a sufficient follow-up of children receiving such treatments to conclude that they have a higher incidence of permanent corneal damage, but my general impression, and that of the local medical authorities, is that they do.

Use of Modern Drugs

The Bambara generally accept the use of both oral and injected varieties of Western medicines — aspirin, antibiotics, and vitamins — in children with measles. They do not view these as impeding the development of the rash.

The attitude of acceptance or rejection of modern medicines either by mouth or by injection among the other ethnic groups, relates directly to beliefs regarding the development of the rash. Those who reject the use of modern medicines do so because they believe they will inhibit the rash from developing. This belief is held by both those who actively try to bring the rash out and those who do not.

Dietary Habits

Large quantities of animal protein are not usually given by the Bambara to their children. After being weaned at about two years of age, children are given a high carbohydrate diet consisting chiefly of cereals, namely millet, corn, and manioc. Parents give their children a small amount of vegetable protein, including *niebe* seeds (*Vigna sinensis*), Sudan beans (*Phaseolus acutifolius*) and Bambara peas, *voandzou* (*Voandzeia subterranea*). Protein malnutrition syndromes and protein-calorie malnutrition syndromes are common in Bambara children between the ages of two and six. The Bambara do not give children protein-containing foods during measles, withholding even the little they may normally give a child. They do not reduce the amount of vegetable protein nor the quantity of fluids, but they do greatly diminish the total amount of food given. This practice is carried out until desquamation is complete.

Among other sedentary agriculturist societies in Mali, including the Bobo-Oule, Dogon, Kassonka, Malinke, Marka, and Minianka, animal protein foods are not fed to children, though they are routinely given to children among three other agricultural sedentary groups, the Senufo, Songhai and Sarakole. The last two groups keep large herds of goats, sheep

DIETARY HABITS DURING MEASLES
AMONG SELECTED ETHNIC GROUPS IN MALI

Ethnic Group	Cercle	Total amount of food	Amount of animal protein	Amount of vegetable protein	Amount of liquids
Bambara	Segou	Diminished	Not given	Normal	Normal
Bozo	Mopti	Diminished	Not given	Not given	Diminished
Dogon	Bankass	Diminished	Not given	Not given	Diminished
Kassonke	Bafoulabe	Diminished	Not given	Not given	Diminished
Malinke	Kangaba	Diminished	Not given	Not given	Diminished
Marka	San	Diminished	Not given	Not given	Increased
Maure	Timbuctoo	Diminished	Not given	Not given	Diminished
Minianka	Koutiala	Diminished	Not given	Not given	Diminished
Peul	Djenné	Reduced to cow's milk	Reduced	Not given	Normal
Sarakole	Yelimane	Reduced to cow's milk	Reduced	Not given	Reduced to cow's milk tamarind juice
Senufo	Sikasso	Normal	Not given	Normal	Normal
Songhai	Gao	Reduced to sorghum	Not given	Diminished	Diminished during eruptive phase only
Tuareg	Dire	Normal	Increased (fish only)	Normal	Normal

and cattle and were semi-nomadic and pastoral until a few decades ago. Among the pastoral Peul, Tuareg, and Maure animal protein is routinely fed to children in the form of dried meat and curdled milk. The Bela, the lowest caste of the Tuareg and their former slaves, do not give their children meat.

An attack of measles in no way induces parents to give their children animal protein in those societies where animal protein is not normally fed to children, and in those groups who usually feed children animal protein, it is purposely withdrawn, the sole exception to this being the Tuareg of Dire who force-feed fish to their measles-infected children.

In contrast to animal protein, protein of vegetable origin is often fed to children in Mali, but many groups withhold vegetables during measles. The reason for this, as for the refusal to give meat, is the fear that both produce diarrhea, a bad prognostic sign. The Songhai of Timbuctoo do not feed vegetables to their children during the eruptive phase, fearing dysentery.

In general, the total food intake during measles infection is reduced among most groups. Exceptions are the Bozo of Djenné and some of the Maure of Timbuctoo. Among the Peul and some Tuareg, food intake is reduced to milk, and among the Songhai to sorghum. Most ethnic groups greatly reduce liquid intake, thinking that fluids worsen the rash.

The dietary restrictions imposed on children with measles extend beyond the acute stage of the disease. The Bobo-Oule continue withholding foods for several weeks after desquamation.

Relationship of Measles to Maternal Menstruation and Parental Intercourse

Certain groups believe that the appearance and worsening of measles are related to maternal menstruation or sexual relations between parents. The Bozo of Djenné, the Kassonke of Kayes, and the Malinke of the same region believe that sexual relations between parents complicate the disease in a child, and parents in general practice abstention. The Kassonke of Bafoulabe believe that sexual relations represent a source of filth and illness and cause complications. The Malinke of this area prohibit parental intercourse if their child has measles. The Peul of Djenné believe that measles can result in a child if its parents have had sexual relations during the mother's menstrual period. Relations are generally stopped once the child contracts measles.

Sayings Concerning Measles

A few ethnic groups have proverbs or sayings about measles which relate to the character of the disease. Some of the more interesting are as follows:

1. *Faroba* — All children get it. (Bambara of Banamba)
2. *Mesquis beuriadasseu* — Thinned like the measled. (Maure or Nara)
3. *Tanrik tassididet* — May measles carry you off. (Tuareg of Goundam)
4. *A ainsi Sadeguere goli dedon in saron* — If your child has not had measles you do not have a child yet. (Dogon of Koro)
5. *Patti n'bia binguelma ana n'gardi so my bettaki* — Never be proud of the beauty of your child as long as we are in this world. (Peul of Douentza)

The last proverb is addressed to mothers during a measles epidemic as a reminder of the possibility of disfiguring complications.

References

Evans-Pritchard, E.E. 1937. *Witchcraft, Oracles and Magic among the Azande.* London: Oxford University Press.

Fofana, B. 1968. Nutrition et Santé au Mali. (Unpublished).

Imperato, P.J. and Traore, D.A. 1969. Traditional Beliefs about Measles and Its Treatment among the Bambara of Mali, *Tropical and Geographical Medicine* 21:62-67.

Morley, D.C. 1967. Measles and Measles Vaccines in Pre-Industrial Countries in *Modern Trends in Medical Virology*, edited by R.B. Heath, and A.P. Waterson. London: Butterworths.

Morley, D.C. and MacWilliams, K.M. 1961. Measles in a Nigerian Community, *West African Medical Journal* 10:246-250.

12

Communicable Diseases of Adults

The communicable diseases are by far the commonest health problems in Africa. They are not necessarily recognized as distinct entities since, as pointed out above, African medical classification is primarily one of symptoms and not of syndromes or of etiologies. In a disease such as onchocerciasis whose symptoms include skin rashes, pruritus, edema of the limbs and blindness, each symptom is viewed as a distinct problem and not as part of the same disease (Imperato 1971). Where symptoms occur successively, as in onchocerciasis, nosology tends to be based on symptoms; only where they occur simultaneously, do they tend to be viewed as part of the same disease process.

In this chapter, the management of a few of the major communicable disease problems will be described. These diseases and their management highlight the essentials of a vast subject and provide insights into the Bambara approach to communicable disease management. The diseases chosen as models are those which are recognized as distinct entities in Western medicine and which are priority health problems because of their high incidence among the Bambara.

The majority of adults in Africa represent cohorts of individuals who have successfully survived the ravages of the childhood communicable disease. Consequently, it is frequently believed that the elderly cannot contract any of these diseases and they are, therefore, often entrusted with the care of young patients. Such a belief is basically correct since African adults have long since built up antibodies to many of the communicable diseases. However, there are some communicable diseases which even adults contract or which begin in childhood and run a chronic course into adult life. Tuberculosis, leprosy, and syphilis are examples of this. In spite of the presence of antibodies, the disease process continues. Then there are, of course, diseases such as tetanus, smallpox, trachoma, and the intestinal parasitic infections which can affect either adults or children.

Leprosy

Leprosy is often confused in its early stages with other dermatologic conditions and it is not until its mutilating effects begin that a clear-cut diagnosis is obvious in the traditional system. Traditional remedies have met with little success in treating leprosy. In many societies the disease is attributed to especially powerful supernatural causes, providing a ready rationale for treatment failure. The demonstrated effectiveness of modern chemotherapy and the existence of excellent anti-leprosy programs for many years all over Africa have lessened dependence on traditional remedies. Many traditional therapeutic approaches are geared toward an alleviation of symptoms and not at cure. Some of the remedies which are still current among the Bambara are as follows:

1. The roots of *Vitex diversifolia* (= *V. simplicifolia*) (*koro*) and *Ximenia americana* (*ntonge*) are mixed in a solution of millet and allowed to ferment for several days. The liquid is then drunk and used as a lotion on the surface of the body.
2. A paste is made from the ground roots of *Indigofera tinctoria* (*indigo*) and *Chrozophora senegalensis* mixed with shea butter. This is applied to skin lesions daily.
3. The leaves of *Bombax costatum* (*dioum*) are mixed with shea butter. This paste is then applied externally to the body.

Cerebrospinal Meningitis

Epidemic meningococcal meningitis is a disease which periodically sweeps across the sub-Saraha zone of Africa and takes a very high toll. It is especially common in certain latitudes of the savanna and sahel of West Africa which form part of the ''meningitis belt.'' In 1969 a very serious epidemic of meningococcal meningitis occurred in Bamako, Mali, with over 5,000 cases being reported and 500 deaths (Imperato 1975). Moslem healers sold a variety of Koranic charms both for treating patients and for preventing the disease. They failed miserably at both and some of these healers were incarcarated by the authorities for charlatinism. Unfortunately, their Koranic treatments, consisting of methods previously described (see chapter 5), retarded the initiation of chemotherapy and directly led to death in instances where early chemotherapy would have easily cured the disease. One of the commonest folk medicines used (aside from Koranic charms) is an infusion made from the leaves of *Cymbopogon giganteus* (*tiekala*). This is drunk and used as a bath lotion.

Traore (1965) cites a remedy which is typical of the magical approaches used by the Bambara. The intestines of a small dog are removed, charred and mixed with shea butter, making a thick paste. This is then spread out over the patient's vertebral column from the neck down to the lumbar region. During my 1969 Bamako experience, many patients who eventually came to us for treatment had already used such traditional remedies without success.

Jaundice

Jaundice is a sign and not a disease per se. The Bambara refer to it as *say* or *saouara*. They do not distinguish between the various disease states which may give rise to jaundice such as yellow fever, infectious and serum hepatitis, and gall bladder disease. During outbreaks of yellow fever, the Bambara used to suspend the aromatic leaves of *Cymbopogon giganteus* (*tiekala*) in their huts. These leaves were thought to prevent the disease from affecting those living in the hut. They may, in fact have some effect, since they might repel the virus-carrying mosquitoes from the hut.

A common remedy used for treating jaundice is an infusion made from the leaves of *Anogeissus leiocarpus* (*ngalama*); this is drunk. (This solution itself has a yellow color and on contact stains cloth yellow.) Another frequently employed folk drug is a solution made from the leaves of *Diospyros mespiliformis* (*sunsun*). The patient bathes in the solution and also inhales the solution as it is being boiled.

Tetanus

Tetanus occurs primarily among newborns as a result of infection of the umbilical stump. However, it is not an infrequent infection among adults. Many of the herbal treatments used are applied externally to the body as salves, lotions, or as baths, and in my experience have no effect on the outcome of the disease. Some of the remedies employed by the Bambara for both umbilical and adult onset tetanus are:

1. The pulverized leaves of *Combretum glutinosum* (*tangara*) are mixed in water and used as a bath.
2. The leaves of *Hibiscus asper* (*tori da*) are pulverized and dissolved in water which is then applied externally to the body as a lotion.
3. A solution is made from the leaves of *Hyptis spicigera* (*nugu*) and taken by mouth. The patient is also bathed with it.

Trypanosomiasis

Trypanosomiasis was once a serious epidemic and endemic disease problem in widespread areas of sub-Sahara Africa. The terminal phase of the disease causes coma and hence it is called African sleeping sickness. (A number of viruses in the United States and elsewhere also cause a coma-producing encephalitis which is not to be confused with African sleeping sickness caused by *Trypanosoma gambiense*, a parasitic protozoan.) About 50 years ago colonial administrations established special anti-sleeping sickness services to combat the disease. For the most part, these special health services were mobile, with teams of doctors and nurses moving from village to village in order to diagnose and treat cases. These services also directed extensive campaigns against the *tsetse fly* which transmits the disease (McKelvey 1973). The end result of these extensive vector-control and chemotherapeutic programs was a dramatic reduction in the incidence of trypanosomiasis. The chemotherapeutic agents then and now available are extremely effective and have resulted in cures in most patients and a reduction of the size of the human reservoir of the disease. Because of this, traditional therapies which were never successful have fallen into disuse and in many regions no generation transfer of them has occurred.

A few of the traditional remedies employed by the Bamana are as follows:

1. A solution is made from the leaves of *Cassia siberiana* (*sinjan*). This is drunk and used as a bath lotion.
2. A solution is made from the leaves of *Strychnos spinosa* (*gongoro ni*) and used as a drink and bath.
3. The leaves of *Detarium senegalese* (= *D. microcarpum*) (*taba*) are boiled in water and the solution used as a bath.

Tuberculosis and Other Bronchopulmonary Disorders

Tuberculosis has become a serious problem in Africa during this century. Among the Bambara it is not recognized very often as a separate entity from other severe bronchopulmonary disorders, and frequently a single name is applied to all such disorders. The Bambara call cough-producing illnesses, tuberculosis included, *kessou*.

Hewat (1906) recorded a large number of remedies for treating tuberculosis and bronchopulmonary diseases. Among these he observed that the leaves of *Lippia asperifolio* and *Clematis brachiata* were burned or smoked in a closed hut and the smoke inhaled.

Among the Bambara many remedies are used, among which are the following:

1. The roots of *Cymbopogon giganteus* (*tiekala*) are mixed in water and boiled. The patient is asked to bend over the pot and breathe in the vapors. When cooked, a portion of the solution is drunk.
2. The bark of *Diospyros mespiliformis* (*sunsun*) is pulverized and mixed with the sap of *Acacia arabica* (*bagana*). This is then eaten.

3. The leaves of *Ostryoderris stuhlmannii* (*kongo dugura ni*) are boiled in water. The patient breathes in the vapor.
4. The bark of *Parkia biglobosa* (*nere*) is boiled in water and the patient breathes in the fumes.

Syphilis

All forms of syphilis are significant health problems in most of Africa. In many areas, as in the dry sahel of West Africa, the disease is endemic. The Bambara recognize the chancre of primary syphilis and call it *da*. Secondary syphilis, characterized by eruptions of the skin and mucous membranes, is called *blenboro*, and in some areas people recognize that it develops in those men who have had chancres. In other areas no association is recognized, the two being considered separate disease processes. Tertiary syphilis, which involves various internal organs, is not recognized, in general. Congenital syphilis is a recognized entity, but people do not know of its relationship to syphilis in adults in children. The folk therapies used for treating both primary and secondary syphilis seem to meet with success since both of these stages of the disease usually go on to apparently spontaneous healing. Unfortunately, despite the apparent healing, the disease process usually continues internally with the eventual development of disabling or fatal tertiary syphilis being likely in patients treated only with folk remedies (or those who are not treated at all).

Some of the therapies used by the Bambara for treating primary syphilis are as follows:

1. A solution is made from the leaves of *Trichilia prieureana* (*ka lubudun*). The patient bathes the lesions with this.
2. The leaves of *Ipomoea rubens* (*Lettsomia rubens?*) (*bugu mugu*) are boiled in water and the lesions washed with the solution.
3. The flowers of *Cymbopogon giganteus* (*tiekala*) are boiled in water and the solution applied to the lesions.

Gonorrhea

Gonorrhea is a major problem in most of Africa. Among females the early disease is usually asymptomatic, although eventually it leads to chronic pelvic inflammatory disease in which the ovaries and Fallopian tubes are infected and scarred, often resulting in sterility. Gonorrhea is easily spread in Africa, for although most societies condemn promiscuity and extramarital sexual relations, both are common. While males come to treatment because of their painful symptoms, females (with no obvious symptoms) rarely do, and the females then serve as an infectious reservoir.

A major problem in treating this disease is that so many of the strains of the gonococcus are resistant to the usually-employed antibiotics.

The Bambara of Mali possess a large number of treatments for the disease, none of which in my experiences are effective, judging from the fact that patients eventually seek care at a dispensary or clinic. Some of the treatments frequently used are the following:

1. The roots of *Acacia albida* (*balanza*) are boiled in water along with the leaves of *Cymbopogon giganteus* (*tiekala*). Once cool, the solution is drunk.
2. The leaves of *Euphorbia convolvuloides* (*dabada*) are boiled in water and the solution drunk.
3. The bark of *Anogeissus leiocarpus* (*ngalama*) are boiled and the solution drunk.

Smallpox

Smallpox was once a serious problem in most of Africa. However, since 1966, a quite successful concerted effort has been made to eradicate the disease from the continent. At the time of this writing, the disease is still present in Ethiopia. When smallpox was common in West Africa, many groups such as the Bambara believed that it was caused by the wind (Imperato 1975). The Bambara employed a number of therapies for treating the disease some of which are as follows:

1. The leaves of *Ximenia americana* (*ntonge*) are soaked in goat's milk and placed on the skin.
2. A solution is made from the pulverized leaves of *Balanites aegyptiaca* and the patient washes with it, drinking some of it at the same time. Members of the patient's family either bathe simultaneously or later on with another portion of the same batch of the solution and also drink it. This therapy is obviously conducive to the spread of the disease (Imperato and Traoré 1968).
3. A mud plaster is made from warm sand and a solution made from the bark of *Boswellia dalzieli* (*nano*). This is applied over the skin and the solution is drunk separately by the patient. If the patient is an unweaned infant, the solution is given to the mother, in the belief that it passes on to the child (Imperato and Traoré 1968).

Yaws

Yaws was once a serious disease of high incidence in Africa, but with the advent of widespread antibiotic use, the disease has become quite rare. It is caused by a spirochete and affects the skin, muscle, and bone and if left untreated results in terrible deformities and scarring. Some of the

traditional remedies used by the Bambara (none of which seems effective)
are as follows:

1. The leaves of *Cassia absus* (*karibono*) are crushed and the dry
   powder applied to the lesions.
2. A bath solution is made from the leaves of *Argemone mexicana*
   (*bozo bo*). The lesions are washed with this solution and a portion
   of the solution drunk.
3. The patient bathes each day in a solution made from the leaves of
   Daniellia oliveri (*sata*).

Trachoma

Trachoma is a major problem in the dry sahelian parts of Africa and
in North Africa. Effective treatment is available from modern Western
medicine. Left untreated, the disease causes scarring and deformity of the
eyelids and can eventually lead to blindness. The Bambara use ophthalmologic drops consisting of a solution made from the leaves of *Polygala
arenaria* (*ntuka ku*). These drops are placed in the eyes each day. This
remedy is not successful, judging from the results I have seen in several
patients who used it.

Schistosomiasis

Schistosomiasis or bilharziasis is a disease caused by several
species of small flatworms which inhabit the blood vessels of the urinary
bladder or intestinal tract. The disease is contracted when people step into
contaminated rivers, streams, and ponds where a form of the parasite is
found. The parasite invades the skin, migrates through the body, and
matures in the blood vessels where eggs are produced after several
months. Depending on the species involved, the eggs are passed mainly
with the urine or the feces. *Schistosoma hematobium* eggs pass out in the
urine, and one of the earliest signs of the disease is bloody urination. The
eggs of *Schistosoma mansoni* are passed out in the feces, but many also
end up in the liver where they create scarring and extensive damage. It is
common practice for people in Africa to defecate and urinate in rivers and
lakes. In so doing, they pass the eggs of these parasites into the water
where they hatch. The organisms then invade a snail host, multiply and
exist, ready to infect a new human host.

Schistosomiasis is a serious health problem along Africa's major
river systems and wherever new irrigation schemes have been developed.
Mild infections often do not cause symptoms and are not recognized. Even
heavy infections of *Schistosoma mansoni* may go unnoticed. The principal

symptom of *Schistosoma hematobium* infection is bloody urine and this is treated by many ethnic groups.

The following are some of the remedies used by the Bambara for treating urinary schistosomiasis:

1. The bark of the tamarind tree, *Tamarindus indica* (*n'tomi*) is soaked in water and then drunk.
2. The leaves of *Argemone mexicana* (*bozo bo*) are boiled in water and drunk.
3. The leaves and flowers of *Cymbopogon giganteus* (*tiekala*) are boiled in water and drunk.

Intestinal Worms

Tapeworm infections due to *Taenia saginata* are very common in Africa since poorly-cooked beef is frequently consumed. *Taenia solium* from pork is also found, but is less common since pork is not frequently consumed in many areas. People are aware that they are infected when they observe the segments of the tapeworm in the feces. Some of the remedies used for tapeworm are also used for other intestinal worms such as *Ascaris lumbricoides* (*roundworm*) and *Enterobius vermicularis* (*pinworm*). Many of the remedies employed are purgatives, the intent being to purge the parasites out of the intestinal tract. Some of these are symptomatically effective against tapeworm, since they cause the lower portion to break off and be expelled; but the head end remains attached to the patient's intestines. It then requires several months for the worm to grow again to the point where segments are again passed in the stools. In the interim, the patient believes himself cured. Occassionally, violent purges cause dislodgement of the attachment head mechanism of the worm and the entire worm is expelled with cure resulting.

Some of these folk remedies are extremely dangerous when given to patients with *Ascaris* infections. They irritate the worms and cause them to migrate. In so doing, they may move into the patient's common bile duct and cause obstruction, or they may form into a bolus and obstruct the small intestine. The latter is not an uncommon complication of heavy *Ascaris* infections even when drugs are not given.

The following are some of the commonly used remedies for tapeworm infections:

1. A solution is made from the roots of *Cassia sieberiana* (*sindian*) and *Afrormosia laxiflora* (*kolokolo*). This is drunk early in the morning on an empty stomach.
2. A solution is made from the leaves of *Ekebergia senegalensis* (*Kusse*) and drunk.
3. The leaves of *Celosia trigyna* (*dotou*) are crushed and boiled in water. The solution is then drunk.

For Ascaris infections the following are used:

1. A solution is made from the leaves of *Annona senegalensis* (*ndanga*) and the leaves of *Scoparia dulcis* (*timitemini*). This is drunk.
2. The leaves and roots of *Opilia celtidifolia* (*koro ngoy*) are boiled in water and the solution drunk.
3. The roots of *Trichilia prieureana* (*ka lubudan*) are pulverized and mixed in water. The solution is then drunk, causing a severe purge.

References

Hewat, M.L. 1906. *Bantu Folk Lore*. Cape Town: T. Maskew Miller.

Imperato, P.J. 1971. Incidence of and Local Beliefs about Onchocerciasis in the Senegal River Basin. *Tropical and Geographical Medicine* 23(4):385-389.

Imperato, P.J. 1975. *A Wind in Africa*. St. Louis: Warren H. Green.

Imperato, P.J. and Traore, D.A. 1968. Traditional Beliefs about Smallpox and Its Treatment among the Bambara of Mali. *Journal of Tropical Medicine and Hygiene* 71:224-228.

McKelvey, J.J. 1973. *Man against Tsetse*. Ithaca: Cornell University Press.

Traore, D.A. 1965. *Médecine et Magie Africaine*. Paris: Présénce Africaine.

13

Chronic Diseases

The high incidence of the acute communicable disease in Africa has overshadowed the chronic disease problems. It is uncommon for any comments to be made about these chronic conditions when the major health problems of African countries are being discussed. Yet these conditions affect large numbers of individuals causing considerable morbidity and mortality. Some, such as hypertension, are relatively asymptomatic for years in most patients and are unknown to Africans in a traditional setting. It was once thought that hypertension was rare in Africa, but in recent years large numbers of studies have shown it to be a fairly common disease. Likewise, peptic ulcer was once thought to be rare, but it is now known that it is fairly common, even in rural areas. Its symptoms are understandably confused by many Africans with other gastrointestinal disorders.

Diabetes mellitus is fairly common, there being variations in prevalence from one area to another (Imperato *et al.* 1976). It is recognized only late in the disease state when polyphagia, polydipsia, polyuria, and extreme wasting occur. Mild cases are not recognized by other patients or traditional healers. Chronic osteoarthritis and rheumatoid arthritis are especially common among the elderly. Their most frequent complaint is either chronic low back pain or joint pain. Goiter due to iodine deficiency is also common in some areas. There are a number of remedies employed for treating it, many of them magical in nature.

Diabetes Mellitus

A number of carefully conducted surveys in different parts of Africa have demonstrated that diabetes mellitus is by no means rare. The data obtained thus far show some differences in age distribution patterns and the types and severity of complications, but it is too soon to draw definitive conclusions about these characteristics. A recent survey of 297 adults from three different socio-economic backgrounds in Mali, showed that 1.4 percent were diabetic and another 8.4 percent probably diabetic (Imperato et al. 1976). The majority of these individuals were asymptomatic and so sought no treatment for their disease.

Clinical cases of diabetes mellitus are not managed with much success by traditional healers. The Bambara use a few herbal infusions, which in my experience exert no influence on the course of the disease. The commonest remedy used by them is an infusion of the bark and leaves of *Sclerocarya birrea* (*n'kuna*). There is some clinical evidence that this drug is a hypoglycemic agent since patients often develop clinical signs and symptoms of hypoglycemia. Its active ingredients and mode of action have yet to be studied.

Goiter

Many of the remedies employed for treating goiter are magical and not herbal. Many Bambara with this condition frequent a well which was formed when a meteor fell near Fana in central Mali in the 1950's. This well, which is considered sacred, is a pilgrimage site for a wide variety of reasons. Patients with goiter obtain some mud from the bottom of the well and smear it over the goiter.

Superficial scarifications are made on the skin overlying a goiter and herbal or mineral preparations sprinkled in them. Talismans consisting of reptile skin or sinew are worn around the neck in the belief they will cause the goiter to disappear. Some Bambara use the leaves of *Balanites aegyptiaca* (*segene*). These are dried and pulverized and then eaten. In my experience, none of these treatments are successful. Young girls and boys living near modern medical facilities, who begin to develop goiters often request treatment with iodine solution, being aware of its efficacy.

Arthritic Conditions

Both chronic osteoarthritis and rheumatoid arthritis are very common in Africa. There are many remedies which are employed, most of them being applied to the surface of the painful joint. The remedies used to treat low back pain are often different from those used for arthritic symptoms in other joints. The Bambara use the following remedies for arthritic symptoms in joints of the extremities.

1. The leaves of *Annona senegalensis* are boiled in water and the solution applied externally to the joint.
2. Shea butter is mixed with pulverized leaves and bark of *Annona senegalensis*. The paste is then applied to the surface of the joint.
3. The leaves of *Ficus thonningii* (*toro*) are tied together in a bundle and heated in water. The packet is then rubbed over the surface of the joint.
4. The leaves of *Carapa procera* (*kobi*) are boiled in water. The joint is soaked in the solution.

Hewat (1906) observed that in South Africa cow dung poultices were applied to the painful joint. *Salix capensis*, the Cape River willow, was also used, the leaves being boiled in water and the solution drunk. Hewat reports that this solution had analgesic effects and provided symptomatic relief.

A number of remedies are used by the Bambara for treating lumbago or low back pain. Often the area is scarified with three small parallel incisions and herbal preparations placed in them. A commonly employed remedy is the rubbing of the oil obtained from the leaves of *Carapa procera* (*kobi*) into the skin over the lower back. The charcoal obtained from burning a number of woods is often mixed with shea butter. The healer then makes three or four parallel lines over the lower back with his finger after dipping it into this paste.

Many of the treatments employed are magical and include the use of animal tissues, such as lizard intestines, hyena brains, fish skin, and chicken feces. Great attention is paid to how these products are applied, the time of day and the position of the patient. Symptomatic relief of a temporary nature is claimed by many who use these remedies. Others state that they have no effect whatever.

References

Hewat, M.L. 1906. Bantu Folk Lore. Cape Town: T. Maskew Miller.
Imperato, P.J., Handelsman, M.B., Fofana, B. and Sow, O. 1976. The Prevalence Diabetes Mellitus in Three Population Groups in Mali, *Transactions of The Royal Society of Tropical Medicine and Hygiene* 70:155-158.

14

Smallpox and Variolation

Variolation is the purposeful inoculation of smallpox virus into the skin to produce immunity against smallpox. It is an age-old practice probably first used in China centuries ago.

An alternative immunizing procedure against smallpox is vaccination, first developed about 1790 in England by Edward Jenner after he observed that people who had recovered from cowpox did not become infected with smallpox. The virus of cowpox, rather than that of smallpox, is used in the vaccination procedure. In man, cowpox is a relatively mild disease. Vaccination, when successful, results in the development of a temporary local cowpox lesion (which, like variolation, leaves a scar) and provides immunity against smallpox. It is safer than variolation because the virus used is not generally dangerous to man, and also because vaccination cannot result in the spread of smallpox from the vaccinated patient to other people.

In the case of variolation, there is a dual danger. The inoculated individual may develop a serious, or even fatal, smallpox infection as a result of the variolation; the smallpox virus may spread from his smallpox lesion, even if it is only a localized one, and cause smallpox infections in other susceptible individuals.

Variolation first became known in western Europe in the early 18th century. In England the first reports appeared in 1700 when Dr. Clopton Havers described the practice in China to the Royal Society of London. That same year, Joseph Lister, a British trader in Peking working for the East India Company, wrote to Dr. Martin Lister, a Fellow of the Royal Society, describing the practice. Shortly thereafter, reports on the practice were

Parts of this chapter were previously published in *Tropical and Geographical Medicine*, 1975, 27:211-221. I acknowledge with thanks the permission of the editors to use this material here.

made by many Europeans, describing variolation as practiced in the Near and Far East. Contrary to popular belief, the son of the British Ambassador to Constantinople, Edward Wortley Montague, was not the first English child to be variolated. The two sons of the secretary to the previous ambassador had been variolated some time in 1716, two years before the well-known Montague case. Five years later, in 1721, Lady Mary Wortley Montague had her daughter variolated in England by a Scottish surgeon, Charles Maitland. Two years previously the first smallpox inoculations had been made in Paris (Miller 1953).

History of Variolation in Africa

The earliest known report of variolation in West Africa was provided by Cotton Mather, who introduced it into the American colonies. He learned of the practice from his African slave, Onisemus, in 1716 (Kittredge 1911). Mather further documented the practice by interviewing other African slaves in America and resolved to try it, well before the Montague report from Constantinople became known. Cadwallader Colden of New York, in writing to Dr. John Fothergill in 1753, explained why knowledge of variolation had not been gained sooner from African slaves, even though they had been in the colonies for almost a century (Colden, 1753).

> It is not to be wondered at, since we seldom converse with our negroes, especially with those who were not born among us: and though I learned this but lately when the smallpox was among us last spring, by some discourse being accidentally overheard among the negroes themselves, I have had the same negroes above 20 years about my house, without knowing it before this time.

Mungo Park, the noted British explorer (and physician) who traveled through much of present day Senegal, Gambia, and Mali in the late 18th century, recorded the existence of variolation in Gambia. Park (1907) states that ''the Negroes on the Gambia practice inoculation,'' and that smallpox epidemics occasionally occurred. At about the same time David Bruce, the Scottish explorer, described variolation in Sennar in what is now southern Sudan. He states that during smallpox epidemics people sought out a child with the disease and wrapped a piece of cloth around an infected arm. They then bargained with the mother about the number of pocks she would sell. The bargain concluded and the money exchanged, the cloth would be removed and wrapped around the arm of the healthy child for whom it was intended. (This variation of inoculation was not uncommon in rural Europe, as well.) Although the skin was not purposely broken, virus often entered anyway, through minute scratches and abrasions.

Denham, an early explorer who visited northern Nigeria, observed variolation in Kukawa in 1823 near Lake Chad (Bovill 1958). He wrote, "They are not ignorant of inoculation, and it is performed nearly in the same manner as amongst ourselves by inserting the sharp point of a dagger, charged with the disease."

Heinrich Barth, the renown German explorer who visited much of what is now Niger, northern Nigeria, and eastern Mali between 1849 and 1855, recorded the existence of variolation in Bornu and Kanuri in Nigeria (Barth 1857).

In the late 19th century, Robert Felkin, a medical missionary in Uganda, reported that variolation was common in the southern Sudan. The inoculum was placed in the skin over the left breast (Wilson and Felkin 1882). Richard Burton who vividly described the ravages of smallpox in East Africa and the eastern Congo basin, reported that the Arabs had introduced variolation and that the current technique was to introduce smallpox pus into an incision on the forehead between the eyebrows (Burton 1860).

David Livingstone has left a graphic description of inoculation among the Bechuana of South Africa (Livingstone 1858).

> For smallpox, the natives employed in some parts, inoculation on the forehead with some animal deposit; in other parts, they employed with the matter of the smallpox itself and in one village they seem to have selected a virulent case for the matter used in the operation, for nearly all the village was swept off by the disease in a malignant confluent form. Where the idea came from, I cannot conceive.

He observed, as this description relates, that the use of material from a severe case resulted in serious disease in those variolated, a fact that had been well-known in Europe since the practice first became common. Generally material was taken from mild cases of smallpox, so it is perplexing that the Bechuana at Livingstone's time used material from severe cases.

During this century, Scott (1960) described variolation in northern Ghana in the early 1900's; Rosenwald (1953) reported on variolation in Tanganyika during epidemic situations; Glokpor (1969) described it in Togo and Dahomey; and Imperato (1975) reported on it among the Songhoi people of the middle Niger. Although variolation was commonly practiced in West Africa in recent years, there is a paucity of documentation of the techniques employed. Colonial medical records in Africa show that medical authorities were aware of the practice, but were more preoccupied with its legal prohibition than with a study of its techniques and results (Gallay 1910). In many colonies and territories, laws were enacted to prohibit the practice. Whether such legislation had the desired effect is doubtful as evidenced by the use of variolation until recently. However, it made variolation a clandestine activity. The British outlawed the Shopana cult in 1917 in Nigeria on the grounds that its priests purposely spread smallpox. This cult is not only concerned with smallpox, but also with a number of other illnesses, including mental illness. (See pp. 99 and 171.) In spite of the ban, the cult has continued to function quite actively on a clandestine basis.

The reasons for such legal prohibitions were not as obvious to the indigenous population as to the administrators who promulgated them. Although the early colonial period witnessed the widespread use of liquid vaccines made from cowpox virus, such vaccines often were subjected to extremely hot ambient temperatures and difficult handling in the bush, and as a result were often inactivated before use and failed to produce immunity against smallpox (Gallay 1910). Assessments of reactions often demonstrated fewer than 20 percent positive. Frequently outbreaks of smallpox occurred in previously vaccinated populations. As a result, the idea gradually took root that variolation protected against smallpox more effectively than vaccination. This was a logical belief considering that most people who were successfully variolated never contracted smallpox, whereas those who were vaccinated often did. It was not until the last decade with the use of heat stable lypholised vaccines made with cowpox that this belief began to change.

Variolation in Mali

A study of variolation was carried out among the sedentary agricultural peoples and the nomadic Peul and Tuareg herdsmen of Mali during the five year period 1966-1971, employing three methods for the collection of information (Imperato 1974). The first was an interview survey which included three types of informants: 24 Bambara who had practiced variolation (variolators); 186 persons who had been variolated; and 237 persons who had witnessed variolation being performed. Secondly, direct observations were made on 129 individuals who were variolated during outbreaks in 1967 and 1968. Thirdly, data were gathered from the concurrent and terminal assessment programs of the national smallpox eradication campaign. During this operation, random samples were taken of sedentary and nomadic populations. These populations were examined for the presence of smallpox, and for variolation and vaccination scars.

During the course of the study information was collected from all of the major ethnic groups in the country. The purpose of the study was to obtain as much documentation of smallpox immunization practices as possible.

The Interview Survey

In the interview survey the majority of variolators (75 percent) were above 45 years of age. Of those who had witnessed variolation, 79.1 percent were over 30 years of age. Of those who had witnessed variolation, 78.2 percent had seen it performed more than ten years previously and 27.8 percent within the last ten years. Of those who had been variolated, 72.6 percent were above 30 years of age.

During the interview survey information was solicited concerning attitudes and beliefs about the dangers and effectiveness of variolation, and about variolation techniques which were familiar to the people interviewed. When asked whether variolation could result in smallpox, the majority of adults correctly replied affirmatively. Children 0–14 years of age either did not know or else had no opinion on the matter. Among the 334 adults who replied affirmatively to this question, 287 (85.9 percent) stated that whenever smallpox resulted from variolation it was usually mild. The majority of adults above 30 years of age believed (incorrectly) that the variolation reaction could not cause clinical smallpox in contacts. However, 31.2 percent of young adults in the 15–29 year age group understood this could occur. The majority of adults above 30 years of age thought variolation better than or at least equal to vaccination in terms of overall effectiveness and desirability. The majority of young adults, 15–29 years of age, thought vaccination preferable.

The various variolation techniques described during the interview survey are presented in the table below. Differences in anatomical site, type of inoculation, and variolation technique exist not only between the various ethnic groups, but also within given groups. With the exception of two groups, the Tuareg nomads of the Sahara and the Bobo-Oule agriculturists of central Mali, all groups exclusively used fluid from the blister-like smallpox vesicles. While the Tuareg and Bobo-Oule did use vesicular fluid, they also used scab material.

In general, variolation has been infrequently practiced in recent years by those ethnic groups, namely, the Bambara and Kassonke, who had regular contact with mobile and stationary health services. The most recent documentation of variolation among these people dates from 1959 when it was practiced by a blacksmith during a smallpox epidemic in the Kolokani District. The recipients' skins were first burned with a hot poker and allowed to cool before the vesicular fluid was rubbed in with a thorn. Eyewitnesses stated that shortly after variolation many people came down with smallpox (Marcoux 1967). The possible exposure of some or even all of

VARIOLATION TECHNIQUES USED BY VARIOUS ETHNIC GROUPS IN MALI

Ethnic Group	Instruments	Material Used for Variolating	Site of Variolation	Variolators
Bambara	Thorn Hot Rod	Vesicular Fluid	Deltoid area Upper extensor surface of forearm	Old Men Blacksmiths
Bozo	Hot Iron Iron Stick Knife	Vesicular Fluid	Upper extensor surface of forearm	Old Men and Women Bela Blacksmiths
Bobo-Oule	Thorn Knife Iron Rod Feathers	Vesicular Fluid Scabs	Dorsum of wrist	Old Men Heads of Families
Dogon	Thorn Knife Feathers	Vesicular Fluid	Periumbilical area Upper extensor surface of forearm	Old Men and Women
Kassonke	Iron Rod Feathers	Vesicular Fluid	Below the knee	Blacksmiths
Minianka	Iron Rod Knife	Vesicular Fluid	Extensor surface of mid-forearm	Old Men
Peul	Thorn Bird Feathers Iron Rod Knife	Vesicular Fluid	Deltoid area Forehead Extensor surface of mid-forearm Axilla	Blacksmiths Old Men
Songhai	Thorn Knife Feathers	Vesicular Fluid	Below the knee Deltoid area	Old Men and Women Blacksmiths
Tuareg	Knife Thorn	Vesicular Fluid Scabs	Axilla Forehead Extensor surface of mid and upper forearm Lateral aspect of knee Shoulder	Old Men Blacksmiths Marabouts

these people to infective cases make it difficult to ascribe a causative role to variolation. Other reports of variolation in the Bambara country describe the almost exclusive use of thorns and vesicular fluid without preliminary burning of the inoculation site.

The Bozo, who are itinerant fisherman in the area of the Niger bend, practiced variolation until quite recently. During a smallpox epidemic in early 1967 several hundred people were variolated in the Mopti region by blacksmiths.

The Bobo-Oule used both vesicular and scab material. Their preferred inoculation sites were either the dorsum or the ventrum of the wrist (see photograph).

The Bobo-Oule are a strongly traditional sedentary society who continued to practice variolation in times of epidemics until the present decade. They have strongly resisted being vaccinated during recent mass vaccination campaigns. In times of smallpox epidemics visitors from

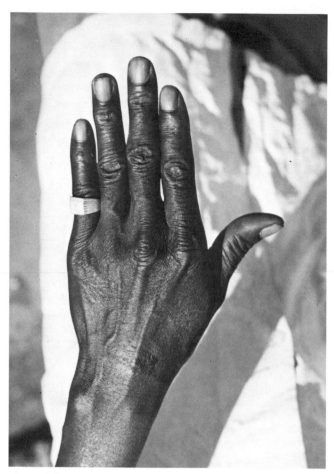

*A variolation scar on the wrist of a Bambara man,
central Bambara country.*

neighboring villages were often examined for a variolation scar before
being permitted to stay. This was done when the visitor arrived and
performed the traditional handshake. The hand was turned over several
times and the wrist examined in the process. The same custom is observed
by the Peul nomads of the same region. It is interesting to speculate about
the influence of this traditional scar assessment process on the choice of a
conspicuous inoculation site.

     Like the Bobo-Oule, the Dogon are a strongly traditional society
among whom variolation continued to be employed in times of outbreaks.
Until quite recently, there were local variations in the inoculation site and
the instruments used.

The Peul pastoralists of the savannah used a variety of sites for inoculation, among them the forehead. The most frequently used site was the extensor surface of the mid-forearm. Vesicular fluid was taken from a mild clinical case of smallpox. The Tuareg nomads of the Sahara have continued to practice variolation until this decade. The actual variolation procedure among these people was performed by their serfs, the Bela. Occasionally old men and marabouts variolated. The Tuareg occasionally employed vesicular fluid and scab material taken from someone's variolation reaction instead of from someone with smallpox.

Direct Observations of Variolated Individuals

In 1967 periodic observations were made on 120 variolated individuals in eastern Mali (Imperato 1968). Twenty-two (18.3 percent) of these people subsequently developed clinical smallpox. The disease in all of these was mild, characterized by a rash composed of discrete lesions. There was no mortality associated with the illness. In 1968, periodic observations were made on nine individuals who had been variolated during an outbreak in central Mali. All of these people subsequently developed smallpox which was clinically mild, and there was no mortality associated with these cases. In the 1967 outbreak the variolation technique used consisted of the application of vesicular fluid with either a thorn or a bird feather to a small round area of 5 mm. diameter on the deltoid area of the arm or the lateral aspect of the leg just below the knee. There was very little tissue destruction associated with this technique and the inoculum was small. When these cases were first seen they were already in the papular stage of their illness. The variolation sites did not show any signs of secondary infection. In 1968 the technique consisted of the application of a large inoculum with a bird feather onto three parallel incisions, each three centimeters long, which had been made on the dorsum of the wrist with a knife. When first examined these cases were already in the desquamation stage of their illness. Seven of the nine variolation sites showed evidence of secondary infection. In both outbreaks all of those who had been variolated and who then developed clinical smallpox had had contact with smallpox cases during the weeks preceding their own illness; therefore, it was not possible to say that their illness was variolation-induced smallpox. All of the 129 observed persons went on to uneventful recovery with no sequelae other than pock marks and variolation scars.

Data Gathered in Assessment Programs

An assessment program was carried out in central Mali between 1967 and 1969. Sedentary villages and nomad camps were randomly chosen as were the compounds and tents within them. The Bambara, who are the largest group in the country, numbering 1.5 million (25 percent of Mali's population), are a sedentary agricultural people who have had many decades of contact with mobile and fixed medical services. Of the 2,068 Bambara people examined, only 3 (0.1 percent) had visible variolation scars. All of these scars were found in persons over 45 years of age. In contrast to this, 19 of 1,188 nomads (1.6 percent) examined had variolation scars. The age distribution of these scars were similar to the age distribution of the nomadic Malian population, indicating that the practice was still current.

Discussion of Variolation

As in many parts of the world, variolation developed in West Africa in response to man's desire to control outbreaks of smallpox. Historically, the practice in Mali was limited to outbreak situations. It survived until quite recently among those ethnic groups whose pattern of life, geographic isolation and/or ties to a traditional culture base kept them from exposure to modern medical practices as well as from the currents of social and economic change sweeping Africa. As the interview survey shows, there are generation differences in attitudes towards variolation and vaccination, reflecting the exposure of the younger generations to education and to modern medical concepts and practices. The data from the interview survey demonstrate that there has been a gradual abandonment of variolation practices. The preference of the older age groups for variolation over vaccination may seem at first sight incompatible with their admission that variolation can result in smallpox. Although there was an awareness among adults that variolation could result in clinical smallpox, there was little awareness among those over 30 years of age that the variolation reaction was infective and could spread the infection among other susceptible people. The development of inoculation-smallpox is not viewed with concern by most adults, an attitude based on their empirical observations that most cases are mild. In many areas variolation is referred to in the local languages as "indigenous vaccination."

All of the variolators were in the older age group. Variolators are either elder members of the village community, heads of families, blacksmiths of the same or different tribal groups, and rarely *marabouts*. Some old men and women have gained respected reputations for their skill in variolating. This stemmed from the empirical observation that those they variolate develop neither inoculation-smallpox nor the natural disease after they have been variolated. The task of variolating was always delegated to the very old, the belief being widespread in this part of Africa that the achievement of old age represents the successful passage through all known killing contagious diseases. Thus the old are thought of as being able to variolate with impunity. This is a fairly accurate observation; most old people have either had smallpox, have been variolated or have been successfully vaccinated. People who variolate are not˙recognized as *variolators*. Rather they are considered as the people who in time of need are capable of inoculating. Even those who gain good reputations for their variolating skill are never thought of as meriting the title of *variolator*. Blacksmiths in most societies in the western Sudan are also magicians, the carvers of fetish statues and masks, and the barber-surgeons. They are often called upon to perform a number of surgical procedures. In many instances where they participate in the variolating procedure they simply prepare the skin by either burning or cutting it. Someone else actually deposits the inoculum into the wound.

While large fees were once charged for variolating, in most instances it is done gratuitously today. Among the Songhai and Peul fees are charged, half going to the variolator and the other half to the donor of the vesicular fluid. The fee is about ten American cents. Among the Tuaregs of eastern Mali, entire camps are often variolated at once, the fee for this being a goat or sheep.

The large variety of techniques and inoculation sites used in this limited area of Africa is indeed impressive. Scott (1960) reported that in Ghana, variolation was performed by the insufflation of dried and powdered scab material. This has not been observed in Mali. Glokpor (1969) has reported on the use of powdered scab material in Togo and Dahomey, variolation being performed by ''healers'' who scarify the forehead and rub the desicated scab material onto the forehead or underside of the wrist.

Variolation among the Yoruba of Nigeria is associated with the cult of *Shopana*, the smallpox goddess. (See above.) The fetish priests of this cult are said to preserve smallpox scabs for long periods of time and can at will initiate smallpox outbreaks through variolation or other means. Similarly in Dahomey, fetish priests care for active cases of smallpox and conduct ceremonies during which the friends and relatives of the patient are variolated on the forehead (Glokpor 1969). This variolation ceremony is performed about four weeks after the onset of the illness when the patient is considered healed.

A great obstacle to discouraging the practice of variolation in Dahomey and among the Yoruba of Nigeria is its association with secret cults, the leaders of which are entrusted with the care of smallpox victims. If the victims die, these healers are entitled to take possession of the personal estate of the deceased. Therefore, it is not in their interest to see smallpox victims survive nor smallpox eradicated. Glokpor reports that a majority of these healers are aware of the consequences of variolation but that for personal gain they continue the practice. However, there is much about the Shopana cult which is not known and it appears that it has perhaps been unjustifiably maligned. In contrast to Togo, Dahomey, and Nigeria, variolation in Mali is not performed by the priests of secret cults as part of sacred ritual.

Variolation poses serious dangers both for those variolated and the community as a whole. Because smallpox virus can survive in scab material for several months, the collecting and preserving of this material constitutes a danger to those susceptibles who may have contact with it. Once these scabs are pulverized into powder, the danger is augmented since the infective material can be carried by the wind. In the absence of clinical cases of smallpox, there exists in effect a reserve of virus in the hands of healers and fetish priests.

Dixon (1962) states, on the basis of analysis of reports on variolation in England in the 18th century, that the development of clinical smallpox from variolation practices was directly related to the technique used. With good technique in which there is a minimum of tissue damage, the smallpox virus replicates at the inoculation site and stimulates antibodies and does not cause systemic infection. Dixon goes on to explain that with extensive deep skin trauma and secondary infection at the variolation site, local response is poor and systemic spread of the virus occurs, leading to clinical smallpox.[1]

During the present study it has not been possible to determine the percentage of those variolated who developed inoculation smallpox. This is because variolation was undertaken during epidemics among people who had known contact with smallpox cases. Although it has been possible to discern how many of those variolated subsequently developed smallpox, some or even all may have developed natural smallpox from contact with infective cases. In 1967 observations in Mali made on 120 variolated individuals in eastern Mali revealed that 22 (18.3 percent) of these people subsequently developed mild clinical smallpox. Among 519 unvaccinated— unvariolated persons in the same village, 65 (12.5 percent) developed smallpox. While more variolated individuals developed smallpox than those not variolated, it must be remembered that they were also a higher risk group, having known contact histories. The technique consisted of the

---

[1]Dr. James Juring and Dr. John Gasper Scheuchzer analyzed the results of variolation practiced in the British Isles, America, and Hanover during the period 1721-1728. During this period 897 individuals were variolated. Of these 845 (94.2 percent) developed severe clinical smallpox after inoculation, 13 (1.6 percent) developed mild smallpox, and 39 (4.2 percent) did not develop smallpox. Of the 845 who developed severe smallpox, 17 (2.0 percent) died. The interpretation of these data is difficult because of the possible exposure of those variolated to active smallpox cases.

inoculation just below the knee of vesicular fluid from a mild case. The inoculum covered a skin area about 5 mm. wide.

The nine variolated individuals observed in central Mali in 1968 also had known contact histories with smallpox cases. Variolation was performed on the dorsum of the wrist using a bird plume. Vesicular fluid was applied over 3 cm. long scratch marks with a knife. In comparison with the first observation made in 1967, the technique in this instance was poorer, a larger area being scarified and a larger inoculum being used. Unlike the technique documented in 1967, herbs and feces were placed over the

Lesions on the head of a child following smallpox vaccination on the arm. (Such lesions may occur if a child touches the vaccination site on the arm and then touches another part of the body.) Four amulets (tafo) are suspended from a cord. The sac on the left contains herbs, while the three others contain verses from the Koran written in Arabic on small pieces of paper. The amulet on the left is the one used frequently by the traditional non-Moslem Bambara. All consist of leather sacs.

inoculation site and secondary infection occurred. All of those variolated later developed clinical smallpox. While the data obtained from these observations is statistically limited, it nonetheless does lend support to what has been previously documented about the relationship between variolation technique and the development of subsequent inoculation smallpox.

Variolated individuals may infect susceptible contacts in the community and initiate outbreaks and epidemics. Individuals with variolation reactions or with mild inoculation-smallpox are not isolated, as is traditionally done by most ethnic groups with smallpox cases. Conditions, therefore, are favorable for the spread of the disease from variolated individuals to susceptibles.

The passage of laws against a traditional practice such as variolation is not likely to have much of an effect in discouraging people from performing it. In the past the health education effort of effective vaccination programs has led to an eventual abandonment of the practice. In those parts of West Africa, such as in Togo and Dahomey, where variolation is an occult practice associated with secret initiation societies, the task is obviously more difficult.

Of the two nomadic groups assessed, the Tuareg had the higher proportion of variolation scars (3.8 percent) compared to 0.7 percent for the Peul. Both of these groups showed a higher proportion of smallpox scars, and a lower proportion of vaccination scars than the sedentary population. Both the Tuareg and Peul, especially the former, have had a paucity of contact with both mobile and fixed medical services. Both are independent and self-reliant and tend to avoid contact with administrative authorities. Their traditional view of government-sponsored medical programs is that they are aimed at better administrative control, an unacceptable concept to a people who see themselves as a separate independent group conducting relations with government in the spirit of an equal. They are also a proud people. Well-intentioned government attempts at setting up assembly points for health services have been unsuccessful because the view of the Tuaregs and Peuls that the person summoned is of slightly less elevated status than those he visits; thus the programs offend them. The topographic harshness of the terrain in which nomads live and their complex system of seasonal movement have posed additional obstacles to the delivery of basic preventive and curative health services. Only recently have vaccination programs succeeded in reaching large members of these people through innovative approaches (Imperato et al. 1975).

There are now great hopes that smallpox will be eradicated from the globe within this decade (Imperato 1975). Routine smallpox vaccination for Americans is no longer advised and vaccination certificates for international travel to certain areas no longer required. Before such optimism many might be tempted to think of variolation as an historical curiosity, long out of fashion, but variolation was still being practiced actively in West Africa until a few years ago. The absence of reported smallpox from West Africa recently holds up the hope that variolation may indeed disappear into the historical past in this part of the world.

References

Barth, H. 1857. *Travels and Discoveries in North and Central Africa*, 1849-1855. London: Longmans Green and Co.
Bovill, E.W. 1958. *The Golden Trade of the Moors*. London: Oxford University Press.
Bruce, J. 1804. *Travels to Discover the Source of the Nile*. Edinburgh: Longman and Rees.
Burton, R. 1860. *The Lake Regions of Central Africa*. New York: Harper and Brothers.
Colden, C. 1753. "Extract of a Letter to Dr. Fothergill, Concerning the Throat Distemper," Society of Physicians in London, I.
Dixon, C.W. 1962. *Smallpox*. London: J. & A. Churchill, Ltd.
Gallay, L. 1910. *Trois Années d'Assistance Medicale et de Lutte Contre la Variole*. Paris: Larose.
Glokpor, G.F. 1969. Seminar on Smallpox Eradication and Measles Control in Western and Central Africa, Proceedings of a Meeting Held in Lagos, Nigeria, May 13–20, 1969. Atlanta: Center for Disease Control, U.S. Department of Health, Education and Welfare.
Havers, C. 1700. *Journal Book*, IX, Royal Society Library.
Imperato, P.J. 1968. The Practice of Variolation among the Songhoi of Mali, *Transactions of The Royal Society of Tropical Medicine and Hygiene*, 62(6): 868-873.
Imperato, P.J. 1974. Observations on Variolation Practices in Mali, *Tropical and Geographical Medicine* 26:429-440.
Imperato, P.J. 1975. The Dubious Gamble against Smallpox, *Natural History* 94(7):8-18.
Imperato, P.J., Fofana, B. and Sow, O. 1975. Strategie et Tactique pour la Vaccination des Populations du Delta Interieur du Niger, *Afrique Medicale* 14(129): 307-316.
Kittredge, G.L. 1911. "Some Last Works of Cotton Mather," *Proceedings of The Massachusetts Historical Society*, Vol. XLV.
Lister, J. 1700 *Lister MSS* 37, folder 15, Bodleian Library, Oxford.
Livingstone, D. 1857. *Missionary Travels and Researches in South Africa*. Longon: John Murray.
Maclean, U.C. 1971. *Magical Medicine*. Long: Penguin.
Marcoux, P. 1967. Personal Communication.
Miller, G. 1953. *The Adoption of Inoculation for Smallpox in England and France*. Philadelphia: University Pennsylvania Press. pp. 45–69.
Park, M. 1907. *Travels in the Interior Districts of Africa—1775–1797*. New York: E.P. Dutton.
Rosenwald (1951) as cited by Dixon, C.W., (1962) *Smallpox*. London: J. & A. Churchill Ltd.
Schenchzer, J.G. 1729. *An Account of the Success of Inoculating the Smallpox in Great Britain for the Years 1727 and 1728*. London.
Scott, D. 1960. *Epidemic Disease in Ghana*. Oxford: Oxford University Press.
Wilson, C.T. and Felkin, R.W. 1882. *Uganda and the Egyptian Soudan*. London.

15

Traditional Surgery

High levels of surgical skills were developed over the centuries in some parts of Africa. The Bambara, however, did not develop surgical skills to a high degree so far as we know. It is certainly possible that individuals practiced sophisticated surgery in local areas at various times; but no established tradition of sophisticated surgery is known to have existed among the Bambara.

In other parts of Africa skillful surgery was generally practiced by a relatively small number of men who learned their techniques through a lengthy period of apprenticeship. One of the earliest and best documentations of high surgical skills was obtained by Dr. R. W. Felkin, an early missionary physician in Uganda. He observed a Cesarean section (described below) carried out with considerable technical skill in the latter part of the last century (Felkin 1884). Such medically trained travelers were few in Africa at that time. The majority of observations of surgical practices were made by laymen who most frequently observed the procedures of lesser-trained surgeons carrying out routine operations. Such reports and the paucity of observations of the work of highly trained surgeons have given the erroneous impression to many people that traditional African surgery was and is both primitive and mutilating (Davies 1965).

It is difficult to know how highly skilled surgery developed in Africa. Davies (1965) in studying surgery among the Banyoro of Uganda presents convincing arguments that such surgical skills developed in two ways. Firstly, surgeons could have learned both anatomy and technique while performing mutilations ordered by ruling chiefs and kings. Secondly, they could have learned a great deal from performing autopsies and postmortem examinations of undelivered mothers. Davies, in the light of his field researches in Uganda, believes that African surgeons could have acquired anatomical knowledge and surgical skill doing these procedures over a long period of apprenticeship. This knowledge was then used in performing abdominal and surgical procedures on living patients (Davies 1965; Roscoe 1921).

Native surgeons practiced in the Kingdom of Bunyoro, a stable state for many centuries and a feudal pastoral society whose economy was based on the plantain, *Musa paradisiaca*. Within an atmosphere of peace and tranquility and social stability, a high level of surgery developed and flourished. Because the Banyoro were a preliterate society, the tradition of their surgical skills had to be handed down orally. Generation transfer of these skills suffered a fatal blow during the latter half of the 19th century when a series of devastating armed conflicts occurred with the recently-arrived Europeans. In the social chaos which ensued, much of the surgical skill and knowledge was lost (Davies 1965).

It is probable that highly developed surgical skills existed in many other parts of Africa, but these were often not documented. Fairly effective management of fractures and dislocations has been widely documented, however, as has the incision and drainage of abscesses. We are less certain about abdominal and thoracic surgery except in a few areas. This does not mean that such operations were not performed, but only that Western observers never learned of them. Scarifying, cupping, circumcision of males and excision of females are still widely practiced and have been dependably recorded by many observers. Trephining of the skull has also been documented among the Kisii of Kenya (Imperato 1966).

Many surgical procedures such as circumcision, excision, and cicatrization (a procedure to encourage development of scars), are carried out as part of *rites de passage*. They are culturally different from procedures like abscess drainage and tumor excision, although the surgical skills required are at least somewhat similar. Whereas an abscess is drained to alleviate pain and heal a disease process, circumcision and scarification are performed in fulfillment of a social requirement. In another sense, the former are emergency procedures and the latter elective procedures.

Bambara Scarification

Scarifying the skin is performed for cosmetic reasons, as part of puberty rites, or for treating illness. The technique is essentially similar in all three cases. Cicatrization is a procedure where a variety of products, herbal or mineral, are rubbed into a scarified area. This creates a foreign-body reaction in the wound, with the production of *keloids* which are areas of heavy scar tissue formation. The end result is a hard elevated area of the skin which follows the outline of the original incision. Cicatrization is more often than not performed for cosmetic reasons.

Bambara surgeons use either knives or razors to scarify. Generally two or three parallel incisions are made over the area considered ill. These incisions range in length from a quarter of an inch to an inch in length. When scarification is carried out for medical reasons the incisions are made to the accompaniment of ritual incantations by healer-surgeons. There is a widespread belief that whatever nefarious agent is at work causing the illness is permitted to escape via the scarifications.

The Yoruba often rub medicines into the scarification sites, whereas the Hausa barber-surgeons do not (Maclean 1971). The latter, however, often sprinkle various powders over the sites to reduce bleeding, much the same as barbers in the Western world do when they nick a client with a razor. The introduction of herbal or mineral preparations into the wounds is viewed as being a direct way of getting at the illness. (Africans often are perplexed when in Western medicine a parentral injection is not made at the anatomic site where the pain is. A patient with pleurisy for example might be given an antibiotic intramuscularly in the buttocks or intravenously in the arm. From the viewpoint of traditional African medicine, it would be better if the drug were injected into the painful area of the chest.)

Bambara Cupping

Scarification with subsequent cupping is a common method of dealing with muscular and skeletal pains and headache. Joint sprains and accidental injury are also treated in this way, as are furuncles and boils of the skin. The usual method is for the surgeon to make a few superficial cuts in the skin overlying the affected area. He then takes a cow horn of the right size and places its wide end over the area. He sucks out the air through a hole in the tip of the horn. creating a vaccuum. Often, the surgeon keeps a piece of bee's wax in his mouth and places this over the hole in the horn, thus sealing the horn to maintain the vacuum. The horn is then left in place for up to a half hour. In Tanzania, I observed healers who placed a substance in their mouths before sucking on the horn. After sucking on the horn, they spit this out, telling the patient that it came out of the scarifications (Imperato 1964).

Cupping is a common practice in Africa. In West Africa, Hausa barber-surgeons enjoy a reputation for being expert at it. Even in countries to which the Hausa are not indigenous, they are highly regarded. In Bamako, Mali, they can be found around the great mosque, seated on straw mats. There they practice both barbering and minor surgery, including cupping. Although these Hausa barber-surgeons are peripheral to traditional medical care among the Bambara people, in Bamako they are an important source of care. (See photo, chap. 6.)

Among many groups, the profession of barbering and surgery is hereditary, passed on from one generation to another. Many of these barber-surgeons also treat fractures and dislocations. But among many ethnic groups there are special groups of some barber-surgeons who treat fractures and dislocations. Frequently, the skill is passed on from one generation to the next.

The Treatment of Fractures And Dislocations

In many areas of Africa traditional practitioners show a high level of skill in the management of fractures and dislocations. Results vary according to the type of fracture, the degree of displacement of the pieces of bone, and the skill of the surgeon. Simple fractures with no displacement of the bone fragments generally heal well provided the area is properly immobilized for a sufficient period of time. Compound fractures, in which the bone protrudes through the skin, are less satisfactorily treated by African surgeons.

The knitting of the broken edges of a bone is a major aim in the modern treatment of fractures, but so is the restoration of function. While traditional African surgeons are often successful at the former, they frequently fail at the latter. To restore normal function the broken bone must be reduced, that is the two or more pieces of bone must be manipulated so that their edges are properly aligned. In certain fractures, such as of the femur of the leg, the muscles tend to pull on the two pieces of bone so that they override. If the fracture heals in this condition, the patients will be left with a considerably shortened leg, a limp, and later side effects on his vertebral column.

In evaluating the success of African surgeons who treat fractures, one must consider what standard of success is used by African clientele. The highly regarded results obtained by some African surgeons might, by standards of Western medicine, be considered atrocious. When these Western standards are applied, one often finds that traditional bonesetters are not what they are reputed to be. An example of this is a woman bonesetter in Bamako who enjoys a reputation for great skill among the general population. The results which the general population are willing to accept are vastly different from those acceptable to Bamako's two hospitals. The general population also does not know of all the cases treated by this woman who find their way to the hospitals for correction of deformities and loss of function.

Where more effective treatment is available, it is difficult to make a strong case for traditional bonesetters. In rural areas where no other options are present, however, they fulfill an important need.

Hewat (1906) reported that Kaffir surgeons called *iggira eloku-qapula* were fairly expert at treating fractures. They reduced fractures by pulling on the limb and manipulating the two pieces back together. Once in position, the surgeons made small skin incisions over the fracture site and rubbed in the ashes gotten from burning certain roots. The limb was then bound with strips of the inner bark of the mimosa tree. Hewat observed that this made an excellent splint. Patients were also given some herbal preparations reputed to promote healing. Maclean (1971) reported that a Sabo postman in Nigeria, who was a recognized expert in setting fractures, used cardboard splints to immobilize limbs. Setting fractured bones is an ancient art among the Luo of Tanzania, but as a result of contact with scientific medicine methods of splinting have changed. Undoubtedly contact with mission and government hospitals has brought this about. Traditionally, fractures were treated with crude splints made of bark, heavy twigs, and sisal leaves, and kept immobilized for several weeks. Some healers still use this method, but most of them have adopted the use of a dung cast containing a moderate amount of clay, closely resembling the classical plaster cast which was no doubt the prototype. Before the cast was applied herbal mixtures were rubbed over the fracture site. As cement is readily available, this is occassionally added to the cast mixture creating difficulties when the time comes to remove the cast!

Luo bonesetters attempt the reduction and casting of most fractures, but not all. The majority would not attempt to treat a fractured clavicle, which is difficult to deal with, although recently one in the North Mara area specialized in clavicular fractures. The bandaging he applies closely resembled that used in modern surgical units, and I suspect that his knowledge was acquired at a hospital. Few attempt to treat a fractured hip, and none whom I observed would try to remove the fragments of a depressed skull fracture. Trephining of the skull is unknown to the Luo in spite of the fact that their Kenya neighbors, the Kisii, practiced it on rather a grand scale. Most Luo do not even seem to know that the Kisii trephined skulls, and I could find no satisfactory explanation for this.

A few jathieth (native doctors) restrict their practice to setting dislocated joints, and one of them near Utegi (in northern Tanzania) recently had a wide reputation for his skill. He would reduce most dislocations by a few quick maneuvers similar to those employed by qualified Western surgeons (Imperato 1966).

Among the Bambara fractures and dislocations are managed by families who possess the necessary skills which are passed from one generation to the next. Splints are similar to those described above, consisting of wrappings of bark and other firm materials. Fractures of fingers without displacement are often not splinted, but simply massaged. Limbs which are splinted are kept in splints from about three to six weeks, a sufficiently long period to permit healing of the fracture.

Treatment of Tumors and Abscesses

Superficial abscesses which can be seen or palpated are viewed as treatable. Once soft and moveable, they are incised and drained. Occasionally they are incised too early, resulting in a spread of the infection beyond its initial localized site. Tumors are generally not touched. Hewat (1906) recorded that in South Africa tumors were thought to be the result of witchcraft. The Bambara do not usually attempt to excise tumors surgically, but often futilely apply poultices made from a variety of herbs in an attempt to make them shrink.

Abdominal Surgery

In 1884, Dr. R.W. Felkin observed a Cesarean section among the Banyoro. The patient was first narcotized with herbal preparations. Bleeding vessels were cauterized with red hot irons, blood drained from the abdominal cavity, and after the uterus was cut open, the baby and placenta carefully removed. The incision in the uterus was now sutured together using iron spikes to which bark-cloth string was attached. The wound was then covered with pastes made from roots, a hot banana leaf, and finally a cloth bandage. The procedure described by Felkin is one which reveals a high level of skill and experience and a good knowledge of anatomy. It has been well established that abdominal surgery became highly developed in what is now Uganda (Davies 1965). It is probable that this skill also existed in other areas of Africa, although there is little precise documentation on this matter for most of Africa.

It is difficult to know what the final results of this type of surgery were. There are no valid follow up reports describing how well patients did. There are no data indicating which of the many possible post-operative complications developed and how often they occurred. What we do know is that considerable operative skill existed. Using local products, these early Uganda surgeons exhibited meticulous care in handling tissues and paid careful attention to small technical details (Davies 1965).

Trephination

Trephination is an ancient surgical procedure in which a hole is made partly through the skull or through the entire thickness of the skull. The word is derived from the Greek *trypanon* meaning a "borer." The operation has been documented in many parts of the world and was very common in prehistoric times in Europe and in South America. Most authorities now believe that trephinations usually were (and are) undertaken for therapeutic reasons. There are a number of illnesses treated by trephination, fracture of the skull being the commonest (Nemeskeri et al. 1965). There is strong evidence that trephination was more common among peoples who employed smashing type weaponry as compared to those who used slashing and stabbing kinds (Moodie 1929; Ford 1937). Clubs are a commonly used weapon in East Africa and depressed skull fractures are frequently encountered. In West Africa, although clubs are used, they are not used so often as in East Africa. The Peul cattle nomads of West Africa carry spears, swords, knives, and clubs, but they rarely employ the latter in combat. When they do, they strike their enemies across the front of the lower portion of the legs. If they strike the head, they attempt to hit their victims across the occipital area (the base of the skull). From experience they know that a blow there will more likely have an immediate fatal result than one delivered elsewhere on the skull.

The sedentary agriculturists of West Africa do not employ clubs as their front-line weapons. In combat they are more likely to use swords, knives, and spears, in that order. This may explain why trephination is unknown in many areas of Africa.

The results of trephination are available to scientists through study of the skulls of both pre-historic and modern men. In most cases, healing can be seen around the edges of the holes. Since such healing requires a considerable time to occur, when it is found it clearly demonstrates that patients survived the surgical procedure.

The commonest techniques used in trephination are scraping, cutting, chiseling, punching, and drilling. In the first, the bone of the skull is slowly scraped away, creating an oval hole. The dura, a tough membrane that covers the brain, is then exposed. The dura is generally not opened and operators take pains not to injure it in any way.

Archaeologists and paleopathologists have found abundant evidence that trephination was extremely common in North Africa. A large number of trephined prehistoric skulls were found by the French General, Faidherbe in the latter part of the 19th century in Algeria. Since that time a number of scientists have documented the practice both in prehistoric and contemporary periods. A number of Berber peoples in the northern and central Sahara practice it today, including the Shawia who live in the Atlas Mountains of Morocco and the Kaluyle nomads who live along the Atlantic coastline of Morocco. The operations performed in these groups have been extensively studied over the past century by a large number of observers and have been described in considerable detail. Margetts (1967) has furnished a list of the most important published documents dealing with trephination in this part of Africa. He also summarizes the procedure observed by Hilton-Simpson in the early part of this century in Morocco. In that procedure, the scalp was opened and a small hole made through the skull using a spinning drill operated by hand. The surgeons took care not to injure the coverings of the brain. Once the hole was made, pieces of bone around it were removed on successive days through the use of saws and elevators. The scalp was not sewn closed, but allowed to heal by granulation. The wound was treated with honey, butter, and herbs.

Dalloni (1935) described trephination among the Teda people of the Tibesti Mountains of northern Chad. The Teda still practice trephination, using the scraping technique. Jean Chapelle (1957), who has studied the Teda for many years, relates that they practice trephination as a treatment for cranial fractures. The pieces of broken bone are carefully removed and the scalp allowed to heal on its own. A light piece of cloth is then placed over the wound. He concludes that most cases recover satisfactorily as evidenced by the large number of people he observed who had healed holes in their skulls.

Talbot (1926) reported that trephination was performed in the Bende District of Nigeria. Patients generally recovered from the operation. Aside from Talbot's report there is virtually no published data about trephination in West Africa. This does not mean that the operation was not performed there, but only that evidence of it is very scarce at this time.

Drennan (1937), reported the existence of a trephination cult among the Bushmen of South Africa and there are several reports describing the operation among the Zulu. It appears that trephination was and perhaps is still very common in South Africa.

In East Africa Brotmacher (1955) and Drake-Brockman (1912) both described trephination among the Somali people. A number of ethnic groups in Uganda treated headaches by cautery, a procedure which is different from trephination, but one which some authors confuse with it. Ruth Fisher (1911), an early missionary in Uganda states, "Headache is cured by inserting a cold knife in the temples as far as the bone, and then applying a hot knife to stop the bleeding." In such a procedure, the bone is not cut as it would be in trephination. Roscoe (1921) observed that the Basoga of Uganda removed bits of bone following a skull fracture and in so doing practiced trephining. The Lugbara of the Lake Albert area of northwest Uganda are well known for trephining. A number of Western medical practitioners have observed the practice among them. The operation is conducted as a cure for headache using a four-inch knife blade with a double cutting edge and awl shaped tip (Margetts 1967). The operation has also been documented among the Topotha of the southern Sudan.

Among two ethnic groups living in the highland region to the east of Lake Victoria along the Kenya-Tanzania border trephination was and is a commonly performed procedure. These groups, the Kisii and the Bakuria are members of the Bantu group who share many cultural traditions. Ever

since the British and Germans set up administrative control over this area
at the turn of the century, it has been known that trephination is a
commonly-performed procedure. The official records of this region, the
District Books, contain numerous descriptions of the practice as do police
reports, medical records, and the minutes of court trials. In brief,
trephination has been well documented in this area. In 1958 Grounds
published the first description of the practice among the Kisii, and in 1962
Coxon published a report covering much of the same materials. A motion
picture of the practice was made by the Warner-Chilcott Laboratories of
Morris Plains, New Jersey, shortly thereafter. It is entitled *Maganga*,
which in ki-Swahili[1] means "doctor." It portrays an operation performed
by a Kisii surgeon named "Kisumu," no doubt an alias borrowed from the
nearby lake city of the same name. Margetts (1967) has summarized Kisii
trephining in great detail.

In 1961, while I worked among the Bakuria of the North Mara
District of Tanzania, I learned about their practice of trephining. The Luo, a
Nilotic people who share this district with the Bakuria, did not trephine and
were unaware that the neighboring Kisii did. They did know of the practice
among the Bakuria, but they were unaware of its details. Because the
practice has been outlawed by the authorities, it was done in secret. The
local administrative authorities in North Mara District estimated that at
least 100 people were trephined a year among the Bakuria (Peoples 1961).
Although precise morbidity and mortality data are unavailable, it was the
impression of most Kuria that people generally survived the procedure.
Occasionally, people died as a result of trephination and often their
families would report this to the local police. A court procedure would then
result, much to everyone's delight, since the Bakuria have a strong
propensity for court litigation.

The Bakuria trephine in order to remove pieces of fractured bone
and to make a hole in the head of patients who suffer chronic headaches
after head injury. The healers who perform the operation are almost always
men, although I was told of a woman who was said to trephine. Margetts
(1967) reports that among the Kisii, men always perform the operation.

Prior to the operation, the healer performs some rituals and recites
some prayers. Often the head is shaven, especially if the patient is a man.
Woman routinely shave their hair and so often appear quite bald. The men
do not routinely shave their heads. Patients most often are made to lie on
the ground with their heads on a log. Margetts (1967) reports that Kisii
patients either sit or lie, and that they are restrained. He observed one
surgeon who placed his patients on a flat bed with his head over the edge;
another bed was then placed on top of him upside down, thus sandwiching

---

[1] *Ki-Swahili* is synonymous with the term *Swahili* when referring to the
language, but is a more precise term, since *ki* indicates *the language of*.

him. Relatives were then made to sit at the corners of the bed! The Bakuria do not restrain patients, unless it is absolutely necessary.

The actual operation among both the Kisii and the Bakuria is virtually identical. A linear or curved incision is made through the thickness of the scalp with a knife. The length of the incision varies but most often it is several inches long. Bleeding occurs freely when the scalp is incised, and herbal powders or charcoal are dabbed into the wound to achieve hemostasis. If a fracture exists under the incision, the broken pieces of bone are removed and blood clots evacuated. If a linear fracture is present, the surgeon starts to scrape away the outer table of the skull along the fracture line. The knives used for the scraping have curved tips so that they will not pierce the brain and its membranes. An oval hole may be made either partially or completely through the skull's thickness. Often patients have successive operations in which the hole is enlarged over a long period. Margetts recorded a case in whom about 30 square inches of bone had been successively removed from the skull, creating an enormous hole. The patient, who was about 50 years old, wore a hat and a plastic plate over his head for protection.

Scraping through the bone requires anywhere from two to five hours. Most operations last for about four hours. Once the hole is made, the wound is flushed out with ordinary water or water containing herbal preparations. Margetts was told of one Kisii operator who spewed water out of his mouth into the wound. The Bakuria do not suture the wound and Margetts reports that the Kisii do so only rarely, using a figure-of-eight suture. Wounds are allowed to heal and herbal preparations or butter are applied to aid the healing.

Fees for trephining ranged from the equivalent of six U.S. dollars to 100 U.S. dollars, depending on who the surgeon was, the nature of the problem, and the ability of the patient to pay. Operations only came to the notice of the authorities if a patient died and the relatives went to the police, or if a dissatisfied patient brought suit against the surgeon. Since the procedure was banned by the British authorities, criminal charges were made against the surgeons by the prosecutors.

Margetts estimated that the overall operative mortality among the Kisii was five percent. Complications include meningitis, brain abscess, and local infections. These cases usually end up in local hospitals such as the Kaplong Mission Hospital in Sotik where I saw a Kisii patient with meningitis secondary to trephination.

Circumcision and Excision

Circumcision is an operation on males in which the prepuce is removed from the penis. Excision or clitoridectomy is an operation performed on females in which the clitoris is removed. These operations are generally performed as part of puberty rites (see chapter 4), but not all African ethnic groups perform them. The Luo of East Africa, a Nilotic people, do not perform these operations. Some societies circumcise males, but do not perform clitoridectomy. Others perform both and among a few only clitoridectomy is performed. Groups who are Islamized generally adopt circumcision and excision (clitoridectomy), but according to the Moslem fashion, the actual surgical procedures remaining the same, but the ceremonies surrounding them following Moslem custom and law.

Where these operations are performed, they form an integral part of the *rites de passage* customs. These puberty rites include the acquiring of knowledge through a period of secluded schooling, the induction into certain cults and societies, and the performance of perscribed activities for a limited period of time. These practices, while extremely important, are peripheral to the focus here which is primarily medical and surgical.

Both circumcision and excision have been widely described throughout Africa by numerous authors. There are subtle variations in surgical technique, positioning of patients, instruments used and time the operations are performed. What is described here are primarily my own direct observations made in both East and West Africa.

Circumcision and Excision among the Bambara of Mali

At one time males were circumcised at 20 years of age, but today most are circumcised at from eight to twelve years. Both circumcision and excision are performed in a community about every three years during the hot dry season. The actual date is set by the blacksmith who makes his decision according to the position of the star *Sirius*. Circumcision is performed outside the village confines in a place in the nearby bush especially set aside for this purpose. Boys are made to sit around the blacksmith with their legs spread open. An adult male supports each one from behind. The prepuce is pulled and twisted by the blacksmith who then ties a cord around it. He pulls the cord firmly so that there is no slack in it and wraps its distal end around his large toe. He places a block of wood between the candidate's legs and puts the penis on it. The edge of the knife is then placed against the prepuce just below the attachment of the cord. The blacksmith then hits the top edge of the knife with a wooden hammer, and in so doing amputates the prepuce. He then scarifies the glans of the penis and the base of the penis with various designs which have a rather complex cosmologic significance (Dieterlen 1950). If a boy has a malformed prepuce which cannot be amputated, the blacksmith inflicts a cut on his thigh which replaces the act of circumcision.

Bambara girls are excised by the women of the blacksmith caste who are also the pottery makers. The operation is performed on the

Recently excised Bambara girls from eastern Bambara country. Both boys and girls today wear their circumcision garb for a month.

outskirts of the village in the presence of assembled adult female relatives of the candidates for the operation. In some villages the operation is done at the site where the women make pottery. The girls are seated on an earthen jar which is turned upside down. Three of their adult female relatives stand behind them and support them. With their legs apart, the surgeon takes hold of the clitoris and amputates it with a swift cut of a knife or razor. The amputated clitoris is buried or else thrown into a rat hole.

There is considerable variation in the disposition of amputated prepuces and clitori in Africa. Among the Dogon of Mali there is wide variation even from village to village. In some areas, the prepuces are mixed in with pounded millet and made into cakes which the circumcised eat on the third day (Leris and Schaeffner 1936). In other villages the prepuces are buried in the ground, burned, or thrown into compost pits.

Very often animal feces are placed over the wounds. The Basembeti and Bakuria of Tanzania frequently did this. Leris (1936) observed that the Dogon employed pulverized goat feces, a practice which I also observed in 1969. Such practices frequently lead to the development of serious secondary infections and tetanus.

Circumcision and Excision among the Basembeti of Tanzania

The Basembeti, also known as the Suba, live in the North Mara area of Tanzania. In 1961 they held circumcision and excision rites for the first

Recently circumcised Bambara boy with a circumcision rattle known as a wassamba.

time since 1955. These rites were performed in August and September. The boys stood during the procedure with an adult male relative standing behind them, holding their shoulders. The circumciser used a knife with a five inch blade and inserted a short stick of about an inch diameter into the prepuce. Once inserted against the glans of the penis, the stick was pushed, drawing the prepuce over it. Holding the prepuce-covered stick with the thumb and index finger of the left hand, the circumciser cut the prepuce off at a level near the base of the stick. The entire operation was fairly quick. The amputated prepuces were given to the boys who in turn burned them. The wound was washed with water and later in the day a herbal paste applied to it.

Whereas the boys were operated on outdoors, the girls were excised in rather dark huts. They were placed on cowskins, in a semi-recumbent position, propped up against a woman who knelt behind them. The female surgeons were then using razor blades, but in former times they had employed knives. They spread the girl's legs apart and then took hold of the clitoris between the forefinger and thumb of one hand. With the other they amputated the clitoris. Stoicism on the part of those being operated on is valued and expressions of pain scorned.

Complications such as tetanus, gangrene, local infections, and hemorrhage are not uncommon. Some of the children, both male and female, die from these operations, but precise statistics are not available. It was my impression that most deaths occurred among girls and primarily from hemorrhage (Imperato 1964).

Circumcision and Excision among the Malinke of Mali

Circumcision and excision ceremonies among the Malinke are held about every three years. Among the animists, the average age of these operated on is 16 years. But among the Islamized most are from eight to twelve years. The boys are circumcised by blacksmiths. Each boy stands during the operation, facing eastward with an adult male relative standing behind him. The blacksmith grabs the prepuce with his left thumb and index finger and pulls it toward him. With the nail of his thumb he makes a visible mark on the surface of the prepuce just distal to the top of the glans of the penis. He then cuts quickly with a knife along this mark. The amputated prepuce is thrown on the ground. The wound is washed with a solution made from the fruits of *Landolphia senegalensis* (*saba*). After this and after all bleeding has stopped the wound is wrapped in a leaf of *Colocynthis vulgaris* (*sana*) and held in place by a piece of string. The circumcised go into isolation for 15 days. On the third day, the original leaf bandage is removed and the wound treated. Thereafter it is treated twice a day until healed. These local treatments consist of a washing in water and soap made from peanut oil. A paste composed of the crushed leaves of *Khaya senegalensis* (*dala*) and *Cymbopogon giganteus* (*tiekala*) is then placed over the wound.

Females are excised inside of their mother's house or else in the house of the blacksmith's wife who performs the operation. Cheron (1933) observed that some girls were excised in the enclosure surrounding the family latrine. The girl sits down on a flat rack with her legs spread apart. Her mother, older sisters, and the family's praise singer surround her. Nowadays, razor blades are frequently used, but formerly knives were employed. The operator siezes hold of the clitoris with the index finger and thumb. Occasionally she stimulates it with her fingers if it is difficult to get hold of. The operator then pulls on the clitoris and amputates it at its base.

It is then given to the girl's mother who traditionally placed it in a rat hole. The actual operation lasts less than a minute. The wound is then washed with water, but no herbal preparations are placed on it.

References

Chapelle, J. 1957. *Nomades Noirs du Sahara.* Paris: Librairie Plon.

Cheron, G. 1933. La Circoncision et L'Excision Chez les Malinke, *Journal de la Sociéte des Africanistes* 3:297-303.

Coxon, A. 1962. The Kisii Art of Trephining, *Guy's Hospital Gazette* 76:263.

Dalloni, M. 1935. *Mission au Tibesti,* Memoires de l'Academie des Sciences de l'Institut de France. Paris: Guathier-Vellars.

Davies, J.N.P. 1965. Primitive Autopsies and Background to Scientific Medicine in Central Africa. *New York State Journal of Medicine* 65(22):2830-2836.

Dieterlen, G. 1950. *Essai sur la Religion Bambara.* Paris: Presses Universitaires de France.

Drennan, M.R. 1937. Some Evidence of a Trepanation Cult in the Bushman Race, *South African Medical Journal* 11:183-191.

Felkin, R.W. 1884. Notes on Labour in Central Africa, *Proceedings of the Edinburgh Medical-Surgical Society* 29:922-931.

Fisher, Mrs. A.B. 1911. *Twilight Tales of the Black Baganda.* London: Marshall Brothers Ltd.

Ford, E. 1937. Trephining in Melanesia, *Medical Journal of Australia* 2:471-477.

Grounds, J.G. 1958. Trephining of the Skull Amongest the Kisii, *East African Medical Journal* 35:369-373.

Hewat, M.L. 1906. *Bantu Folk Lore.* Capetown: T. Maskew Miller.

Imperato, P.J. *Doctor in the Land of the Lion.* New York: Vantage Press.

Imperato, P.J. 1966. Witchcraft and Traditional Medicine among the Luo of Tanzania, *Tanzania Notes and Records* 66:193-201.

Leris, M. and Schaeffner, A. 1936. Les Rites de Circoncision Chez les Dogon de Sanga, *Journal de la Société des Africanistes* 6:141-161.

Maclean, U.C. 1971. *Magical Medicine.* London: Penguin Press.

Margetts, E.L. 1967. Trepanation of the Skull by the Medicine Men of Primitive Cultures, with Particular Reference to Present-Day Native East African Practice. In *Diseases in Antiquity,* edited by D.R. Brothwell and A.T. Sandison. Springfield, Illinois: Charles C Thomas.

Moodie, R.L. 1923. *Paleopathology: An Introduction to the Study of Ancient Evidence of Disease.* Urbana, Illinois: University of Illinois Press.

Nemesken, J., Kralovansky, A. and Harsanyi, L. 1965. Trephined Skulls from the Tenth Century, *Acta Archaologia Hungarica* 17:343-367.

Peoples, J. 1961. Personal Communication.

Roscoe, J. 1921. *Twenty-Five Years in East Africa.* London: Longmans.

16

Traditional Dentistry

Dental problems in Africa follow the same spectrum observed in Europe and in the United States. Many of these problems are left untreated, particularly the cosmetic and orthodontic ones, since there are no means available to remedy them and because they do not produce pain and discomfort. In most African societies teeth are generally cleansed daily by most people and a variety of things done to them in keeping with tribal custom. Teeth are often filed into points as part of the *rites de passage* and among certain peoples a fixed number are removed during these same puberty rites. Tatooing of the gums and interior of the lower lip is practiced in many areas, often as an integral part of puberty rites. By and large, dental caries are not treated until a tooth becomes painful. And for toothache there exist a large number of medical remedies — and established techniques for extraction when other remedies fail.

Cleansing of Teeth

Good oral hygiene is held up as a positive quality by most ethnic groups, with children being taught after their puberty rites to clean their teeth. Behavior patterns do not necessarily follow a culture's accepted norms and so there are always a certain number of people who do not bother to cleanse their teeth.

Across much of Africa, teeth are cleansed with short sticks of wood measuring about six to eight inches in length and an inch in diameter. In rural areas, people can cut the appropriate stick to suit their needs. In large urban areas, they are sold by peddlers on the street for a small sum. The bark is usually removed from these sticks prior to their being sold. The stick is inserted into the mouth and its side and tip rubbed both horizontally and vertically across the surfaces of the teeth. The tip of the stick is frequently bitten during the process so that it becomes frayed and the user spits out the small pieces frequently during the process of cleansing. Once cleansing is begun it may be kept up for as long as an hour with the user taking frequent respites. The stick is not taken out of the mouth but held between the buccal mucosa and the teeth, sticking out much as a cigar would. These indigenous teeth polishers are not used daily by most people, but many employ them several times a week. Their use has been described by a number of authors and they have been variably described as *chewing brushes*, *chewing sticks*, *toothbrushes* and *brush sticks* (Lagercrantz 1946; Meyerowitz 1951; Monod 1953; Lemmet 1918; Monteil 1915).

In addition to cleansing teeth in this manner, after eating many Africans wash off the surface of their teeth with a finger dipped in water. This is regularly done by Moslems when they wash themselves for prayers several times a day. At the same time the mouth is washed out with a small quantity of water.

Among the Bambara and Malinke of Mali, indigenous toothbrushes of this kind are used by men only after they have been circumcised and by women after they have been excised. Their use was once closely intertwined with cosmologic beliefs which in recent decades have gradually disappeared under the influence of Islam and modern Western technology.

Zahan (1963) has described in great detail the cosmologic significance and symbolism of these sticks in the traditional Bambara religion. He relates that there are 44 categories of plants whose branches or roots can be used as tooth polishers and that each category has a special significance. These 44 categories correspond to the 44 teeth in the human mouth. Those in the first category symbolize force and power, characteristics which the Bamana believe can be transmitted to their spoken words by using a tooth polisher from this category. Each type of stick imprints on the mouth certain abstract characteristics which are taken up by the saliva and absorbed by the user and imprinted on his spoken speech (Zahan 1963). They impart such characteristics as good fortune, success, acquisition of knowledge, courage, facility of speech, wisdom, etc.

The Bambara call these sticks *gwese dalaso*. At one time certain species of wood were used at specific times of the year, during the rainy season for example or at harvest time. Others were used at the end of the cool season in January, just after the harvests when the Bamana devote themselves to renewing their social relationships. When planting peanuts and peas a certain stick cut from a branch of *m'peku ba* (*Lannea acida*) was used. It is a symbol of plenty and bountiful harvests. During battle, sticks of *n'garo* (*Cissus populnea*) were used since this tree was believed to protect against bullets. The heads of the Bambara secret initiation societies employed preferentially certain categories as did the blacksmiths, village chiefs and other notables, categories symbolizing quality characteristics desirable for their specific social roles. Thus, these sticks of wood were not mere toothbrushes. The user was believed to gain from them a number of qualities desired and needed to fulfill his role in society (Zahan 1963).

Uncircumcised individuals never use these sticks, since culturally no significance nor importance is attached to what the uncircumcised say. Also, these sticks are not used at night since the trees from which they are cut function primarily during the day. Night use is viewed as a perversion. Although most of these beliefs are no longer held and customs no longer observed the above two observances (i.e., use only by the circumcised and only in daytime) are still common.

The wood most commonly used in the Bambara country today for tooth polishers is *sana* (*Daniellia oliveri*), a wood which is a symbol of long life and esteem. Heads of families often commence the Bambara year using a specific wood and then successively use several others, each with its own significance. Some of these woods are used in medicinal preparations for such diverse problems as abdominal cramps and infertility.

These sticks obviously act to clean teeth through the mechanism of friction, but they may also act chemically to dissolve dental debris and alter the bacterial flora of the mouth, thereby preventing dental caries. The active ingredients of these woods and their role in decay prevention have yet to be studied.

Ceremonial Alterations of Tooth Form

The filing of teeth as part of the rites of puberty was once a common practice in many parts of Africa. It was a procedure carried out as part of a group of bodily alterations which included cicatrization, tatooing, stretching ears, and placing holes in lips. Generally the upper incisors were filed, but the number of teeth filed and their final shape varied from tribe to tribe. In the early 1960's the practice was still in use among several small Bantu-speaking peoples in northern Tanzania where I observed it being performed. The Basembiti and Bakuria filed six upper front teeth of both boys and girls after circumcision and the completion of puberty rites. The operation was performed by both men and women, each working on patients of the same sex. The person having his teeth filed would lie down in a supine position on a straw mat with his head lying on the thigh of the operator. If the operator were right-handed it was preferable for the patient's head to be in his left thigh, so that the maxillary teeth were approached from above. A thin slate stone was used to do the actual filing, the operator rubbing it gently at first and then more vigorously as he removed the lower lateral surfaces of the teeth. All of the teeth could not be done at one time and in general it required several sessions for all of the teeth to be filed.

The Luo, who are Nilotes living along the eastern shores of Lake Victoria in Kenya and Tanzania, did not circumcise; but as part of their puberty rites, they removed the lower six front teeth from the mandible. In the 1960's the practice was falling into disuse, but was still being performed in some locations. The absence of the lower six front teeth confers a pronunciation quality on the spoken Luo language which cannot be duplicated by those who do not have this dental defect. Luo who have not gone through puberty rites and who are not considered adults obviously cannot speak the language correctly, a fact which is immediately apparent. As among many African peoples, little significance is attached to the words of the pre-pubertal.

The Luo do not pull the teeth out. Rather they pry them out with a pick-like instrument. All six teeth are pried out at one sitting, an operation which is surprisingly rapid, taking about an hour in uncomplicated cases. Quite a bit of bleeding occurs as a result of this procedure and secondary infections are common. The operators observe no antiseptic techniques and the pick is laid on the ground or anywhere else without regard for its being dirtied.

Many educated Luo I met were extremely embarrassed by the absence of their lower six teeth and frequently sought my help in having dentures made. Some even traveled up to Nairobi in Kenya or down to Dar Es Salaam in Tanzania to have dentures made.

Tatooing of the Mouth

The tatooing of gums and the buccal mucosa of the lower lip is a widespread practice in Africa. In West Africa, the practice is generally restricted to women who view tatooed gums as a sign of beauty. While many beautification practices, such as cicatrizing and the stretching of ear lobes and lips, have fallen into disuse over the past several decades, tatooing of the mouth has not. It is still widely practiced, even in large urban centers like Dakar, Senegal (Grappin et al. 1975).

Among the Bambara, a woman is not considered beautiful unless her mouth is tatooed. The operation was once carried out in two distinct phases, the first at a young age, before a girl underwent excision and the second after this rite was performed. Previously excision was usually performed at the age of 14 years. Nowadays, it is performed at the age of four or five years, and tatooing is now done several years after excision when a girl is about 15 years of age. In large urban centers girls often opt not to have it done and their parents do not force them to do so.

Tatooing among the Bambara is performed by old women who belong to the caste of leatherworkers, the *garanke*. They use a black dye which is made from the ashes of *Prosopis africana* (*gwęle*) mixed with butter made from cow's milk. This dye gives the gums and mucosa a gray-black hue. To inject the dye, they once employed thorns from *Balanites aegyptiaca* (*n'zegene*), but today sewing needles are routinely used, having almost completely replaced thorns.

Tatooing of the gums is called *nyi-susu* which literally translated means "pounding the teeth." It was at one time carried out before a girl's puberty rites, but nowadays it is done afterwards. Ritual offerings were given by the client to the operator—40 cowrie shells, four basins of water, and four basins of crushed cereal (Zahan 1963), but this is no longer done. At one time the thorns were furnished by the client and the dye by the operator, but today the operator provides both.

The client lies supine on a straw mat with her head on the operator's thighs. The dye, which is a thick paste, is rubbed over the upper gums and then the operator takes several needles and with a rapid pounding action sticks the gums. This in effect injects the dye onto the sub-epethelial layers of the gums. The operator starts on the right side of the mouth and moves to the left. Traditionally, operators then did the lower gums going from left to right and repeated the process a total of four times the same day. Today, they often do it once and then have the client return several times after intervals of a few days and re-tatoo the gums until the desired hue is obtained.

Grappin et al. (1975) recently observed in Dakar that the gums are tatooed in about two minutes time. There, the operators spread a black dye over the gingiva with their fingertip while putting away the lip with the other hand. By multiple puncture, three punctures per second are made for about two minutes. Then the operator rests for about a minute. During these rest periods a piece of cotton cloth is applied against the gums with the fingers to stop bleeding. Finally, when the gums have been tatooed, some dye is placed on the gums and left there for as long as possible. No rinsing is done and no foods are eated which might remove the dye. Clients return for several sessions until the desired hue is obtained.

Grappin and his colleagues had one patient rinse her mouth after the first round of tatooing in order to see how much dye had been impregnated in the gums. They found that the degree of coloration was considerable. In Dakar the black dye used is either soot gathered from cooking pots or ash obtained from burning cotton cloth that has been soaked with peanut oil and shea butter.

Tatooing of the buccal mucosa of the lower lip is called *da wolo susu* by the Bambara, "pounding the lip." This is less frequently done today than before. When such tatooing was a common custom, the client went to the operator's home in the company of her brother's wife or the sisters of her fiancé. The ritual payment consisted of a white rooster, two hundred cowrie shells, and two balls of soap. The family of the girl's fiancé provided these items of payment (Zahan 1963). Such payments are no longer made.

The client is placed in the same position as described above and the dye applied to the lower buccal mucosa. The tatooing is accomplished by the same multiple puncture technique. During the procedure, those who accompany the girl tap on her abdomen with their hands and chant. Grappin et al. (1975) described the same activity in Dakar. The purpose of this is to distract the client from the obvious pain of the procedure. Zahan (1963) relates that the girls used to chant "*Ka dusu da,*" "calm your heart." Traditionally, after the lower lip was tatooed the operator tied an indigo-colored strip of cloth around the girl's mouth. She remained in seclusion for seven days and was not permitted to speak to anyone. These practices are no longer widely observed today.

Sterility is completely lacking during tatooing, and infections of both a minor and major nature are frequent. Grappin and his colleagues (1975) observed in Dakar that the needles were placed anywhere—on the dirt or on a table or straw mats—and were grossly contaminated. Considering that the instruments are so unsterile and the procedure an extremely septic one, it is a wonder that the consequences are not more severe than they are.

In the traditional Bambara religion, the tatooing of women's mouths had special significance (Zahan 1963). It was believed that by nature women were not masters of their language. They could not control what they said, they related all they heard and guarded no secrets. (A similar belief can be found in the Talmud: "What is said to a woman is announced to the city.")

Tatooing imparts a discipline to the organs of speech. The lower lip, according to the traditional Bambara, is the last control point before the words exit. Tatooing it imparts reserve and discipline and enables women to control what they say (Zahan 1963). The tatooing of gums is thought to impart control over the pronunciation of words since the gums hold the teeth whose action is believed to give words their final sound (Zahan 1963). These beliefs may have emerged out of a desire to give a cultural rationale to an accepted custom.

Teething

Remedies are used for teething when in the opinion of the mother and others the teeth are late in coming out or when the child is irritable and in apparent pain. Many of these remedies are not applied to the gums, but to the child's body or head. Some of the commoner remedies used among the Bambara are as follows:

1. The leaves of *Mitracarpus verticillatus* are boiled and the child washed with the solution.
2. The stems and leaves of *Ipomoea rubens* (= *Lettsomia rubens?*) are boiled and the child washed in the solution.
3. The leaves of *Afrormosia laxiflora* (*kolokolo*) are boiled and the child washed with the solution.
4. The leaves of *Alternanthera repens* (*sien goni*) are boiled and the child's head washed with the solution; some of the solution is also rubbed on the gums.

The Management of Toothache

Dental caries are a major and neglected public health problem in Africa. Because of other health priorities, dental problems have in general been either ignored completely or else paid scant attention. There exists the mistaken notion among westerners that Africans have good teeth and few or no caries, but this is simply not true. Dental caries is a major problem often leading to serious complications such as abscess formation and osteomyelitis of the jaw. The epidemiology of dental caries has not been extensively studied in Africa and thus there exist little baseline data on the disease.

As a general rule, Africans pay little attention to dental caries until a cavity begins to produce pain. It is widely believed that cavities are caused by small insects burrowing through the teeth, creating the types of holes and erosive destruction caused by wood borers, insects which made analogous holes in fresh wood. The aim of many forms of treatment is the destruction and/or removal of these "teeth-boring insects."

Medicinal Treatment of Toothache

The first approach to the treatment of toothache is the initiation of medicinal therapy. If this fails an attempt will be made to extract the tooth. Most remedies are applied topically to teeth, used as mouthwashes, or inhaled through the mouth as a vapor.

Hewat (1906) reported that the Bantu of South Africa often applied small doses of *Acokanthera venenata* (= *A. oppositifolia*) to the offending tooth. This plant was also used for treating snakebite. It was observed that this plant had a distinct anesthetic action. They also used several other plants which he states had a similar anesthetic action. These were placed as a powder or paste into the tooth cavity. Some of these were *Blepharis capensis*, *Solanum capense*, and *Indigofera meisneri*.

Some of the remedies employed by the Bambara are as follows:

1. A stalk of *Sclerocarya birrea* (*n'Kuma*) is heated and then placed into the tooth cavity.
2. The mouth is rinsed several times with a solution made from boiling the bark of the baobab tree, *Adansonia digitata*.
3. The flowers of *Cymbopogon giganteus* (tiekala) are pulverized along with the grains of *Aframomum melegueta* and the powder obtained placed in the cavity of the tooth.
4. The bark of *Fagara xanthoxyloides* (*goro n'gua*) is pulverized and the powder placed in the tooth cavity.
5. The leaves of *Daniellia oliveri* (*sana*) are boiled in water. The patient stands over the boiling pot and breathes in the fumes with with mouth open.

For dental abscess, the Bambara commonly employ two remedies. The bark and leaves of *Parkia biglobosa* (*nere*) are boiled in water and the boiling solution placed in a narrow neck calabash, the end of which is placed on the mouth. It is believed that the fumes produced cure the abscess. The leaves of *Tribulus terrestris* (*mousso-koroni-ni*) are boiled. The patient breathes in the vapor produced by the boiling liquid.

The Luo of Tanzania often placed a hot metal rod into the tooth cavity which, while painful, often resulted in an ablation of pain due to destruction of the tooth's nerve.

Tooth Extraction

When medicinal therapies fail, as they often do, an attempt is made to extract the tooth. Hewat (1906) observed that Kaffir surgeons did this by pulling the tooth out by means of a leather thong attached to it. The Luo in Tanzania pry teeth out with a metal pick. The Bamana use a similar technique but try to loosen the tooth first by placing pressure on it from all available surfaces. The tooth is sometimes pounded with a piece of metal and not infrequently the crown is broken off. The roots are then left in place, which causes complications later on. The Kikuyu of Kenya used to extract teeth with the aid of the tip of a spear. The tooth was pried out, much the same way as in the procedure used by the Luo (Cagnolo 1933).

Tooth extraction is easier among older adults than among adolescents and young adults because older people often have peridontal disease which makes the teeth loose and easy to pull out. Often people pull their own teeth out, with assistance from friends if necessary. If unsuccessful they go to a tribal surgeon.

Other Treatments for Toothache

A number of healers have taken advantage of the belief that small insects cause cavities. They engage in charlatanism, which earns them a considerable income. In both Senegal and Mali, where this insect theory of tooth decay is especially common, Moslem Koranic healers pretend to remove these insects from the teeth of patients, and in a most convincing way. The practice in Dakar, Senegal, described by Leye (1962), is identical in neighboring Mali. The healer obtains a number of small caterpillars which are wrapped in their cocoons. The ones used are from the family *Psychidae* (bagworm moths) which are found in large numbers dangling from their threads from the branches of Flamboyant trees. These caterpillars measure less than a quarter of an inch in length. The charlatan then places a number of these in the hollow stem of *Sesbania pachycarpa* (*mbalambala*).

The patient is made to sit down and open his mouth. Reciting passages from the Koran or simply cryptic Arabic texts, the healer places the tip of the stem on the affected tooth, taking care to hold the stem horizontally. He then sucks on the opposite end and in so doing easily brings the cocooned caterpillars up into his mouth. These he spits out and hands over to the patient who frequently believes they came out of his tooth. For this service Koranic healers are paid the equivalent of a daily wage.

Surprisingly, patients often say they feel better after this procedure, although within a few hours the pain usually returns. There are always ready explanations for the return of a toothache such as more worms in the tooth, and not infrequently patients return to the same healer over a period of several days.

References

Cagnolo, C. 1933. *The Akikuyu*. Nyeri: Consolata Mission Press.
Grappin, G., DiPasquale, C. and Thiam, T. 1975. Description d'Une Pratique de Tatouage Gingival à Dakar, *Afrique Medicale* 14(130):433-434.
Hewat, M. 1906. *Bantu Folk Lore*. Cape Town: T. Maskew Miller.
Lagercrantz, S. 1946. The Chewing Brush, Especially in Africa. *Ethnos* 1–2:63-70.
Lemmet, J. 1918. L'Hygiene de la Bouche Chez Les Indigenes du Senegal, *Bulletin du Comité d'Etudes Historiques et Scientifiques de l'A.O.F.*, 3–4:400-404.
Leye, T. 1962. Chenilles et Charlatanisme Dentaire, *Notes Africaines*, 95. Juillet.
Meyerowitz, E. 1951. *The Sacred State of the Akan*. London: Faber and Faber.
Monod, T. 1953. Autour du Batonnet Brosse à Dents Ouest Saharien, *Notes Africaines* 60:117.
Monteil, C. 1915. *Les Khassonke*. Paris: Lerous.
Zahan, D. 1963. *La Dialectique du Verbe Chez les Bambara*. Paris: Mouton.

17

Snakebite and Other Bites and Stings

Snakes and scorpions are greatly feared in most of Africa and with good reason since many of them are highly poisonous. Poisonous snakes are especially feared. In many areas, the fear of snakebite is far greater than objective facts warrant, much the same as the fear of being mugged in many an American city today is disproportionate to the actual risk. Specific cases of snakebite followed by disability and death are faithfully remembered in all their details in local areas, but the many instances when people are bitten by poisonous snakes and survive are quickly forgotten. When the victim does survive, the bite is often attributed to a non-poisonous snake, although a poisonous one may have been responsible. If people accept that the bite was indeed inflicted by a poisonous snake, survival is often attributed to the indigenous treatments used.

Within recent years, the epidemiology of poisonous snakebite has been carefully studied in many areas of the world, and especially in Asia. One of the ranking authorities in this field, Dr. H.A. Reid of the Liverpool School of Tropical Medicine, has observed large numbers of individuals bitten by venomous snakes in Asia. He found that only 15 to 40 percent of patients bitten by poisonous snakes are actually poisoned systemically. Local poisoning (without systemic spread) was observed in 30 percent of viper bites and 35 percent of cobra bites. Among those who are clinically poisoned, the severity of the poisoning varies from trivial to severe. In a series of 58 patients bitten by poisonous sea-snakes off the coast of northwest Malaya between 1957 and 1961, only 11 (22 percent) were poisoned. In the remaining 68 percent of these unequivocal bites, no poisoning ensued (Reid 1975).

Patients in Dr. Reid's various series were observed for the specific signs and symptoms of clinical poisoning. Where these became apparent, appropriate antivenom was administered. When they did not appear, the patients were not given antivenom. For the types of snakebites he has studied, clinical observation of the patient is possible during which antivenom is withheld without jeopardizing the outcome even if poisoning does occur.

These observations have had an impact on the clinical management of snakebite inflicted by specific snakes that he studied. Antivenom is not an innocuous substance and can itself cause serious and even fatal reactions in allergic individuals. It need not be given then in cases of bites due to certain Asian snakes unless specific signs of clinical poisoning appear.

Less work has been done with reference to African snakes, but the same principles carry over for most types of bites. In light of these facts, one must judge with great caution the stated efficacy of various traditional treatments for snakebite. Only a small proportion of those bitten by poisonous snakes are actually poisoned to a life-threatening extent. A significant proportion are not even envenomated during the bite. These cases either never develop symptoms at all or if they do they recover without the use of antivenom or indigenous remedies. In short, the odds are in favor of traditional medical practitioners who treat snakebite, since most of their patients will recover even if left alone.

Snake venoms are poor antigens, so it is difficult to make effective vaccines out of them. Many snake handlers mistakingly think that they are immune because they are frequently bitten without any symptoms developing. What they do not realize is that the snake has bitten without injecting its venom (Reid 1975). This same principle applies to numbers of snake cults in Africa or magicians and healers who claim the ability to handle snakes with impunity. Again, the odds are in their favor.

Snakes in Africa

Snakes in Africa are more often thought and dreamt about than seen by most people. There are, of course, regions where snakes are commonly present and there are seasonal variations in their population densities. People generally have a fairly good notion of the sort of habitats that some snakes prefer, and they either avoid these areas or proceed through them with caution. During my years in Africa, when I was traveling extensively in rural areas, I would not see a single snake for a year or two and then suddenly I saw several in a few days.

Along the banks of the Niger River, snakes frequently inhabit rocky crevices which are flooded by the rising river during the rainy season. As the waters flood them out, the snakes move inland away from the river. This accounts for their frequent presence in areas adjacent to rivers in cities like Bamako during the rainy season. During this season frogs and toads hatch and are numerous and often move on land away from the river. Since these are snakes' principal food source, snakes are attracted further away from the river. Rocky hills are another environment in which snakes abound, since crevices afford excellent sites for them to rear their young. A striking example of this are the two rocky mountains behind the city of Bamako, Mali, known as Koulouba and Point-G. The principal government ministries are located on the former and the national hospital on the latter. Together there are not more than 30 buildings on these mountains; yet a week scarcely goes by that a poisonous snake is not killed around one of the buildings. The spitting cobra, *Sepdon haemachates*, is the principal snake sighted on these mountains. In 1969, the Ministry of Finance was obliged to keep a mongoose in its building because of the continual presence of spitting cobras. An effective remedy employed against snakes in such high density areas is the spraying of powdered dieldrin insecticide around the bases of the buildings. It kills large numbers of snakes, but unfortunately is very toxic for domestic animals.

The densities of snakes tend to be high on the peripheries of bush fires since they are driven out along with other animals by the advancing fire. Some escaping the flames, remain behind in burned out areas, but because of habitat destruction they surface during the day. A common sight in Africa is the presence of birds of prey hovering over bush fires with snakes and other small mammals in their beaks.

African snakes can be grouped into two large categories, the vipers and the elapids. As a general rule the former inject a venom which causes disruption of the blood-clotting mechanism, and the latter a venom which is neurotoxic. Among the vipers (*Viperidae*, as they are scientifically called) are *Bitis gabonica*, the gabon viper, *Causus rhombeatus*, the night adder, *Bitis arietans*, the puff adder and *Bitis nasicornis*, the horned adder. Among the neurotoxic *Elapidae* are *Dendraspis viridis*, the green mamba, *Dendraspis angusticeps*, the black mamba, *Naja nigricollis*, the cobra, *Dispholidus typus*, the boomslang and *Sepedon haemachates*, the spitting cobra.

Most of these species are nocturnal or semi-nocturnal, although cobras frequently bite during the day. Puff adders are slow-moving and are often found lying on bush trails at night; many bites result when people accidentally step on them. The green mamba is especially feared along the coastal rain forest of West Africa where it frequents palm trees where men often go to collect palm nuts (Harley 1941). During the mating season it attacks without provocation. Mambas also frequent termite mounds, areas approached with caution by most Africans. Many poisonous snakes are arboreal and strike from trees, and in many areas Africans avoid sitting beneath certain types of trees for this reason. Baobab trees are especially avoided since they frequently develop large holes in the trunks which harbor spitting cobras and mambas.

Snake Cults

The widespread fear of poisonous snakes in Africa is alleviated among some groups by institutionalized snake cults and societies that supposedly confer immunity to snakebite and subsequent poisoning. In Liberia, the *Ba Kona* is a snake cult, a secret society whose purpose is primarily the treatment of snakebite. The members also learn about the habits of snakes and how to handle them with apparent impunity. Harley (1941) relates that the members of this society catch and tame any type of snake except spitting cobras. Pythons, green mambas, gabon vipers and other snakes are caught and tamed by a variety of techniques. Harley states that the men rub the leaves of a climbing fern on their arms before attempting to catch snakes. They reach into holes and pull snakes out by their tails, hit them on the head a few times, and then hold them by the neck. The gabon viper is captured by the neck first. Accordingly to Harley, captured snakes are tamed through the use of the leaves of *Microdesmis puberula* which is chewed and then spit onto the snake's head. He observed that this herb made snakes lethargic and if used too frequently it killed them. To avoid this toxic effect, the members of the cult wash their product off with water and counteract it with the leaves of *Scleria barteri*. A variety of other herbal preparations are also used for capturing snakes. Snakes captured by the members of the *Ba Kona* cult are kept in boxes in the cult house. When the snakes are initially caught the chewed leaves of *Microdesmis puberula* are kept on their heads to make them easy to handle.

In Mali, snake cults exist among the Minianka people and the Bobo. Pythons, whose bites are non-poisonous, are kept in special cult houses and special sacrifices made to them. Among the Bobo-Ule there are individual snakebite healers who capture poisonous snakes, much as Harley observed in Liberia; however, they also capture spitting cobras with apparent impunity. I once witnessed the capture of a spitting cobra in the cercle of San by a Bobo snakebite healer who removed the snake from a hole in a termite mound. Prior to capturing the snake, he rubbed a herbal preparation on his hands and arms. A snake cult also exists among the Nyamwezi of Tanzania whose members are extremely adept at handling poisonous snakes (Moffett 1958).

In a cultural sense, snake cults institutionalize the treatment of snakebite and invest the snakebite healer with credibility. Confidence in these individuals runs high and, given the now-known epidemiology and pathogenesis of snakebite, success is almost guaranteed, whatever they do. This does not mean that some of their techniques and herbal preparations and are not effective. More than likely they are, but objective investigation must still be carried out to separate myth from fact. Given their ability to stupefy snakes with herbs and to do it so effectively, it is likely that many herbs used by them in treating snakebite are excellent antidotes.

The Treatment of Snakebite

There is considerable variation in the treatment of snakebite in Africa. In Liberia, treatments are specific for each individual snake although there are some remedies which are good for any kind of snakebite. When the identity of the snake is not known, the healer places a few buds of *Mareya spicata* (= *M. micrantha*) in his mouth, chews them and then sucks the wound directly, spitting out the poison. A paste is then made of the same buds, placed over the wound and held on place by a bark bandage (Harley 1941). An integral part of treatment in many areas is inducing vomiting. This is the practice of ethnic groups in Mali, Tanzania, Liberia, the Ivory Coast, and many other areas. There is a belief generally that the poison lodges in the stomach of a snakebite victim and can be expelled by vomiting.

In Liberia the members of the *Ba Kona* society treat snakebite. Vomiting is first induced by giving the victim any one of many emetic preparations. Once this is done a tourniquet is tied above the wound using *Dichrostachys glomerata* or some other vine (Harley 1941). In Mali, tourniquets are not used and I wonder if the use observed in Liberia by Harley was recently introduced. The healer routinely sucks out the wound, according to Harley, but I have not been able to document such a practice among other groups in either West or East Africa. Harley does not state how long such practices had been going on. Presumably the practice was rather recent. These practices are so similar to those used in Western medicine that one is led to presume that they were borrowed from the latter in view of the significant presence of American medical missionaries in the country before Harley recorded these practices.

In South Africa Hewat (1906) recorded that tourniquets were tied around the affected limb immediately. A thong or anything else available was used, the wound incised with a knife and bled. A cupping horn was then applied over the wound, with the healer sucking on the other end. This treatment is similar to that in use in Western medicine practiced in South Africa, and one wonders about its adoption from there. Hewat also relates that certain individuals always pursued snakes when they saw them and killed them, often being bitten in the process. The gall bladder and venom sacks were mixed with clay and then swallowed in the belief that this gave the person immunity to snakebite.

Among some groups in South Africa, a pit was dug and filled with bushes which were then burned. The ashes were raked out and the bitten man laid on a skin and was covered with the ashes. He was then rolled in the skin and given herbal infusions by mouth. The end result was excessive perspiration.

Among the Pondo and Zulu of South Africa, healers used different herbs for bites inflicted by different snakes. Hewat recorded that the commonest plants used for treating snakebite were *Leontis iconurus* (= *L. leonurus?*), *Teucrium africanum* and *Melianthus comosus.*

In Tanzania, the Luo and Bakuria believe that the snake's fangs remain in the wound after the bite, much like the sting of a bee. Their traditional healers incise the wound to remove the fangs. Patients who I treated for snakebite in Tanzania always requested that the fangs be removed. Else they left dissatisfied. In order to please them, we kept puff adder fangs in a jar and would show these to our patients who then felt pleased they had been removed (Imperato 1964). It may well be that the practice of incision of the wound observed by Harley in Liberia and Hewat in South Africa was for this purpose.

In Liberia green mamba bites are treated with the buds of *Dichrostachys glomerata* (*tene*) which are beat up with white clay and rubbed into the wound. Black cobra bites are treated by sucking the wound out, the healer first placing the buds of *Mezoneurom sp.* in his mouth. Then the beaten leaves of *Smilax kraussiana* are mixed with white clay and applied to the wound. Bites of the gabon viper are treated by first sucking the wound, the healer first chewing the buds of *Ageratum conyzoides* (*da vo*). The fruits of *Ficus vogeliana* are then crushed with white clay and applied to the wound, four figs for a man and three for a woman. A strong emetic is given for this bite because the gabon viper's venom is believed especially dangerous because of its long fangs (Harley 1941).

Harley concluded that the treatment of snakebite in Liberia was difficult to evaluate since it was a mixture of the magical and the rational. The leaf poultices applied to the wounds apparently relieved pain in the cases observed by him; but they did not alleviate the other effects of the venom.

Among the Bambara of Mali, the treatment of snakebite is likewise a mixture of the rational and magical. Incisions are made to extract the serpent's fangs that are believed to remain in the wound. Remedies consist of salves applied to the site of the bite, infusions which are drunk, and solutions which are applied to the wound. Other remedies are chewed and some inhaled. Combinations of various kinds are often used.

A few of the many treatments employed are as follows:

1. A stem of *Hymenocardia acida* (*gregeni*) is chewed.
2. A salve is made from the pulverized roots of *Cussonia barteri.* (*bolokouro*) and applied to the wound.
3. A salve made from the pulverized green leaves of *Ipomoea rubens* (*bugu-mugu*) is applied to the wound. When the snake involved is the small red viper, called *fofoni* by the Bambara, this salve is applied to the entire body.

4. The leaves and shoots of *Combretum ghasalense* (*tiangara*) are chewed and the juice swallowed. The chewed leaves and stems are then applied as a salve to the wound.
5. The leaves of *Pterocarpus santalinoides* (*diao*) are boiled and the liquid drunk. This acts as a purgative. The remainder of the liquid is applied to the wound (Traoré 1965).

Many remedies consisting of salves or solutions applied to the wound are made from herbs and animals such as rats, lizards, frogs and antelopes. Formulas often call for the addition of a toad's head or a rabbit's paw to the herbs which form the basis of the treatment.

The Prevention of Snakebite

In Liberia individuals who must go out at night protect themselves from snakebite by rubbing the juice squeezed from the leaves of *Scoparia dulcis* (*bela*) on their arms and legs. Adepts of the snake cult carry a medicine horn containing the leaves of *Mareya spicata* (*wana*) which is believed to ward off snakes (Harley, 1941). The Bambara believe that attacks from snakes can be warded off by taking a daily dose of a powder made from the pulverized buds of *Ximenia americana* (*ntonge*) and the root of *Annona senegalensis*. This is taken for a week and its effect is supposed to last for ten lunar months (Traore 1965).

Individuals, such as snakebite healers, who handle snakes cover their arms and hands with a salve made from the pulverized green leaves of *Ageratum conyzoides* (*nungu*) and *Cyathula prostrata* (*norna ba*) prior to picking up snakes. This concoction is said to prevent the snake from attacking.

Scorpion Stings

Scorpions are found in most parts of Africa. Their stings are extremely painful, but they are rarely fatal except in small children. The toxic symptoms encountered in scorpion stings are muscular cramps, profuse sweating, fever and convulsions. In the Sahara several especially dangerous species are found, *Adnroctonus australis*, *Buthus occitanus* and *Buthacus arenicola*. The Bambara distinguish between the various species of scorpions. *Dyonkomi* is a large, brown scorpion considered to be especially poisonous. *Kosson* is the name applied to small flesh-colored scorpions. Scorpions figure prominently in many legends and stories. Twins, who are considered special beings by the Bambara are believed capable of handling scorpions without risk of being stung.

For stings of the *dyonkomi* scorpion, the pain is alleviated by applying the pulverized leaves of *Euphorbia hirta* (*daba du ble*). The dry feces of a donkey are soaked in water and applied to the wound for stings of smaller scorpions. The leaves of several other plants are also employed, applied as a salve to the wound. These include *Ficus thonningii*, *Cissus populnea*, *Ceratotheca sesamoides* and *Vigna sinensis*.

Insect Stings

Very little concern is expressed for the bites of mosquitoes, tsetse flies, and other biting insects, although many of these are extremely painful, especially tsetse fly bites. African honey bees and wasps are exceptionally aggressive and often sting without provocation. Honey bees are raised in cylindrical shaped straw structures which are coated inside with a cow-dung solution. This odor apparently attracts them to set up a hive in these structures. Honey and bee's wax are in high demand in Africa and so rural farmers suspend a large number of these straw cylinders from the upper branches of large trees. Periodically they remove the wax and honey and are not infrequently stung.

Bee and wasp stings are viewed as a nuisance and nothing more, there being no knowledge of the potential danger of severe and fatal allergic reactions. Anaphylactic reactions secondary to bee stings are viewed as a disease apart, having no association with the sting. The Bambara use the leaves of *Cassia siberiana* (*sindian*) as an infusion and apply it to the stung site to relieve the pain. For wasp stings they apply the crushed leaves of *Annona senegalensis* to the stung site.

Africans make no apparent effort to avoid bee and wasp stings, even in situations where it is obvious that they will be stung if they don't get out of the way. Mud wasps often hover inside of houses and huts or at their doorways and are in close contact with humans, increasing the risks of being stung. In areas where surface water is scarce, bees congregate in the early morning hours around village wells where they obtain water. This brings them into contact with the women who draw water at this time. Although women are frequently stung, they make no effort to avoid the bees and treat the entire matter lightly.

References

Harley, G.W. 1941. *Native African Medicine, with Special Reference to its Practice in the Mano Tribe of Liberia*. Cambridge, Massachusetts: Harvard University Press.
Imperato, P.J. 1964. *Doctor in the Land of the Lion*. New York: Vantage.
Moffett, J.P. 1958. *Handbook of Tanganyika*. Dar es Salaam: Government of Tanganyika.
Reid, H.A. 1972. Clinical Notes on Snakebite, in *Manson's Tropical Diseases*, edited by C. Wilcocks and P.E.C. Manson-Bahr. London: Balliere, Tindall, and Cassell.
Reid, H.A. 1975. Epidemiology of Sea-Snake Bite, *Journal of Tropical Medicine and Hygiene* 78(5):106-113.
Traoré, D.A. 1965. *Médicine et Magie Africaines*. Paris: Présence Africaine.

18

The Traditional African Pharmacopeia

For the most part traditional African drugs are herbal preparations. The roots, barks, leaves, branches, flowers, and seeds of the African flora are employed in remedies that are generations old. Minerals and animal products are also used, but less frequently. Many questions arise with regard to this group of drugs. The specificity, modes of action (if any), and efficacy of most of these medicines generally are not established in such a way as to satisfy modern pharmacologic standards. Similarly, the margins of safety, the short and long term toxicities of most preparations are unknown. The traditional system includes beliefs about the specificity and efficacy of certain products, but such impresssions do not prove that herbal preparations are really effective. Too many other variables can explain a patient's recovery after treatment.

When traditional medicines are toxic, the toxicity is generally not associated with them in the minds of the traditionalists, a fact that is confirmed by their continued use of preparations demonstrated by modern medical scientists to be toxic. The use of such preparations sometimes continues even when the poisonous effects are immediate, dramatic, and fatal! Una Maclean (1971), for example, found that 50 prcent of all households in Ibadan, Nigeria, used *agbo tutu* for treating convulsive disorders in children, even though this concoction (which contains green tobacco leaves, together with either human or cow urine, and other herbs) not infrequently causes coma and death. (See also pp. 136 and 217.)

By definition, a pharmacopeia is a book containing an official list of medicinal preparations, their uses and effects. By and large such books do not exist for most ethnic groups in Africa. However, medicinal preparations, their uses and effects are memorized and passed on from one generation to the next, and for a number of years this information has been recorded by investigators who have studied traditional medicine in Africa. Earlier investigators often recorded only the local language name for a herbal medicine and not the scientific name. Preparation and usage were frequently described in only a sketchy fashion and at best only vague impressions of efficacy were provided. Long-term toxicity and even short-term toxicity were not easy to assess, nor are they now from a purely observational perch.

In the past few years, a number of investigators have carefully recorded portions of some local pharmacopeias and published them primarily as articles or as part of articles and books covering broader aspects of traditional medicine; but these only provide us with the tip of an iceberg, for the African pharmacopeia is enormous. At present, the bulk of Africa's traditional pharmacopeia is still unwritten; it is stored in memories from Dakar to Capetown.

Recent years have witnessed an intensification of interest on the part of African scholars in their own traditional pharmacopeia. In some countries, this interest has emerged against a background of revalorization of traditional institutions and practices. National campaigns, often termed ''return to authenticity,'' have been launched in several African countries. Those in Zaire, the Central African Republic, and Chad have been the most sweeping. An important part of these campaigns is the revival of use of many traditional medical practices which had fallen into disuse. Scientific and medical personnel are often intimidated by indirect and direct political pressures into making statements about the quality, safety, and efficacy of herbal preparations which have not been substantiated scientifically. Changes in national leadership, usually by military coups, have resulted in an abandonment of some of these socio-political programs and retractions of statements made by medical and scientific personnel about the characteristics of national traditional pharmacopeias. Unfortunately, this serves to destroy credibility in whatever else might be said in the future by these qualified individuals about their country's traditional pharmacopeia.

This linkage to a political process makes whatever is written or said about a traditional pharmacopeia suspect in the minds of many scientists. Within given countries, sides are chosen early on between proponents and opponents, the latter being most often Western-trained medical personnel. Those who support a revival of use of herbs often set forth the appealing economic argument that their countries cannot afford to buy imported pharmaceuticals on the market in the Western world. They then go on to say that one should use those remedies which have proven their efficacy to previous generations (Koumare 1972). They also state that these remedies are in abundance (which they are not) and that they can be made available to most patients free or at low cost (Koumare 1972). Actually, in urban areas in Africa traditional herbal remedies are often more expensive than modern drugs on the open market, and in rural areas the prescribed plants often are rare enough to require a day's search to find them. Thus, opponents are quick to point out the obvious inaccuracy of statements made by the proponents and to view with suspicion not only whatever else they say, but also the conclusions of whatever studies they publish (Emmanuel 1976).

Health care administrators in Africa are often in more politically-sensitive positions than the cadres of Western-trained African physicians who deliver medical care. It is not surprising that they often pay at least lip service to traditional medicine. There is a tendency for many politicized health care administrators rhetorically to embrace traditional medicine and the traditional pharmacopeia because in their minds these institutions stand in opposition to Western medicine which is closely associated with colonialism. The traditional African pharmacopeia is thus being studied in an emotion-charged atmosphere. Politics, national pride, and xenophobia often cloud these studies and make their results of questionable value.

Those who view this contemporary scene in Africa often do not realize that a similar sequence of events occurred in Western medicine. An understanding of the origins and development of the modern Western pharmacopeia offers insights into the past history of Africa's pharmacopeia, its present state, and what its course of development is likely to be.

Origins and Development of the Western Pharmacopeia

Three hundred years ago, Western medicine had at its disposal only a score of drugs that are considered to be effective today. The medicinal armamentarium included cathartics, castor oil, figs, aloe and senna. Alcohol, opium, and the leaves of the hyoscyamus plant were used as pain relievers and for sleep as they had been for centuries. Mercury was used as a diuretic and purgative. Intestinal worms of different kinds were treated with three products, roots of aspidium, bark from the pomegranate tree, and with an oil obtained from the leaves and fruit of the American wormwood, known also as chenopodium (Dowling 1970). Some of these products, such as oil of chenopodium and aspidium were widely used until rather recently.

Colchicum was used by the Arabs as far back as the sixteenth century and later used in Europe for rheumatic joint pains. We know now that this product, derived from the stem of meadow saffron, is a drug of choice for treating gout. Quinine, which comes from the bark of the cinchona tree was widely used before the beginning of the 18th century, as was ipecac for amebic dysentary, and chaulmoogra oil for leprosy. The former comes from the root of a Brazilian plant called *ipecacuanha* and the latter from the seeds of trees from the Far East. Ipecac is still used today to induce vomiting. There were several other drugs that were used and that have been shown to be pharmacologically effective and safe, but these were used along with many other remedies which are now viewed in Western medicine as having been worthless, just as the ancient Egyptians used such effective remedies as opium for pain and senna as a cathartic, and yet used ink and cerebrospinal fluid for baldness (Dowling 1970). Animal excreta and viscera were mixed with herbal preparations, as they had been for centuries. Such remedies were in widespread use in Europe well into the 19th century. Local pharmacopeias in Europe and America contained a large percentage of remedies of vegetable and of animal origin and a few minerals.

During the first half of the 18th century medicine and magic were still closely intertwined in Europe. Nostrums, or secret remedies, were frequently prescribed by physicians. The French tried to deal with this problem in 1728 by issuing a series of decrees which empowered the Lieutenant General of Police of Paris to keep secret proprietary medicines under surveillance. At the same time, the French created scientific commissions to investigate these remedies since there had been what we would call today "consumer complaints" about them. Control of these preparations moved successively from the Royal Commission of Medicine to the Faculty of Medicine and then to the Royal Academy of Sciences. The government asked individual pharmacists to analyze secret remedies and entrusted their control and supervision to commissions and scientific bodies. From the outset, chemical analysis was viewed as the most important screening test for assessing the value of nostrums. Once active ingredients were found, clinical trials were undertaken under the supervision of either specially appointed scientific commissions or the Royal Society of Medicine (Berman 1970). These initial investigations were not very productive, but, as the century moved on, modern chemistry developed and it became possible to analyze these preparations for their active ingredients.

In 1758 the Faculty of Medicine of Paris published the *Codex Medicamentarius*, a printed pharmacopeia which had previously been published earlier in the century. They deleted from it such items as hair, placenta, urine, human blood, and skull bone powder and other bizarre items. However, the Faculty of Medicine still approved the inclusion of cow dung, serpent skin, dog hair, and pigeon feathers. The 1758 edition of this pharmacopeia represents an important milestone in modern medicine because an attempt was made to standardize and unify drugs used in a given locality. There were other pharmacopeias in use in France at the time, but they gradually fell into disrepute as learned scientific concensus came to endorse the official *Codex*.

Parallel events occurred in other countries in Europe. Essentially the process of pharmacopeial evolution was the same everywhere. Patients started questioning the alleged efficacy of traditional remedies. They simply observed that they did not work. The Renaissance and the Age of Reason had turned men into questioning empirical observers. Governments moved to analyze traditional remedies with the tools newly available through an infant science of chemistry. Official pharmacopeias were published, standards for drugs established governing preparation, dosage, and administration, and magical and useless preparations were prohibited.

As traditional medicines were scrutinized, scientists searched for new and useful medications. Edward Jenner demonstrated the usefulness of vaccination with cowpox as a preventive measure against smallpox. In 1752 James Lind conducted well-designed experiments which demonstrated that scurvy in sailors could be prevented by citrus fruits. In 1785 William Withering published his book, *An Account of the Foxglove and some of its Medical Uses*; thus did digitalis come into the modern pharmacopeia. During the 19th century, chemists succeeded in isolating alkaloids such as morphine from crude opium, atropine from belladonna, caffeine from coffee and tea, nicotine from tobacco, and strychnine from *nux vomica*. These were important milestones because they meant that the active ingredients were available in a pure form and could be carefully and accurately studied for dosage, mode of administration, and side effects (Dowling 1970).

Governmental regulation of the drug industry intensified in the Western world during the 19th century, but in spite of this patent medicines containing secret ingredients proliferated in Europe and America. Pharmacies were regularly inspected by teams composed of members of medical school faculties, pharmacists, physicians, and the police. Drugs which did not meet standards were confiscated and fines were imposed. The development of synthetic organic chemistry late in the 19th century made possible the mass production of quality controlled drugs and this went a long way toward reducing the use of patent medicines and nostrums. These concoctions did not die out easily, even when it was demonstrated through analytical chemistry that they were useless. "Theriaca," for example, was a concoction containing 71 separate ingredients. It contained only one important active ingredient, opium. "Theriaca" had been in use for so long that removing it from the French *Codex* was a long and tedious affair. It was finally removed in 1908 (Berman 1970).

In Britain and the United States, government legislation controlling the manufacture of drugs intensified towards the end of the 19th century. Successive editions of the *British Pharmacopoeia* and the *U.S. Pharmacopoeia (U.S.P.)* reflect the progress of biological and chemical standardization and careful chemical analysis. In Britain, as elsewhere, adulteration was a chronic problem which government legislation sought to control

(Stieb 1970). At the beginning of the 20th century, standards for blood products, vaccines and even surgical dressings were introduced and published in official pharmacopeias.

It was not until the 20th century that legislation established and enforced standards for drugs and biologicals in the Western world. In the United States private professional groups set the standards which were recognized by the Federal government. The *U.S. Pharmacopoeia (U.S.P.)* was first published by the United States Pharmacopeial Convention in 1820 and was recognized as an official compendium by the Federal government in 1905. In 1888, the American Pharmaceutical Association published the *National Formulary (N.F.)* which established standards for drugs not included in the *U.S.P.* (Dowling 1970). Gradually the Federal government became more and more involved in drug control. In 1902, the Congress passed the Biologicals Act, in 1906 the Pure Food and Drugs Act, in 1938 the Food, Drug and Cosmetic Act and the Drug Amendments Act of 1962.

The Food and Drug Administration (FDA) had its beginnings in 1927. Over the years its powers were widened by Congress as well as the scope of the products it evaluated and licensed. Following the tragic deaths which resulted from the use of elixir of Sulfanilamide, the FDA was given the power to require proof of safety before any new drug could be marketed (Dowling 1970). Today, this is an important function of the FDA.

Before drugs are licensed they must first be chemically standardized. Experiments in animals must demonstrate their efficacy, margin of safety, potential toxicity, absorption, biologic and chemical actions, distribution in plasma and tissues, breakdown and excretion. This screening procedure in animals is Phase I in the evaluation procedure. Once a drug has passed through Phase I, it is evaluated in small human populations. This is Phase II of the FDA's screening requirements. Again, efficacy and potential toxicity are carefully monitored. If a product meets the standards of Phase II, it is screened in large population groups in a Phase III (DeFelice 1972). Even once licensed, drugs are monitored by their manufacturers and long term effects, if any, are noted. The appearance of potential toxic effects results in the issuance of warnings to the general public. Occasionally, certain drugs are either temporarily or permanently withdrawn when toxic effects are reported. Many drug manufacturers routinely issue warnings to physicians about the use of certain drugs during pregnancy, not because any ill effects have been observed, but because the effects are unknown.

Paralleling the history of the regulation and standardization of drugs in Western medicine has been a dramatic shift in the sources of drugs. Dowling reports that of the 286 therapeutic or preventive drugs listed in the 1965 Seventeenth Revision of the *U.S.P.* 179 (63 percent) were synthetic organic chemicals and only 19 (7 percent) of vegetable origin. In the Fourth Edition of the *U.S.P.*, published in the mid-19th century, 80 percent of the drugs were of vegetable origin (Dowling 1970). The general trend has been the synthesis of new drugs in the laboratory. At one time drugs came primarily from natural sources and physicians and/or pharmacists discovered them. Plants were, of course, a major source of new drugs. Out of the thousands of such products which were once in Western pharmacopeias, only about a score have survived the rigors of chemical analysis, double-blind control studies, and standards for quality, efficacy, and margin of safety.

These few plant products are often held up as glorified examples by those who champion plant sources as a fertile area of search for new drugs, yet little effort is expended today in screening plants as a source of new drugs since past efforts have yielded little or nothing of value. In recent years only a few new drugs have been found this way, such as the anti-hypertensive agent *Rauwolfia serpentina*. It was discovered by an Indian physician, Dr. Vakil, in the early 1950's (Dowling 1970). The active ingredient of this plant, called reserpine, was later extracted from it and is now widely used today. Naturally-occurring products are rarely extracted today. Instead they are synthesized in laboratories all over the world. Epinephrine, for example, was first extracted from the adrenal gland; now it is synthesized. Likewise, other drugs are made in bulk by synthesis. Often the parent compound is manipulated molecularly and analogues made which are less toxic and more potent.

Origins and Development of the African Pharmacopeia

In a sense, an African pharmacopeia has been around for countless centuries, but only now is it being recorded. Many authors have recorded the names, both local language and scientific, of herbal preparations and how they are prepared and administered for various illnesses (Traore 1965; Bouquet 1972; Keita 1975; Van Peuyvelde *et al.* 1975). Several nations are attempting to systematically record the names, method of preparation, administration, and stated specificity of herbal preparations (Koumare 1972). In many respects, this situation resembles the origins and development of the *Codex* in France, the *British Pharmacopoeia* in Great Britain, and the *United States Pharmacopeia*. This enormous task has only just begun in Africa. As was the case earlier in Europe and the United States, those who record this pharmacopeia often offer editorial endorsement of efficacy based on rather sketchy impressions and observations.

From the vantage point of modern science, little is known about the pharmacology of most of the herbal preparations used in Africa. No doubt useful active ingredients may be isolated from the many herbs used now in Africa. Their future worldwide use will to a great extent depend upon their uniqueness. If they are merely naturally occurring analogues of products already being synthesized in modern laboratories, they will have no great worth, except in demonstrating that the indigenous pharmacopeia contains something of value. The great thrust of the modern pharmaceutical industry towards drug discovery via synthesis dims the chances of Africa's pharmacopeia being carefully screened. Because of this, some African countries have initiated their own pharmacologic screening programs.

Recognizing the importance of traditional medicine and indigenous pharmacopeias, the Executive Board of the World Health Organization recommended the worldwide study of the feasibility of training and utilizing traditional healers in the modern health care delivery system (WHO 1975). WHO has also recommended laboratory investigations into the pharmacologic and other properties of herbs and controlled clinical trials of therapeutic substances as part of this broader undertaking.

In some countries, such as Mali, national institutes of traditional medicine have been established. In Mali this institute is known as the *Institut de Phytothérapie et de Médecine Traditionnelle*. It has the following objectives.

1. The preservation of traditional herbal preparations by recording their use.
2. The improvement of certain preparations (by means not yet determined.)
3. The instruction of modern medical personnel in the use of certain herbal medications.
4. The establishment of collaboration between traditional and modern practitioners and the pointing out to the latter that they are not superior to the former.
5. The encouraging of young people to become traditional healers.
6. The establishment of a national pharmacopeia of traditional herbal preparations.

This institute, which is headed by a pharmacist trained in Europe, does not enjoy major support from the country's medical establishment. Trained as they are in the Western scientific mode, they respect standards established by modern science. Unfortunately, many of the studies carried out by this institute and others like it deviate so far from accepted modern standards in design and controls that the results are meaningless. In effect, then, such studies even though published are viewed with skepticism and summarily dismissed by those who demand proper study design.

An additional element serving to alienate the modern medical segment of the health care delivery system is the questionable ethics of some of these studies, as when traditional remedies being tested are given directly to volunteers, without any animal studies being performed first. Little thought is given to possible adverse and toxic reactions, as evidenced by the following research policy.

> As for our study approach, it is adapted to Malian conditions both for the inventorying of medicinals used in popular recipes and for the establishment of their pharmacologic properties. To speak only of the latter, our policy, although having raised at the beginning certain concerns, seems the best. It permits us to avoid the interminable and onerous toxicity studies. Certainly there is a certain risk involved but it is a calculated risk such as that involved in all therapies and . . . it is an honor for our profession to accept such responsibilities. (Koumare 1972).

This policy, flawed in its reasoning, goes against accepted scientific research standards. It would probably result in criminal indictment if carried out in many parts of the world. Expedient in the short term, it destroys credibility in the long term and does considerable harm to the perceived value of the traditional pharmacopeia.

Most authorities would agree that the African pharmacopeia possesses some valuable and useful products. There is an important need to elucidate the pharmacology of these preparations to the satisfaction of modern science. Indeed, we already know the pharmacology of some, which gives strong testimony to the value of Africa's pharmacopeia, but pseudoscientific endeavors will contribute little or nothing to our knowledge of the pharmacology of these herbal preparations.

National pride and revalorizing traditional medicine do not create an atmosphere in which critical analyses can be made and objectively valid conclusions drawn about the efficacy and safety of herbal preparations. Today even benign expressions of doubt about the efficacy and safety of herbal medicines are violently and emotionally denounced along with those who dare to make them (Koumare 1976). In many ways, the current course of events in Africa is similar to what occurred in Europe and the United States in the 19th century when those who voiced doubts about the efficacy of certain herbal preparations were denounced by the defenders of these drugs. Heated debates took place and later there were protracted court cases over the question of pharmacologic efficacy and safety (Berman 1970).

Toxicity Studies

It has long been observed by both laymen and health professionals that traditional herbal preparations sometimes cause untoward reactions, severe toxicity, and even death (Koumare 1972; Gueye *et al.* 1972). Many preparations are quite impure and contain several pharmacologically active ingredients. In addition, dosages are not controlled. So toxicity may result from one or more of the ingredients in a given herb and may occur only when certain amounts are used. The prescribed methods of preparing herbs, by boiling, drying, charring, and soaking may detoxify them in much the same way as manioc, a staple food in Africa, is detoxified of its lethal prussic acid. Little has been done by modern science in this area, so our knowledge is quite scanty.

The majority of reports about the toxicity of herbal medicines stem from clinical observations of patients who have been seen in modern dispensaries, clinics, or hospitals. Most often the exact nature of the toxicity cannot be elucidated because of the absence of a toxicologic laboratory. In Bamako, Mali, the most frequent cause of chemical intoxication seen in patients at the main hospital is the ingestion of traditional herbal medicines (Koumare 1973); but the offending agents are rarely identified (Gueye *et al.* 1972).

In countries like Nigeria, where sophisticated medical services are available in urban centers, toxicity from traditional herbal preparations is frequently diagnosed. In recent years an effort has been made to study the basic chemical modalities responsible for the clinical toxicity of plants used as medicinals. The poisonous effects of many African plants have been known for quite some time (Watt and Breyer-Brandwijk 1932).

An example is a plant known by the Yoruba of Nigeria as *amunimyae* (*Senecio abyssinicus*) which is widely used for treating a variety of illnesses (Williams and Schoental 1970). It is also used in many other parts of Africa by various ethnic groups, including the Bahaya of Tanzania, who employ it as a treatment for syphilis and yaws (Watt and Breyer-Bradwijk 1932). In laboratory studies using white rats, Williams and Schoental (1970) have demonstrated that this herb produces significant liver damage including cirrhosis and tumor formation. This type of toxicity is not acute and consequently is not perceived in the traditional setting. The probable reason for this plant's toxicity is the presence in it of a number of alkaloids. The high incidence in Africa of primary carcinoma of the liver and cirrhosis give these findings an added significance.

Acute nicotine poisoning has been widely documented in Nigeria from the use of *agbo tutu* (see p. 208). It is primarily used as an anticonvulsant in children but in large doses results in coma and death (Maclean 1971). Cow urine is a common constitutent of this and many preparations used by the Yoruba of Nigeria and has resulted in a variety of toxic manifestations. At the present time, its mode of action is being studied at the University of Ibadan.

References

Berman, A. 1970. Drug Control in Nineteenth Century France: Antecedents and Directions, in *Safeguarding the Public: Historical Aspects of Medicinal Drug Control*, edited by John B. Blake, Baltimore: The Johns Hopkins Press.

Bouquet, A. 1972. La Pharmacopée Traditionnelle du Congo-Brazzaville, *Afrique Médicale* 11:99, 349-352.

Clarke, F.H. 1973 *How Modern Medicines Are Discovered*, Mount Kisco, N.Y.: Futura Publishing Co.

DeFelice, S.L. 1972. *Drug Discovery*, New York: Medcom Learning Systems.

Dowling, H.F. 1970. *Medicines For Man: The Development, Regulation and Use of Prescription Drugs*. New York: Alfred A. Knopf.

Emmanuel, G. 1976. Les Guerisseurs: Un Mythe, *Jeune Afrique* 811: 10-11.

Gueye, S. Koute, P., Sylla, O. and Zarouf, M. 1972. Intoxication par un Medicament Indigène d'Action Cardio-Vasculaire, *Afrique Médicale* 11(104): 911-914.

Keita, S. 1975. Tisane Aux Cinq Plantes, *Afrique Médicale* 14(130):423-426.

Koumare, M. 1972. Pharmacopie, Médecine Traditionelles et Médecine Moderne, *Etudes Maliennes* 2:54-56.

Koumare, M. 1973. Note Preliminarie sur les Intoxications Aigues au Mali, *Etudes Maliennes* 5:55-59.

Koumare, M. 1976. Pharmacopie Africaine: Le Professeur Mamadou Koumare Répond au Dr. P.J. Imperato, *L'Essor* No. 7273, p. 6, No.7274, p. 6.

Maclean, U.C. 1971. *Magical Medicine*. London: Penguin Press.

Stieb, E.W. 1970. Drug Control in Britain, 1850-1914, in *Safeguarding The Public: Historical Aspects of Medicinal Drug Control*, edited by John B. Blake, Baltimore: The Johns Hopkins Press.

Traoré, D.A. 1965. *Médecine et Magie Africaine*. Paris: Presence Africaine.

Van Puyvelde, L., Pagezy, H. and Kayonga, A. 1975. Plantes Medicinales et Toxiques au Rwanda, Alcaloides, Saponosides et Tannins, *Afrique Medicale* 14(135):925-930.

Watt, J.M. and Breyer-Brandwijk, M.S. 1932. *The Medicinal and Poisonous Plants of Southern Africa*. Edinburgh: R. and S. Livingstone.

Williams, A.O. and Schoental, R. 1970. Hepatotoxicity of *Senecio abyssiniais*, *Tropical and Geographical Medicine* 22(2):201-210.

World Health Organization. 1975. Health Manpower Development, Training and Utilization of Traditional Healers and Their Collaboration with Health Care Delivery Systems. Executive Board Publication 57/21.

Appendix A

A Synopsis of Major Disease Problems in Africa

Communicable diseases are by far the greatest health problem in all of tropical Africa. The second major problem is that of under-nutrition. Both of these are closely related to one another. Improved nutrition increases resistance to disease, reduces both adult and infant mortality, and increases the desire and ability to deal with sanitation problems that play a key role in disease transmission. Sub-Sahara Africa has been the scene of some of the most lethal epidemics known to man. Trypanosomiasis eradicated populations in many areas and decimated them in others (Jamot 1924). Meningococcal cerebrospinal meningitis killed a sixth to a quarter of the population in the savanna region of West Africa in cycles which took place before the introduction of antimicrobial agents (WHO 1963). Other diseases such as yaws, guineaworm, and onchocerciasis have occurred and continue to occur on a scale unparalleled in any other part of the world. Malaria, leprosy, yellow fever, relapsing fever, schistosomiasis, typhoid fever, the dysentaries, and other communicable diseases are also endemic to this part of the world.

Statistics and Their Meaning

It is often said that published health statistics coming out of most of Africa are inaccurate. The accuracy of such data is dependent of course upon completeness of reporting and accuracy of diagnosis, factors which vary from place to place and from time to time. Figures based upon attendance at hospitals and dispensaries can be very misleading because they reflect illness only among those who come to seek treatment. Fixed medical facilities draw people from a limited distance beyond which the population does not bother to come simply because it is too far. Also, only those come who think that their illness is treatable at such a facility. Statistics from fixed medical facilities only mirror a selected fragment of the disease picture in an area. Because of this, certain serious disease problems have been present on a large scale for decades without medical authorities being aware of their existence. Such diseases do not show up in official statistics until someone actively begins to look for them. The statistics which are reported by fixed medical facilities are the result of what in epidemiologic terms is known as passive surveillance. Active surveillance, in which medical authorities go out on a regular or periodic basis and systematically examine the entire population of an area for the signs of specific disease, gives a more accurate picture of disease problems than that coming out of fixed medical stations.

The two former major colonial powers in Africa espoused different philosophies of disease prevention and treatment. The British placed the emphasis on establishing numerous fixed medical facilities, whereas the French developed a remarkably efficient autonomous mobile health service for all of French West Africa and French Equatorial Africa. This mobile health service, which was known as the *Service des Grandes Endemies*, was centrally administered and divided into a number of *secteurs* in which were located mobile teams of infirmiers (nurses) and other para-medical personnel headed by physicians. The service established a regular schedule of visits to all villages in the sectors during which the entire population was examined and treated for the major endemic and epidemic diseases including trypanosomiasis, onchocerciasis, leprosy, malaria, trachoma, treponematoses, and cerebrospinal meningitis (Richet 1958). In addition, these mobile teams immunized against smallpox and yellow fever. After independence, the former French colonies retained the *Service des Grandes Endemies*. They presently coordinate their activities through a supra-national regional health organization in West Africa known as the O.C.C.G.E., *Organisation de Coordination et de Cooperation Pour la Lutte Contre Les Grandes Endemies*, which has its headquarters in Bobo-Dioulasso, Upper Volta. A similar organization exists for the central African states with headquarters in Yaounde, Cameroon. These organizations coordinate disease prevention and treatment among all of the French-speaking states of West and Central Africa (Richet 1965).

The British and the French did not develop their respective major health systems to the exclusion of any other. In the French colonies a network of curative medical facilities was set up to handle disease problems not managed by the *Service des Grandes Endemies*. These facilities were few compared to their counterparts in the British colonies. Since independence, however, individual Francophone countries have greatly expanded the medical dispensary system and some have integrated it and the mobile medical service. In the Anglophone colonies, teams did go out from their dispensaries into rural villages to diagnose, prevent, and treat illness, but the regularity and the efficiency of this activity was not comparable to that of the *Service des Grandes Endemies*. In these territories mobile teams have been formed for the purpose of administering categorical immunization programs, such as those against smallpox and measles and more recently against cholera.

Because active surveillance is an inherent characteristic of mobile health services, the statistics generated by this operation are obviously superior to those which are collected in fixed dispensaries. For the most part, the West African savanna lies in the French-speaking areas and consequently we possess some accurate knowledge of what the main disease problems are. Data from this region illustrate the general health problems present in Africa. Morbidity statistics are more accurate than mortality data because deaths are often not reported. We know from well-planned and well-executed surveys for measles morbidity and mortality that the fatality rate varies from 10 percent in urban areas to 50 percent in rural villages. The reported fatality rate of 1.1 percent reflects gross under-reporting of deaths.

Climatic and topographic zones have distinct disease characteristics and these are clearly mirrored in the data that the *Service des Grandes Endemies* has accumulated over the years. Although communicable disease problems dominate, this does not mean that such non-communicable conditions as cardiovascular disease, diabetes mellitus, peptic ulcers, and malignancies are not present. Certainly these and other chronic disease problems are present in the African population. However, the diagnosis of these conditions is often difficult without the assistance of confirmatory laboratory and X-ray procedures. Such tests are not usually available to rural populations and consequently many of these conditions go undetected. In urban centers where health services are well-developed and sophisticated techniques for diagnosis present, these conditions are often found. Therefore, one sees an apparently higher incidence of chronic disease in urban African populations. While this does reflect detection in the cities compared to the lack of it in rural areas, it may also reflect a real difference in incidence between urban and rural populations. Certain diseases such as diabetes mellitus may actually occur more frequently in urban populations because of dietary habits. Likewise, peptic ulcers and coronary artery disease may occur in the elite segments of African city populations due to a combination of dietary and stress factors.

Most of the degenerative and chronic illnesses become clinically apparent in middle and late adult life. Because the average life expectancy in Africa is so low, the population does not live long enough to develop these problems to the degree that they constitute a source of medical concern.

Both traditional and industrial societies have developed systems of medical prevention and care that address themselves to the major disease problems encountered in their respective societies. In Europe and America one finds coronary care units in hospitals, but such hospitals do not have wards for managing typhoid fever because the incidence of this disease is extremely low in the developed world. The institution and its personnel are oriented toward the management of the most commonly-encountered problems. Likewise in Africa, the traditional medical establishment is oriented toward the management of the common disease problems. Although the traditional medical system is geared toward the handling of what is most frequently encountered and as a result becomes most competent at this, it is, like its counterpart in the developed world, flexible enough to deal with the entire spectrum of illness. This is another of the parallels to be found between Western medicine and traditional African medicine. (See chapter 2, above.)

CASES AND DEATHS FROM FIVE
CHRONIC DISEASES, REPUBLIC OF MALI, 1971*

Disease	Number of Cases	Number of Deaths	Fatality Rate
			%
Hypertension	1,331	34	2.5
Cerebro-Vascular Disease	70	25	35.7
Myocardial Ischemia	272	26	9.5
Diabetes Mellitus	143	7	4.8
Peptic Ulcer	2,466	19	0.9

*Ministry of Public Health Archives

The statistics for Mali in 1971 show a low incidence of trypanosomiasis and onchoceriasis, but one must be cogniscent of the fact that such figures reflect the situation in one particular year and do not show long-term disease trends nor the true magnitude of diseases. The low figures for these two diseases reflect the large-scale control measures undertaken to interrupt transmission. Without these constant control measures, these figures would be a hundredfold greater, similar to those encountered by the *Service des Grandes Endemies* when it began its activities in the 1930's. The value of statistics is very.much dependent upon informed and intelligent interpretation, without which it is impossible to draw correct conclusions.

In 1968 there were 1,129 cases of cerebrospinal meningitis reported in Mali. In January, 1969, a serious epidemic of the disease began in the western savanna near the town of Kayes and swept eastward into Upper Volta and Niger. During this epidemic, 11,636 cases and 1,221 deaths were

PRINCIPAL CAUSES OF MORTALITY
BY AGE GROUP
REPUBLIC OF MALI, 1972*

Infants Less than 1 Year	1-4 Years	5-14 Years	14 Years +
1. Malaria	1. Malaria	1. Malaria	1. Malaria
2. Measles	2. Measles	2. Dysentaries	2. Tuberculosis
3. Gastroenteritis	3. Malnutrition	3. Trypanosomiasis	3. Dysentary
4. Bronchitis and pneumonia	4. Gastroenteritis	4. Malnutrition	4. Trypanosomiasis

*Ministry of Public Health Archives

reported in Mali, a dramatic contrast to the 1968 figures (Ministry of Public Health, Mali, 1972). Similarly, in 1970 and 1971, a cholera pandemic reached West Africa where the disease was unknown before. During late 1970 and early 1971, a total of 2,877 cases and 288 deaths were reported in Mali.

Many of the other communicable diseases also have epidemic cycles. Measles has an annual cycle in cities and a two- to three-year cycle in rural areas. When smallpox was present it had a five- to seven-year cycle in the savanna (Imperato et al. 1972).

In interpreting statistics one must be aware of a number of characteristics about disease, otherwise false interpretations result. Also, national statistics show the number of cases and deaths for a country as a whole. With certain diseases, such as onchocerciasis, the disease morbidity is confined to limited geographic areas where the number of cases per thousand population is much higher than for the country as a whole. The epidemiologic characteristics of the communicable diseases are well-known to medical authorities in this part of the world. Some of these diseases such as malaria are ever-present endemic problems, reflected in annual statistics. Others such as trypanosomiasis and onchocerciasis are potential endemic and epidemic problems kept under control through a large investment in personnel, material, time, and effort. Still others such as yellow fever and meningococcal meningitis are cyclical epidemic problems which sweep through the savanna population at intervals.

Diarrheal Syndromes

Diarrheal syndromes are especially common among young children and often carry a high mortality. Poor levels of hygiene create a favorable environment for the spread of these infections. Among young children below four years of age, weanling diarrhea is a major cause of morbidity and mortality. This disease is caused by a number of different pathogenic organisms. For reasons which are poorly understood, it does not respond well to antimicrobial therapy. It is usually found among children who are either overtly malnourished or in a state of marginal malnutrition.

A number of diarrheal syndromes are caused by protozoan organisms, bacteria, and viruses. Many of these are self-limited but have a high mortality when contracted by children who are marginally nourished. The lack of adequate supportive measures to correct dehydration and electrolyte imbalance contributes to the high mortality.

Typhoid fever is widespread in Africa as is paratyphoid fever. Since 1970, cholera has been a major problem in most of the continent, having occurred as an explosive pandemic in 1970 and 1971. The disease is now endemic in most of Africa.

Nutritional Deficiencies

In Africa protein malnutrition (kwashiorkor) and protein-calorie malnutrition (marasmus) are extremely common among young children around two years of age who have been recently weaned. In many regions of Africa, both of these syndromes have a seasonal incidence, being highest when food supplies dwindle just before the new planting season. Nutrition surveys throughout Africa over the past several decades have revealed marked seasonal variations in total caloric intakes that reflect food availability, with generally low to marginal caloric intakes, and a deficient intake of animal and vegetable proteins and essential vitamins. Thus the average rural African diet is lacking in both quantity and quality (May 1968). Against such a background, communicable diseases prosper.

Severe malnutrition, particularly marasmus, occurred on a wide scale throughout the sahel (semi-desert) area of West Africa and in Ethiopia during the drought which lasted from 1972 through 1974, illustrating how precarious a subsistence existence is led by most of the people in this part of the world (Imperato 1974).

Arthropod-Borne Diseases

Malaria

The main vectors of malaria in Africa are the mosquitoes *Anopheles gambiae* and *Anopheles funestus*, both of which are efficient transmitters of the disease. The overall efficiency of a vector depends on two factors, its life span and its man-biting habits. A species which is short-lived and zoophilic is unlikely to transmit malaria to man except when the mosquito population becomes extremely great. In such areas the disease is cyclical in nature, rare in some years and during the dry seasons. On the other hand, the two vectors in the savanna, especially *A. gambiae*, are long-lived and anthropophilic, capable of maintaining transmission at saturation levels throughout the year except during the dry season when levels drop somewhat (Hamon and Coz 1966). Epidemics of malaria do not occur under these circumstances. Rather the situation is endemic — malaria is present all the time. Attempts at controlling malaria through residual spraying with insecticides and chemoprophylaxis with chloroquine salts have been attempted unsuccessfully in the savanna. The mosquitoes' resistance to the chlorinated hydrocarbon insecticide, dieldrin, has developed in some areas and is transmitted as a semi-dominant gene. Hybrid mosquitoes with one resistant parent are sufficiently resistant to survive doses of this insecticide which are practicable for field use and those inheriting the gene from both parents are resistant to almost any dose. Resistance to DDT on the other hand is inherited as a recessive gene so that hybrid mosquitoes can be fully susceptible; however, *A. gambiae* tends to avoid surfaces covered with residual DDT because they are irritating (Hamon and Mouchet 1961).

Because of such problems, residual spraying alone will not control malaria, and therefore attempts have been made to eliminate the reservoir in man by mass treatment with the antimalarial drug chloroquine. Attempts were made to mix chloroquine with common salt in a well-executed WHO project in Ghana, but were unsuccessful because chloroquine has a very bitter taste which makes it difficult to achieve a balance between effective prophylactic levels and palatability. It was thought that if chloroquine were taken by everyone, malaria could be eradicated, since man is the only reservoir for the species which cause human illness. However, it is quite clear now that certain species of malaria can develop resistance to chloroquine. There is little prospect therefore that malaria will be either eradicated or greatly controlled in the savanna at present.

Fortunately malaria engenders a high degree of immunity in the indigenous population. Maternal antibodies are passed on to African infants and by the age of three years the children develop sufficient levels of their own so that they are virtually immune to the effects of malarial infection. The highest mortality from the disease occurs in exposed children below the age of three years whose immune responses are not yet fully developed. African adults may suffer several days of fever a year as a result of constant challenge by malarial parasites but these are generally mild attacks. A single dose of an anti-malarial drug will cut short such episodes. While the administration of anti-malarial drugs to children below the age of three years greatly reduces the mortality from malaria, it also interferes with the development of antibody levels. Thus, when these children reach adulthood they do not have the immunity present in those who have not taken chloroquine prophylaxis. The widespread presence of the sickle cell trait in Africa also protects a proportion of the population since malaria parasites in abnormally sickle-shaped cells are easily removed and destroyed by the body's reticuloendothelial system.

It is now agreed that unless some new discoveries offer genuine prospects of eradicating malaria carried by *A. gambiae*, the problem can be dealt with by protecting young children with regular chemoprophylaxis and by making anti-malarial drugs readily available to the population.

Trypanosomiasis

In Africa, two major species of trypanosomes affecting man are found, *Trypanosoma gambiense* and *Trypanosoma rhodesiense*. In West Africa only the former is present and man is the principal resevoir. The disease is transmitted by the bite of tsetse flies of the *Glossina palpalis* group which require a blood meal for survival. Tsetse flies need a certain amount of shade and atmospheric humidity and for this reason are primarily found along river banks where there are shrubs and trees and around water holes and pools. In the forest zones where their humidity and vegetation requirements are usually met, tsetse flies have a much wider flight range and their contacts with man tend to be casual. In the savanna, however, where water sources are scare, man-fly contacts are intense since both are obliged to use the same limited rivers and streams, water holes, and river crossings. In taking a blood meal, the tsetse can become infected if the parasites are present in the blood of the person bitten. During the next two weeks the organisms undergo development within the fly and finally lodge in its salivary glands. The fly then passes on the infection to the next person it bites. The incubation period of gambian trypanosomiasis is very long — two years and more — and during this time an infected person may have the parasites in his blood without suffering from any severe clinical symptoms. He may travel long distances by road, on rivers, or through the bush with herds of livestock; and as he goes along he may cause sizeable outbreaks along the way. These asymptomatic carriers may be the source of epidemics in areas which had been cleared of the disease. The disease is fatal in 80 percent of those who are infected and not treated.

As the 20th century began, epidemics of trypanosomiasis broke out in the Congo basin and along the western and northern shores of Lake Victoria (Duggan 1970). Many have presumed that the disease was introduced into the region by Arab traders, by Henry Stanley's expedition of 1888, or by the Sudanese refugees accompanying Emin Pasha, but scientific studies now attribute the epidemic situation to the general disruption which took place in the African ecology at that time. From the Congo basin and Lake Victoria, the epidemic spread westward and north eastward across Africa. In the Cameroon, Jamot, the French physician who established the first mobile medical teams, uncovered 105,902 cases among 335,000 persons examined. In Nigeria, 300,000 cases were uncovered in a period of six years, and in French West Africa over half a million cases were diagnosed in the 1930's.

Trypanosomiasis can recur in epidemic form if a scrupulous search is not maintained for cases. Control measures are no longer as efficient as they once were in the colonial era because of a paucity of funds for mobile medical work and the lack of African physicians willing to engage in the difficult effort involved in this type of medical service. The reappearance of epidemic sleeping sickness is one of the greatest hazards facing the savanna countries. Certain occupational groups are most likely to introduce it into the savanna from the forest foci to the south where man-fly contacts are close enough to maintain a continuing low-level rate of infection. Laborers from the savanna often work on plantations for the season in such foci and then return home and, infected with the disease, they constitute one of the chief causes for concern. The control of trypanosomiasis is achieved through the treatment of all cases and carriers, and the prophylactic administration of the drug pentamidine to the entire population. With the implementation of such measures, the human resevoir is greatly reduced and the tsetse flies become non-infective (Waddy 1970). Other successful measures used are the clearing out of shade-producing vegetation along river banks and at river crossings, and the use of insecticides. The latter method is extremely expensive for large areas, but has been used successfully in local schemes such as in Bamako, the capital of Mali, which is an endemic focus of trypanosomiasis.

Onchocerciasis

Onchocerciasis is a helminthic infection due to *Onchocerca volvulus* and transmitted by black flies, *Simulium damnosum* and others. These flies lay their eggs in running water, and larvae and pupae develop where rocks break the water's surface, creating turbulence which results in oxygenation. These flies range in size from two to six millimeters in length and bite primarily at dawn and at dusk. Often, they gather in great swarms and their bites alone make them one of the world's worst insect pests, not only where they transmit onchocerciasis. (Black fly control programs exist in the Adirondack Mountains of New York State and in Canada where the insects do not transmit the disease.) Onchocerciasis is found in Africa and in Central and South America wherever conditions favor the breeding of these insect vectors.

The mature adults of *Onchocerca volvulus* migrate freely in the human subcutaneous tissues for a while, but eventually settle down in pairs and create fibrous subcutaneous nodules especially over bony prominances such as the rib cage and the iliac crests. They produce thousands of microfilariae per day which migrate in the skin giving rise to a severe itching and a variety of dermatologic lesions. Eventually they migrate into the eyes where they damage the anterior segment and the retina and cause blindness. Blindness rates as high as 50 percent are found in many foci inflicting devastation both on the sufferers and on the social and economic fibers of society (Imperato and Sow 1971).

The combined effects of mass blindness and fly nuisance forces a progressive retreat of men from river valleys in the savanna. After each such retreat more and more trees are cut down and more grass burned in order to creat new agricultural lands. Soil erosion also progresses further into the watersheds and results in a drying up of the permanent rivers which then contain water only after a heavy rain (Budden 1956).

The traditional approach to the control of onchocerciasis, as with most vector-borne diseases, has been twofold, an attack on the vector and a reduction of the reservoir of infection through mass treatment. The immature microfilariae are extremely sensitive to diethylcarbamazine, but in heavily infected people their mass death causes severe allergic and often fatal reactions; thus the drug must be used with caution. This drug, however, does not have any effect on the adult worms and so relapses in a year's time are inevitable. Suramin kills the adult worms, but its untoward effects demand that it, too, be used with extreme caution. In spite of these drawbacks, large numbers of infected persons are treated each year through the concurrent use of the above-mentioned drugs and antihistamines and steroids which decrease the frequency and severity of allergic reactions. Large scale treatment programs have been launched in the Volta River Basin where it is estimated that three million people out of the total population of five million are infected and a hundred thousand are blind (Richet 1968).

The larvae of black flies are extremely sensitive to DDT. One part of DDT to thirty million parts of water has been found sufficient to clear streams of the fly. But the fly has a long flight range that becomes even longer during the rainy season, meaning that successful vector control hinges on the treatment of the entire river system of an area (Richet 1968). The dangers of continued DDT use in such river systems is another factor which must be weighed in vector control programs. At the present time the World Health Organization is setting up an onchocerciasis control program in the Volta River Basin focus which lies in the savanna in Mali, Upper Volta, Dahomey, Ghana, and the Ivory Coast.

Diseases Transmitted through Contact

The principal contact diseases are leprosy, yaws, endemic syphilis, and trachoma. All of them readily respond to appropriate treatment and so control is primarily a matter of planning and executing effective programs.

Leprosy

Although leprosy is still prevalent, there being a half million patients in the savanna zone in former French West Africa, the disease can be controlled and cured through the use of a variety of drugs. Where mobile teams are operative, case finding is effective since the disease is easily diagnosed because of its distinct and visible features. Patients are either sent to regularly-held leprosy clinics not too far from their villages or visited by auxilliaries as in many of the Francophone countries. These auxilliaries travel from village to village on bicycles in order to examine and treat patients.

Yaws and Endemic Syphilis

Yaws and endemic syphilis are non-venereal treponemal infections which are usually acquired between the ages of three years and fourteen years. The treponemes are difficult organisms to differentiate because they cannot be cultured in the laboratory. All of them, including *Treponema pallidum* which causes both endemic and venereal syphilis, give identical serologic reactions. There is no complete cross immunity between these infections and so a person with yaws can be infected with syphilis. Both yaws and non-venereal syphilis can be transmitted by simple contact. Yaws transmission is facilitated in the humid forest country of the coast where wet skin provides easy passage of the organisms. Until the advent of penicillin, yaws was a great problem in the savanna. The widespread use of antibiotics in the pediatric age groups has served to control the disease and to eradicate it in some areas.

Endemic syphilis is found primarily in the northern savanna and in the sahel among ethnic groups whose level of personal hygiene is poor because of a lack of sufficient water supplies. Its transmission is facilitated by the use of common eating and drinking vessels. The disease responds well to penicillin therapy and this drug when used on a mass scale effectively interrupts transmission. In some areas of the northern savanna and sahel over 80 percent of various population groups have been found to be sero-positive, indicating either past or active infection. At the present time an intensive survey is being conducted in the savanna and sahel for cases of endemic syphilis.

Venereal Syphilis and Gonorrhea

Venereal syphilis and gonorrhea are growing public health problems in Africa. The actual incidence of both these infections is difficult to know because many cases go undiagnosed, especially in women, and many others which are treated go unreported for the same social reasons which exist in other parts of the world. In recent serologic surveys conducted in Bamako, which is far from endemic (non-venereal) syphilis areas, 25 percent of those tested were found to be positive. In 1968, there were 6,840 cases of venereal syphilis registered in Mali, but local medical opinion holds that this figure represents a small fraction of actual cases.

Trachoma

Trachoma is found throughout the savanna and also in the sahel and desert. It is caused by a virus which can be easily transmitted where levels of personal hygiene are low and flies are abundant. Flies transmit the infective virus mechanically. It can also be transmitted by contact with clothing or other materials which have become contaminated. The virus causes a conjunctivitis and inflammation of the cornea which if not treated leads to extensive scarring and eventual blindness. The disease can be treated with a variety of antibiotics and with surgical techniques that can correct the anatomical deformities caused by scarring. The table below presents some of the most recent statistical data on trachoma and onchocerciasis in the Francophone areas of West Africa. The higher figures for Upper Volta reflect both higher disease incidence and more efficient case finding.

TRACHOMA AND ONCHOCERCIASIS
IN FIVE WEST AFRICAN STATES, 1969*

Country	Population Examined by Mobile Teams	Trachoma Cases Diagnosed	Onchocerciasis Cases Diagnosed
Ivory Coast	970,448	665	9,206
Upper Volta	1,615,341	44,010	54,650
Mali	584,154	673	2,939
Niger	71,681	415	25
Senegal	493,586	2,587	1,949

*Institut d'Ophthalmologie Tropicale d'Afrique, O.C.C.G.E.

Other Diseases

Measles, cerebrospinal meningitis, schistosomiasis, and filarial infections other than onchocerciasis are important causes of morbidity and mortality. Tuberculosis is also a serious problem which is being given more and more attention by government health services (Blanc 1970). Skin test surveys and radiologic surveys conducted in a number of countries have shown that the incidence of both past infection and active disease is appreciable. Skin test surveys in Upper Volta showed 29 percent to be positive. In the Ivory Coast, 50.5 percent were positive and in Chad 57.8 percent. In Mali, 10,204 individuals chosen randomly were X-rayed and active disease was found in 88. Surveys of cattle at abbatoirs have revealed tuberculosis infection in 20 percent of the animals, indicating that non-pulmonary bovine tuberculosis in humans may be more prevalent than once was thought. In the past several years many nations have undertaken active BCG immunization programs[1] against tuberculosis aimed at all those below the age of ten years.

The list of disease problems in Africa is indeed long. In this section an attempt has been made to focus attention on the most important of these and to explain in very general terms their chief epidemiologic and pathologic characteristics. Many diseases not specifically covered in this discussion are responsible for appreciable levels of morbidity and mortality, but in a relative sense they are of less public health concern than the major problems discussed here. Although traditional medical practitioners do not view disease prevalence with a statistical eye, they do form general impressions about the relative frequency of well-defined disease processes. It is not surprising then that they are often able to indicate what the principal diseases in an area are and convey some notion of their relative prevalence. Likewise they are often able to describe changes in disease prevalence and the cyclical nature of some of the epidemic diseases.

---

[1]BCG vaccine is named after two French scientists, Calmette and Guerin, who first developed the vaccine from special strains of tubercle bacilli in the 1920's.

References

Blanc, F. 1970. Histoire de la Tuberculose en Afrique Noire Francophone, *Rapport Final de la Dixième Conference Technique de l'O.C.C.G.E., Tome I*, Bobo-Dioulasso, pp. 97-108.

Budden, F.H. 1956. The Epidemiology of Onchocerciases in Northern Nigeria, *Transactions of the Royal Society of Tropical Medicine and Hygiene* 50: 233-248.

Duggan, A.J. 1970. An Historical Perspective, in *The African Trypanosomiases*, edited by H.N. Mulligan. New York: Wiley-Interscience. p. XIVI.

Hamon, J. and Mouchet, J. 1961. La Résistance aux Insecticides Chez les Insectes d'Importance Médicale, Methods d'étude et Situation en Afrique au Sud du Sahara, *Médecine Tropicale* 21:565-596.

Hamon, J. et Coz, J. 1966. Epidemiologie Générale du Paludisme Humain en Afrique Occidentale, *Bulletin de la Société de Pathologie Exotique* 59: 466-483.

Imperato, P.J. 1974. *Report of a Health and Nutrition Study of the Sahel Relief And Rehabilitation Program in the Republic of Mali.* American Public Health Association, Document No. 125.

Imperato, P.J. and Sow, O. 1971. Incidence of and Beliefs about Onchocerciasis in the Senegal River Basin, *Tropical and Geographical Medicine* 23:385-389.

Imperato, P.J., Sow O. and Fofana, B. 1972. The Epidemiology of Smallpox in the Republic of Mali, *Transactions of the Royal Society of Tropical Medicine and Hygiene* 66:176-182.

Jamot, E. 1924. Etat Sanitaire et Depopulation au Congo, *Bulletin de la Societe de Pathologie Exotique* 12:32.

May, J. 1968. *The Ecology of Malnutrition in French-Speaking Countries of West Africa and Madagascar.* New York: Hafner.

Ministry of Public Health Archives. 1972. Bamako, Mali.

Public Health Problems in 14 French-Speaking Countries in Africa and Madagascar, Volumes I and II, prepared by Z. Deutschman and B.B. Waddy. Washington, D.C.: National Academy of Sciences. 1966.

Rapport Annuel du Service de Sante, Annee 1971. Bamako, Mali: Ministere de la Santé Publique. 1975.

Richet, P. 1965. L'Histoire et l'Oeuvre de l'O.C.C.G.E. en Afrique Occidentale Francophone, *Transactions of the Royal Society of Tropical Medicine and Hygiene* 59:234.

Richet, P. 1968. Le Problem de l'Onchocercose, *Médecine d'Afrique Noire* 15: 63-66.

Richet, P. 1958. "Le Service Commun de Lutte Contre les Grandes Endemies de l'Afrique Occidentale Francaise." (Unpublished.)

Tropical Health 1962. *A Report on a Study of Needs and Resources.* Washington, D.C.: National Academy of Sciences.

Waddy, B.B. 1970. Chemoprophylaxis of Human Trypanosomiasis, in *The African Trypanosomiasis,* edited by H.N. Mulligan. New York: Wiley-Interscience.

WHO Chronicle 17:256-263. 1963.

Appendix B

Glossary

Alfa — a term for marabout

Arrondissement — smallest administrative unit in Mali; several combined *arrondissements* constitute a *cercle*

Ba Kona — a secret society in Liberia whose primary purpose is to treat snake bites

Babalawo — Yoruba diviners

Bagi — leprosy

Barah — Islamic charms, usually worn in leather sacs

Baraka — holiness; the nyama inherent in all beings; supernatural power

Basi — charms

Basitigui — diviner-healer

Belee — small stones used in divination

Bemba — the Bambara name for the supreme being; also called Ngala

Bilakoro-dogoma — the age set including boys between the ages of six and ten years

Bilakoro-dogomani — the Bambara age set encompassing boys below the age of six years

Bilakoro-koroba — the age set encompassing boys between ten and fifteen years

Blenboro — secondary syphilis

Boboya — deaf-muteness

Boli — material supports for the nyama (q.v.) of ancestral spirits

Calabash — a gourd

Cercle — government administrative unit; there are 42 cercles in Mali

---

NOTE: African names for plants are omitted from this Glossary.

Cwezi — ghosts of ancient folk heroes and kings (among certain African groups such as the Banyoro)

Da — syphilis

Da wolo susu — tatooing of the inside of the lower lip

Dabarey futu koy — ''master of evil''; sorcerer (Timbuctoo)

Damadyala — gonorrhea

Danga — curses inflicted by certain 'Moslem clerics (morijugou)

Dangu — a communal protective spirit

Dassiri — a communal protective spirit

Demba gnouma — ''good mother''; also used to mean measles

Dingaka tsa dinaka — herbalists who also are diviners (among the Botswana)

Dingaka tsa ichochwa — herbalists who also sell herbs (among the Botswana)

Donkono — plant poisons

Dolo — millet beer

Dougou — village, country; also spelled *dugu*

Dougou-tigui — village chief

Dozoboli — a talisman worn by hunters

Dugu — (*see* Dougou)

Dya — the double of the soul

Dyeli — bard class

Dyide — a spirit medium cult once common among the Malinke and Bambara in the 1930's

Dyoli — skin ulcers

Dyon — slave class; slave

Dyonkomi — a large, brown scorpion

Dyow — secret; secret initiation society

Endemic syphilis — syphilis spread by use of common eating and drinking utensils or other non-sexual means

Fa — the head of an extended family; father

Fa — psychotic disorder

Fama — king

Fanu m'ba — edema of the entire body; generalized body swelling

Fari-gouan — fever

Faro — a supernatural being who played an important role in creation; he is an androgynous being who lives in water

Finyabana — diseases believed carried by the wind, e.g., meningitis, measles, smallpox

Fla-n-bolo — the age set of recently circumcised boys and excised girls; traditionally one was formed every three years

Fla-n-ton — the grouping of three fla-n-bolo (q.v.)

Flani — twins

Flanitokele — twin statue

Flelikela — sorcerer

Fofoni — a small red snake

Folo — thyroid goiter

Furatigui — herbalist

Garanke — leather worker caste

Gla — the void out of which everything was created

Gnanzani — measles

Gne-fla — a spirit medium; also known as *nyabouin* and *soma* (q.v.)

Golongise — cowrie shells used in divination

Gorou — acne

Guessedala — weaver group

Gulli — charms of braided or knotted string (Timbuctoo)

Gwese dalaso — chewing stick, used to clean teeth

Hakili wili — anxiety

Horon — freemen class; free person

Igqira elokuqapala — Kaffir surgeons expert at treating fractures

Imam — local chief Moslem cleric

Infirmier — male nurse

Jathieth — Luo healer (Tanzania)

Jinn — genies; spiritual beings

Jinoro — hydramnios

Ka sisi — laryngitis

Kaba — ringworm

Kafo — a traditional geographic and political unit composed of several villages

Kafo-tigui — an area chief

Kambu — metal tweezers; a fetish made of tweezers and used to cause illness (Timbuctoo)

Kana — a ball of shea butter used as amulets by herbalists

Karamoko — "literate man," the name by which Moslem clerics are sometimes known

Karaw — the most important class of the Kore society

Karwwa — an infertile woman (among the Hausa of Niger)

Kenke — granules that remain after korte is made

Kessou — cough-producing illness

Kilikilimacien — epilepsy

Kilisi — magical formulas of words pronounced over herbal medicines

Klani — prickly heat

Klodimi — earache

Kolidohi — *Rauwolfia vomitoria*, a tranquilizing herb (Bambara)

Kolochi — arthritis

Kolokari — fracture of bone

Komo — one of the major initiation societies

Kono — bird; name of a major initiation society

Kono dimi — abdominal cramps

Kono dya — constipation

Konon-dale — prolonged pregnancy

Kore — a major initiation society and the final one into which men are inducted, also spelled Kwore

Kore-dugaw — a class of the Kore society whose members dress and act as buffoons

Koro dimi — low back pain

Korte — material element or charm used in sorcery

Korte koni — sorcerer who uses korte to cause illness (Songhoi)

Kossan — a small, flesh colored scorpion

Koule — calabash and woodworker caste

Kulusi dyala siri — impotence

Kunandi — the parents of twins; "privileged ones"

Kungolo dimi — headache

Kwashiorkor — protein-deficiency disease

Kwore (*see* Kore)

Maganga — doctor (Swahili)

Maniamaga mousso — traditional midwives (Bambara)

Marabout — a term used by the Bambara for Moslem clerics who are Koranic teachers and who diagnose and treat diseases believed to be due to supernatural causes. They also make talismans to ward off illness. They are also known by the names *alfa*, *karamogo*, and *moriba*.

Marasmus — protein-calorie deficiency disease

Matrone — midwife assistant

Medecin chef — chief medical officer of a cercle

Messemani — small spots (= measles) (northern Bambara)

Missimani — same as *messemani*

Morijugou — the name given to those Moslem clerics who practice sorcery

Moson — a ball of bud used as amulets by herbalists

Moura — coryza

Mousso-ka-dyiri — the tree of a woman's cult

Moussa Koroni — "little old woman"; the name given to the female supernatural being created by Pemba (q.v.)

M'soron — yaws

Nama — an initiation society whose chief purpose is to control sorcery

Ndormadyiri — a supernatural being who is the heavenly blacksmith

Nenkenieblenke — schistosomiasis

Neone — measles

Ngala — (*see* Bamba)

N'garo — poliomelitis

Ngoyo — a species of wild tomato used in sacrifices to Faro

Ni — the soul

N'kenyede — a system of sand-reading divination

N'tomo — the first initation society into which young boys are inducted

N'Toro — tapeworm

Numu — blacksmith caste

Nyabouin — a spirit medium

Nyama — man's character after death, acting as a spiritual force

Nyamakala — guild artisan; casted person

Nye dimi — conjunctivitis

Nyenyini — sorcerer; sorcery

Nyi-susu — tatooing of the gums

Onchocerciasis — river blindness, a disease caused by parasitic roundworms (filaria) that are carried by certain biting insects

Onishegun — Yoruba herbalists

Osanyin — god of the herbalists, among the Yoruba

Oullokobana — eclampsia of pregnancy

Pemba — a supernatural being who played an important role in creation. He transformed himself into an acacia tree

Pembele — an altar to Pemba

Quinnekilila — spirit medium who may also control spirits for malevolent purposes

Sahel — transition zone of dry scrub bush between the savanna and the southern Sahara

Saouara — jaundice

Say — jaundice

Segele — dracunculiasis (Guinea worm), a parasitic disease

Shea butter — a pasty butter extracted from the fruit of the shea tree (*Vitellaria paradoxa*)

Shetani — spirits who do not assume a corporeal form; can cause illness

Sinzin — twin cult; sometimes used to mean twin statue (*flanitokele*)

Sirikoun — an oracular fetish

Soma — a spirit medium

Souba — witch

Soubaka — (*same as* souba)

Soubara — (*same as* souba)

Soumon — dental caries

Soumoni — abscess

Souya-maou — (*same as* souba)
Sunoko bana — trypanosomiasis

Tafo — kilisi (q.v.) which are material-
ized
Tana — (*same as* tne)
Teliko — the spirit of air
Tere — man's character
Tiqui — chief or master
Tne — totem
Tokotokoni — dysentery
Ton — the name given to all male and
female age sets in a Bambara vil-
lage; also means an association or
set of rules
Ton-tigui — chief of a ton
Toumoni — pinworm
Trypanosomiasis — African   sleeping
sickness
Tynibibi doy — "master of black talk";
Gabibi magicians (Timbuctoo)

Tyi wara — an initiation society whose
focus is agriculture; the name of the
deity who taught farming to men

Uvula — part of the soft palate that
hangs down above the back of the
tongue

Wanzo — a nefarious force which resides in the prepuce and clitoris.
Woklo — small elf-like spirits; also
called *woklani*
Woloso — person born into enslaved
condition

Yegerou — hiccups

Zo — smallpox

Index

Names of places will be found in this index. Proper names of authors cited and of other people mentioned in the text will be found in the Name Index, below.

Schistosoma hematobium, 156
Schistosomiasis, 16, 156-157
Schizophrenia. *See* Mental illness
Sclerocarya birrea, 131, 160, 198
Scoparia dulcis, 134, 158
Scorpion stings, 206, 207
Sculptures, 120-121, 123, 124-125. *See also* Masks
Sebeke, 98
Secret societies. *See* Cults
Securinega virosa, 136
Sedatives, 96
Segene, 160
Segou (kingdom), 3, 4, 39
Segou (town), 5, 7, 13, 40, 140
Sehei (people), 93
Senegal, mental illness in, 101-102
Senecio abyssinicus, 100, 217
Senegal River, 2, 5, 14
Senility, 93
Senufo (people), 8, 147
Sepdon haemochates, 202
Service des Grandes Endemies, 89
Sexual relations, 41, 42, 112, 154; drives, 107; and measles, 149; taboos in, 108; of twins, 123
Shawia (people), 181
Shea butter, 64, 73, 151
Shea tree, 64
Shetani, 27, 37
Shopana cult, 99, 165, 171, 172
Shopana spirit, 95
Sickness. *See* Illness; Disease; Treatment of disease
Sien goni, 197
Sierra Leone, 102, 103, 108
Sikasso (town), 3, 7
Sindian, 157
Sinjan, 111, 153
Sinzin cult, 118, 125, 126
Sirikoun. *See* Oracle; Fetish
Slaves, in Africa, 41, 84, 148; in America, 163
Sleeping sickness. *See* Trypanosomiasis
Smallpox, 95, 155, 162-175
Smallpox cult. *See Shopana*
Smilax kraussiana, 110, 111, 125
Snake cults, 203-204
Snakebite, 204-206
Snakes, 200-206
Solanum capense, 197

Soma (spirit mediums), 37, 58-61, 74, 79, 80. *See also* Spirit mediums
Somono (people), 8, 11
Songhay (empire), 3; people, 3, 8
Songhoi (people), 83, 84, 86, 144, 146, 147, 164, 171
Soninke (people), 12, 14, 15, 16
Sorcerers, 28-30, 35, 59, 86, 87, 95
Sorcery, 28-30, 35-37, 52, 62-63, 109, 142
Souasousa. *See* Coughing
Souba, 34, 74
Soubaka (witches), 34. *See also* Witches; Witchcraft
Soubara (witches), 34. *See also* Witches; Witchcraft
Souma-Koumaou. *See* Malaria
Souroukou-gningnin, 136
Sourwood, 147
Souya-maou (witches), 34. *See also* Witches; Witchcraft
Spirit agents, 36, 37
Spirit medium cults, 61, 74, 99
Spirit mediums, 34, 35, 37, 58-61, 74, 79, 95, 102. *See also* Diviners; Healers; *Soma*
Spirits, 27-28, 63; ancestor, 102; Islamic, 37, 102; protective, 32, 34, 47, 97, 110, 112; *Shopana*, 95
Spoken formulas. *See* Verbal formulas
Sterculia setigera, 97
Stimulants, 96
Strophanthin (poison), 36. *See also* Poisonous plants
Strychnos spinosa, 111, 153
Suber, *See* Basembeti (people)
Sudan beans, 147
Sunsun, 152, 153
Surgery, traditional, 176-190
Suruku n'domo, 98
Suruku n'tomo, 97
Swahili language, 184
Syphilis, 15, 102-103, 112, 154

Taba, 153
Tafo, 64
Talisman, 33, 63-64, 160. *See also* Amulets; Fetishes
Tamarindus indica, 111, 135, 157
Tana, 33
Tangara, 134, 152
Tanzania, 55

Name Index

Also by Pascal James Imperato

Doctor in the Land of the Lion
(1964)

Last Adventure
(1966)

The Treatment and Control of Infectious Diseases in Man
(1974)

The Cultural Heritage of Africa
(1974)

A Wind in Africa
(1975)

What to Do about the Flu
(1976)

Historical Dictionary of Mali
(1977)

About the Author

Dr. Pascal James Imperato is a physician with broad training and much experience in medicine, public health, and tropical medicine. He has spent several years in Africa, including over five years as a medical officer in Mali. His role as a physician gave him unusual opportunities to observe and communicate with the people in Malian villages and nomad camps, and he has worked closely with Malian medical workers who have a profound knowledge of their country. As a result, Dr. Imperato has been able to gain a much deeper insight into Malian culture, particularly with respect to medical practices and beliefs, than most foreigners ever attain.

Dr. Imperato is on the faculty of Cornell University Medical College and is the author or co-author of over 68 medical publications. At the time of publication of this book he is New York City's Commissioner of Health.